James Baldwin Brown, Elizabeth Baldwin Brown

Stoics and Saints

Lectures on the later Heathen Moralists and on some Aspects of the Life of the

Mediæval Church

James Baldwin Brown, Elizabeth Baldwin Brown

Stoics and Saints
Lectures on the later Heathen Moralists and on some Aspects of the Life of the Mediæval Church

ISBN/EAN: 9783337336721

Printed in Europe, USA, Canada, Australia, Japan

Cover: Foto ©Lupo / pixelio.de

More available books at **www.hansebooks.com**

STOICS AND SAINTS

*LECTURES ON THE LATER HEATHEN MORALISTS, AND
ON SOME ASPECTS OF THE LIFE OF THE
MEDIÆVAL CHURCH.*

BY THE LATE

JAMES BALDWIN BROWN, B.A.,

MINISTER OF BRIXTON INDEPENDENT CHURCH.
AUTHOR OF 'THE HIGHER LIFE,' 'FIRST PRINCIPLES OF ECCLESIASTICAL TRUTH,'
ETC., ETC.

'The fountain of all human progress, of all human
hope, is the living presence of God in and
with the world.'

J. B. B.

GLASGOW
JAMES MACLEHOSE AND SONS,
Publishers to the University.
1893.

NOTE BY THE EDITOR.

THE Lectures contained in this volume were delivered at different times and in various places during the later years of Mr. Baldwin Brown's life, and if that life had been prolonged he would himself have prepared them for the press. They are now published at the earnest desire of many who heard them, with but slight alteration, the characteristic freedom of a spoken address being purposely retained. Though not originally given in one course, the Lectures are essentially related in their leading ideas and method of treatment, and are arranged chronologically as a consecutive series.

Certain portions of the fifth Lecture were included in an essay on 'The Religious Life,' in 'Ecclesia' (first series), and are reproduced here by kind permission of the publishers. With that exception all that is contained in the book appears now for the first time.

E. B. B.

St. Lawrence-on-Sea, Kent,
October 1893.

CONTENTS.

I.

THE LATER AGE OF GREEK PHILOSOPHY AND THE EPICUREAN AND STOIC SCHOOLS.

THE LATER AGE OF GREEK PHILOSOPHY AND THE EPICUREAN AND STOIC SCHOOLS.

IT needed the insight of a consummate genius like Socrates to see that man was really the centre of the world. The Cosmos is on so grand a scale, its spaces are so immense, its forces are so terrible, that man seems but a helpless, noteless pigmy in its midst. It was but natural that the first beginnings of Philosophy, that is, of man's thought about things, including himself, should be concerned with the universe; with the mystery of its genesis, the secret of its order, the meaning of its life. The earlier sages set themselves to guess the solution of the mystery. One thought fire was the fundamental principle, another moisture, and so on through the elements. Each sought to discover the secret of the unity of the creation, persuaded that under infinite variety such unity existed, if man could but discover its principle; and this, the earliest quest of man, is the quest of science through all the ages, which it is painfully pursuing still. Man still has before him in his path of discovery the vision of

> 'One God, one law, one element,
> And one far-off divine event,
> To which the whole creation moves';

and this vision, science and theology, working together not in impious antagonism but in holy concord, will one day make real.

It is significant that these early sages mostly dwelt under the sceptre of the great Asiatic despotism, where man was but a human atom, of slight account for all the higher purposes of intelligent and responsible existence, and where speculations on the vast system of the Cosmos around him would be the first natural exercise of man's intellect and imagination, the despot assuming the whole outward government of his life. Socrates marks the dawn of a new era. He transferred the centre of gravity of Philosophy absolutely and finally to Man. He saw that, as far as this earth was concerned, man was the final end of the creation; man who, while he could search the secret things of the Cosmos around him and master the key to its methods, could himself become creator in the intellectual and political spheres. And Socrates, it must be remembered was a citizen of a free political community, as men understood freedom in those days, when all the hard work of the world was done by slaves. Socrates as a thinker made man the centre of his system, but Socrates, as the citizen of Athens, found man the centre of a very large, free, and noble activity, and developed to a pitch of individual culture and dignity, which, as characteristic of a whole community, is still un-matched in the history of the world.

Man was of slight account individually on the sea boards of Asia Minor, when Thales began his speculations about the world-system around him. Man individually and in his political relations was of immense account in Athens, and Athens was herself the free and energetic head of a great movement which was changing visibly the destinies of the civilised world. When Socrates was born, the excitement of that splendid struggle for human liberty, which at Salamis wrested the sceptre of civilisation from Asia and transferred it to Europe, was still vivid and inspiring. Athenian freemen had done a deed unmatched for daring heroism in the earth's annals, and it was a deed that, as Socrates grew to manhood, was clearly giving a new form to human history. The century which followed the crowning victory of Salamis was at Athens, in point of political activity and intellectual and imaginative production, the most brilliant upon record. The world has never seen a community, each member of which was cultivated to such a pitch of intellectual acuteness and political judgment as that commonalty of Athens. An Athenian in those days, the days of Æschylus, Sophocles, Euripides, Aristophanes, Pericles, Pheidias, Socrates and Plato; a citizen of a city in whose life he was not only expected but as a rule able to take part; one who was called to sit in judgment on the most brilliant leaders, thinkers and artists of the world, might well deem that there was something in man, in his faculty, in his energy, in his capacity for development, in his manifest destiny, through which he could claim all the forces of the physical creation as his ministers, and which gave him the right and the power to examine all external things in the light of the ideas which were enshrined within.

Socrates, born and nursed in the midst of the splendid energy and activity of that Athenian commonwealth, gathered and expressed the great lesson of its life. He busied himself entirely with man. With the physical theories which occupied his predecessors he had no concern. They were mere guesses having their main interest in the search after unity which they revealed. Man, as a being with a capacity for knowing the truth, for discriminating the real nature of things from the false or partial conceptions which uncultivated human nature is prone to form of them; man, as a being capable of entering into very high and noble relations with his fellows, and of living by the help of wisdom a very perfect and beautiful life, was the theme of his constant investigation; on this he bent the energies of one of the keenest and most subtle intellects that man was ever endowed with, and the force of a moral nature, a will and a conscience, which are peerless in the heathen world. To make men wise was his life-long endeavour; to destroy the *idola*, the false ideas of things which he found them cherishing, and to substitute the true. The discovery of truth with a view to conduct, so as to make the individual worth more to himself and to the State, was the aim of his wonderful dialectic; for man was always conceived of and treated by him as a member of a community, a being in relation to his fellow beings, whose line of duty was marked out by the public life of his day. The condition of such a career as that of Socrates, with such an aim, was the existence of a very noble, free, and large public life in the community which he sought to lead into the ways of wisdom; a life full of energy, purpose and hope.

His country, teeming as it was with brilliant energy and activity, could not bear his searching uncompromising examination of its ideas, its principles, and its aims. As befell a greater than Socrates, it cast him out and slew him. Thenceforth the story of Athens is a story of decline and decay. It need not be thought that the decay of Athens was the judgment of God on the martyrdom of her great teacher. God's most dread judgments are the stern execution of His laws. But as a fact, from the days of Socrates the course of Athenian history was one of rapid degradation; then followed the rise of Macedon to supremacy in Greece, the victories of Alexander, the division of his vast empire among his generals, and the final extinction of the liberties of Athens, which lost all political dignity and independence, while remaining the intellectual centre of the world.

There are few things in history more humiliating than the life of Athens as a State during the Macedonian era, tossed about as she was from conqueror to conqueror, and indulging in slavish adulation of them all. There are passages in Plutarch's Life of Demetrius Poliorcetes, the most brilliant, though the most inconstant and profligate of the Graeco-Asiatic rulers, that afford graphic illustrations of the degradation to which Athens had sunk in the days in which the Epicureans and the Stoics arose. We have even preserved to us a hymn of divine honour addressed to this prince by the Athenians.[1] By this time the public life of Athens, which had been her glory, had utterly perished. Men were cut rudely adrift from that which had been their guide and law, the public opinion of their State. There was no State; the brutal hand of war had abolished all political independence throughout the whole world of which Greece was the centre; there was no fixity in any political arrangements; one day Athens belonged to Demetrius, the next to Cassander, just as the fortune of war decreed, while the citizens, who once wielded a wide and splendid empire, were the sport of the caprices and the insults of their despots. The wealth too of the city was dissipated by the constant inconstancy of the political combinations in which it was included. Its trade decayed, its genial youth was drawn off, not for patriotic expeditions but to man the mercenary armies which for many generations filled the Graeco-Oriental world with confusion and slaughter.

In such a condition of society, amid the clash of arms and the struggles of contending despots, the noble quest of the elder Philosophy for the True, the Beautiful, the Good, passed utterly away. Within a generation of their deaths, the works of Plato and Aristotle had almost ceased to occupy the attention of their countrymen, and new Schools, new Sects as they were well called, with new questions and new dogmas, were in possession of the field. The man of whom and with whom Socrates discoursed was emphatically a citizen, a man in whose thoughts devotion to the State was uppermost. These were days when Athenians were too busy with the duties and

---

[1] Athenæus, vi. 63.

responsibilities of their absorbing public cares to think much about happiness, or indeed to think much about themselves at all. They were citizens first and men afterwards; the individual in those days had hardly disentangled his individuality from the State of which he was a member, so as to realise that he was a *man*, with personal responsibilities, experiences, and destinies, which no one else could share. In the palmy days of Athens, when Pericles ruled and Socrates taught, a man thought as a citizen, wrought as a citizen, and philosophised as a citizen; and except in his relations as a citizen he would have found himself utterly at sea in the conduct of his life.

In still earlier stages of civilisation, in the tribe, a man is hardly a person. He is like the limb or organ of a greater body, his tribe; and out of that unity he is nought. Now there is something which is not without beauty and nobleness in this earliest form of human society, in which the man hardly realises his 'self' except in relation to his fellows. But as society progresses and rises towards the higher stages, this primitive order of things breaks up and vanishes. Man has to be placed under the strongest stimulus to personal development; he has to be stirred and trained to understand his relations and duties as a personal being, as the condition of his entering into the highest and most fruitful relations with his fellow men in the State and in the Church. He must be made to feel his individual relations, primarily to God and then to his fellows, and thus only can State life and Church life put on their finest forms and bear their most perfect fruits. This is the end at which Christianity aims. It will isolate men first, press on them the duties and responsibilities of their individual being, lead them to cry, as if it were the one concern for them in the universe, ' What must I do to be saved,' and then, when their whole nature, body, soul and spirit, is in full development and activity, it will create out of the union of these individuals a higher condition of society than the primitive form of human relations could possibly have secured. The highest state possible to a community is attained when there is a principle brought to bear that, on the one hand, gives to the man the strongest stimulus to individual development, and, on the other, compacts most closely his relations with his fellow men. The Jew in the old world made an approximation to this condition within the limits of his national life. God's commandment was addressed to him from the first as a person, one who had personal relations with the invisible and eternal, while the tie which bound together the individuals of the race, remains the strongest nexus of man to man which even to this day is known to history. The problem, How this condition is to be realised for humanity at large, is the problem which has been solved by Christianity. The object of Christianity is to 'present every man perfect,' while at the same time it links him closely to the brotherhood of the Universal Church.

That process of individualisation, if we may so call it, which was accomplished nobly for the Jew by the Revelation of the Divine law, and for man at large by the Advent, was achieved more painfully for the Greek by all the strife, degradation and misery of the generations of Hellenic decay. When the liberty of Athens was destroyed, the citizen had no longer a State to live for; patriotism died down for want of a country to love. It was in Athens that a teacher of the New Academy declared that a philosopher would not much trouble himself if his country were enslaved. Athens *was* enslaved, or such a thought would never have occurred to an Athenian moralist. But liberty being lost, political life being utter humiliation, the strong hand and the brutal will ruling everywhere, mercenary soldiering having supplanted patriotic military service, there being no principle anywhere to fight for, and no empire of tolerable dignity to serve, men fell back upon themselves. At any rate, they said to themselves, amid the universal impoverishment and misery, I am here, a living being, with a wonderful capacity for enjoying and suffering, and I must look to myself, and enjoy, as far as I may, my own individual life. Then arose that new philosophical question as to personal conduct and happiness which gave birth to the Epicurean and Stoic Schools, and for the next three hundred years occupied the whole field of Philosophy; for even with the Sceptic, who asserted that nothing could be certainly known, the fundamental consideration was a quiet life.

The question of happiness as the aim of life first comes to the front in the Ethics of Aristotle, and its appearance is the sign of the changed condition of public affairs. In Aristotle's days, in fact, the State was already in decadence. But Aristotle's 'happiness' was a noble and beautiful idea. It was the energetic play of all man's best and highest powers in their proper tasks. The strain of effort and the sense of victorious achievement were its factors; the happy man was the man whose whole nature was in full activity about its noblest work. But the question had come to have a much narrower meaning in the days when the Epicureans and the Stoics appeared. Noble work was then a hard thing to find; great ideas had been banished from the minds of men; great principles ceased to influence the movements of societies. On all sides there was a scramble of selfishness, and it was the selfish idea of happiness, the passive idea, that was uppermost in the minds of men when these sects arose. How a man could get his bit of happiness for himself and enjoy it—it was all that was left to him—was the main theme of Philosophy till the Gospel 'Whosoever will come after me, let him deny himself, and take up his cross, and follow me,' was preached to the world.

Let us understand that it is a very necessary process,

this distinction of the individual man from the community—his extrication as a being with personal responsibilities and destinies, from the family, tribe, or state, with which in the earlier stages of his development his life is bound up. This extrication from the communal life, this differentiation, so to speak, is the first condition of man's advance to the higher grades of civilisation, in which with his fully realised and developed manhood he will enter into higher forms of political combination with his fellows, and fill a larger and nobler sphere. It may be said this is a development of selfishness; in a sense, yes. It is the full unfolding of Self, but not for Self. The man who, under a strong sense of personal misery, is moved to cry out for his own salvation, is the man who comes ultimately to think least of self, and to devote his powers most resolutely to his fellow men. This disentanglement of the individual man with his personal interests and needs, was distinctly in the Divine order of the progress of Society. But at first it took a low and selfish form. Neither Stoic nor Epicurean could carry the development up to its ultimate stage, in which the higher self becomes the servant and minister of man, in which the happiness of the personal being is found in ministering to the happiness of others. For that another and a better Gospel was needed, and that too was sent. It is Christianity alone, which, while applying the strongest possible impulse to man's individual development, and pressing on him most solemnly the interests of his own being, binds him in bonds of closest brotherhood to his fellow men. Nevertheless, though under conditions they understood not, Stoic and even Epicurean were preparing the way for the Gospel.

It has been remarked that Plato and Aristotle were themselves soon well nigh forgotten in that Greece of which they were the intellectual glory; and yet it is wonderful to note, how the Sects lived upon the crumbs of the table of the Socratic School. Socrates was the starting point of all the younger philosophies.

The first in order of the Sects was that of the Cynics, whose founder Antisthenes appeared soon after the death of Socrates, and of whom Diogenes in his tub is the far-famed representative. We can hardly call Cynicism a philosophy, it was rather a habit of life, and it was founded on the well-known contempt of Socrates for external things, his indifference to ease or pain, want or fulness, life or death. But in Socrates this noble contempt of externals was but the accident of his intense pursuit of higher things. The Cynics took the accident, as the Quakers took what was accidental in George Fox's life, and made it the basis of their discipline. In their hands it became a hard ascetic doctrine, which continued to attract its votaries for 500 years, and handed down some legacies to the ascetic school in the Christian Church.

The next in order of development were the Sceptics, founded by the celebrated Pyrrho of Elis, who has been the eponymus of the Sceptic schools through all time. It is probable that a misinterpretation of the Socratic method was at the root of Pyrrhonism in its first inception. The form of the Socratic dialogue suggested how much was to be said on both sides of a question, and how hard it was to come at the truth. To every statement there is an answer; to every reason a counter reason; while Socrates constantly professed that he knew nothing, and bent the whole strength of his keen intellect to prove to all who conversed with him that they were in the same case. Pyrrhonism could not see that it was just the intensity of his conviction that truth might be known, which made him so ruthless in destroying refuges of lies and refuges of half-truths in himself and others. Pyrrhonism *did* see that Socrates found very much to be said both for and against the propositions he discussed; that the great master Aristotle had set himself in many vital points against Plato, and that both had passed away and had left no settled body of truth. Pyrrho too had travelled far; had been in India with Alexander; had talked with Brahmins, and studied the manners of distant lands. It appeared to him as the result of all that the safest way was to doubt of everything; to adhere to the maxim that to every reason an equal reason may be opposed; to keep the mind in absolute suspense about all propositions, and absolutely imperturbable by all the influences of the external world. We know nothing about anything. This thing is white, we say—we mean that it seems what we call white, but what it *is* who can tell. And as to imperturbability, it was said that nothing would make Pyrrho halt or hasten; he would not leave the road to escape being run over by a carriage or bitten by a dog—this is doubtless a joke at his expense, but it shews the temper which he set himself to cultivate. His manner of life was much admired; his fellow citizens made him high priest, which reveals something significant about them as well as about him. His doctrine was however too deathly cold, and his manner of life was too utterly cheerless for anything like wide acceptance among his fellows. It is true that the same dreary asceticism makes itself seen in Christendom, but then it had at the heart of it a burning enthusiastic love, which made it, in the monk, a thing of quite another sphere. Pyrrho could see nothing within him, above him, around him, to kindle enthusiasm. His system was, as has been said, deathly cold, and the multitude shrank from it, though it continued to reappear in force, at intervals, in the history of Philosophy, and was found, nay is found—we have not done with it yet—an instrument of no little power in breaking down and breaking up systems of thought that have outlived their work. An age of dogmatism never fails to lead on to an age of scepticism, which does judgment on its dogmas and torments its disciples: but in the 'everlasting No,' no age can rest. Pyrrho himself confessed 'It is hard to strip off the man.' On the humanity of human nature, which is constant through the ages, many a proud system goes to wreck.

It was in the midst of this Cynicism as to manners and morals, and Scepticism as to truth, that the Epicureans and Stoics began to rebuild the lapsed structure of Philosophy. It is to be noted that with Pyrrho too, as with them, the one question was happiness. He doubted of everything and maintained an impassive imperturbability—we will not call it serenity, serenity belongs to a higher sphere—because he thought he should be happier in doing so. It was the one attraction of Scepticism : it freed him from the pain and the trouble of any overmastering, imperious thought. Indeed this concern about the every day interests and happiness of men, which became the key note of the philosophy of the Sects, ran through the whole scale of life in those days. Men turned their thoughts in upon themselves. Imagine the horror with which an Athenian of the noble days of Athens would have heard Carneades tell Clitomachus that he thought a philosopher would not be greatly troubled if his country were conquered! In the dramatic literature of the time the same spirit reigns. In the old comedy Aristophanes had the citizen always on the stage; all the interest of the drama was political : all the jokes and sarcasms were pointed at political persons or political doings. Aristophanes is a sealed book to those who are not familiar with the public life of his day. But in Menander, in the comedy of the time of which we are now speaking, politics are never alluded to. All is personal and domestic; the woes of lovers, the tricks of slaves, the knaveries of tradesmen, the intrigues of wives occupy the whole stage. We have already seen that in one sense this was a development; a development provided there was a further progress beyond. If it had ended there, if it had only substituted the self-enfolded man for the citizen prepared to serve as judge, to legislate, to fight and to die for his country, it would have been an utter and fatal degradation. But if the man thus isolated and made conscious of his personal interests and responsibilities, could be taken hold of by some loftier discipline, if educated in this way to a higher point he could be brought into new and more fruitful relations with his fellows, then it might be a very valuable step in the unfolding of the destinies of the human world. That 'if' Christianity answered; that discipline the Gospel of Jesus and the Resurrection supplied.

Epicurean and Stoic occupied themselves with this same question, How shall a man secure his personal happiness? So far they were twin shoots out of the same stem. And let it be added that there was a latent scepticism in both of them, though they rose in protest against Scepticism, and tried to supply a positive rule of life to man, based on a certain view of the order of the world. They were both in their main attitude defensive. They had no deep belief in the rightness and the goodness of the system of things around them; and their secret thought was to arm themselves against it to the utmost of their power. Possessed by this inner scepticism about the capacity of man to arrive at truth, and the duty of man to search for it, they neither of them cared for the pursuit of truth for its own sake. Dialectic they utterly despised. They sought to know what would make for happiness, and cared for nothing beyond. But yet they were not sceptics. An utter sceptic may have a rule of life, and a very good one as far as it goes. But when a man bases his rule of life on what he can discern of the order of the world, however insufficient, however false, his notion may be, he rises out of Scepticism, and has earned a title to the sacred name of Philosopher. Epicurus even did not say nothing can be known, he believed that something could be known; a miserable something, we feel, but still he believed it to be truth, and on it he grounded his system and his life.

One cannot help finding considerable charm in what is known of Epicurus and his company. It is little enough; but it differs generically from what we know of the other philosophers. Epicurus, it will be remembered, is the only one of the old heathen teachers who gave his name to his Sect. They were always known as Epicureans. It is not without meaning that we speak of Epicurus and ' his company.' He gathered a body of friends around him, with whom he lived in the closest fellowship and who regarded him with reverential love. In the Garden where they met were gathered what in outward aspect looked more like a company of Christian Cœnobites in the early monastic days, than anything which we meet with in Greek society. Epicurus must have been a man of singular charm of manner, and singular moderation of temper His disciples loved him with a perfect affection, and it is said that they had pictures of Epicurus in their rooms and their bed chambers, and even on their rings and their plate. One ' fell down at his feet,' and did him reverence. Even to Lucretius, a man of the loftiest genius, his master Epicurus seems a grander and more beneficial being than any of the gods whom his countrymen held in reverence. The personal devotion of the disciples to the master was conspicuous and beautiful ; we find nothing parallel to it in the history of the Stoic School. ' When the stranger,' writes Seneca—himself an ardent Stoic, though he always does justice to Epicurus— ' comes to the garden on which the words are inscribed, " Friend, here it will be well for thee to abide, for here pleasure is the highest good," he will find the keeper of that garden a kindly hospitable man, who will set before him a dish of barley porridge and water in plenty, and say 'Hast thou not been well entertained? These gardens do not whet hunger but quench it; they do not cause a greater thirst by the very drinks that they afford, but soothe it by a remedy which is natural and costs nothing. In pleasure like this I have grown old.'[1] 'Epicurus,' said Ælian, 'cried and said, "To whom a little is not enough, nothing is enough. Give me a barley cake and water and I am ready to vie even with Zeus in happiness."'[2] 'Send me,' he writes himself to a friend, 'some cheese of Cythnos, that when I will I may fare sumptuously.'[3]

That these temperate habits were honest and well-authenticated, the comic poets by their jokes at them testify. 'Your water drinking,' says a character in a play, 'makes you useless to the State; whilst by my potations I increase the revenue.' Another says, 'This fellow is bringing in a new philosophy, he preaches hunger and his disciples follow him. They get but a single roll, a dried fig to relish it and water to wash it down.'

Now as the avowed principle of Epicurus was pleasure, and the sensations were all that he knew in man, it is natural that there should have been animated controversy about the temperance and purity of the life in that Garden of Epicurus, where 'pleasure was the highest good.' There were women there too belonging to the company, women it would seem of considerable grace and attractiveness. Scandal was busy with their names. There was a curious collection of letters published by a certain Stoic, a bitter enemy of the Epicureans, purporting to have passed between Epicurus and Leontium, the best known of the women who frequented the Garden, and others, and these suggest grave doubts as to the morality of the association. But the genuineness of these epistles has been severely questioned, and we should probably be safe in believing them forgeries.

---

[1] *Epist.*, 21. 10.　　[2] *Variæ Historiæ*, IV. 13.　　[3] Diog. Laert., X. 11.

The question can never be decisively settled; and a garden which has over its portal the words, 'here pleasure is the highest good,' gives at once some colour to scandal. On the other hand, the morality of the sect was always stoutly asserted by the Epicureans and seems to have been generally believed by their contemporaries. It appears indeed clear that if sensuality, in the coarse sense of the term, had been the 'pleasure' of Epicurus, and excess the law of the life in the company of the Garden, the beautiful reverent homage which they rendered to their master when living, and to his memory when dead, would have been poisoned in its springs. The community could never have held together so long in unity on the basis of indulgence; and there are moreover some unquestioned letters of Epicurus which seem to be conclusive against the darker charges urged against him by his foes. There have come to light at Herculaneum certain mutilated documents relating to Epicurus and his school, and in a portion of a letter thus recovered there are some words addressed apparently by Epicurus to the daughter of his chief disciple Metrodorus and this very Leontium, a young girl for whose welfare he took thought on his death-bed. It runs thus:—'We have arrived safe and sound at Lampsacus, I and Pythocles and Hermarchus and Ctesippus, and there we found Themista and the rest of our friends safe and sound. I hope that you, too, are well, and Mamma, and that in all things you are obedient to her and to Papa and Matro, as you used to be. For remember, my bairn, that we are all of us very fond of you—so be obedient to them.'[1]

We can hardly think that a man of impure heart and impure life would have written that letter. In the epistles of Epicurus too, as given by Diogenes Laertius, there are the most gentle and wise rebukes of errors and faults, which

---

[1] Translated in Wallace's *Epicureanism*, Lond. 1880, p. 60.

shew a tenderness, a courtesy, and yet a firmness, which negative the supposition that the Garden was the home of vicious delights. In truth the letters of Epicurus must have been very remarkable documents. There was a collection of them extant in the second century of our era, and its loss is very deeply to be regretted. They were preserved and handed down by the disciples from generation to generation, as carefully as the letters of St. Paul were handed down in the Christian Church. Many acute scholars have observed some outward similarity between the two sets of documents. In one sense, the highest, St. Paul and Epicurus are at the opposite poles; but there is noticeable likeness in the manner of their letters. There are the same urbanity, the same playful irony, the same mixture of exhortations about the smallest personal and the largest moral questions, and the same earnest desire for the welfare of those addressed, according to the conception of each as to the true conditions of the welfare of the human soul. The likeness must not be pressed too far even as to externals; still it is there; we may say that as a writer of pastoral epistles Epicurus has a certain superficial likeness to St. Paul.

And yet, on the other hand, there was nothing in his doctrine, or rather in the principles on which his doctrine rested, however much there may have been in his personal influence, to withhold his followers from the basest sensuality. His doctrine was one of temperance, of a very noble temperance; but there was nothing behind it to sustain it but the individual nature and will of the man. Pleasure is the chief good, sensation is the only guide to reality, the only assurance of truth. There is no law or rule above us, we have simply to guide our course by what we feel, though we must interpret our feelings by our faculty of judgment that enables us to compare experiences and conclude which is the best. In a letter addressed to Menœceus, which is very valuable as giving his own exposition of his system, he lays down in the following words his doctrine about pleasure :—

> When we say then, that pleasure is the end and aim, we do not mean the pleasures of the prodigal, or the pleasures of sensuality, as we are understood by some who are either ignorant and prejudiced for other views, or inclined to misinterpret our statements. By pleasure, we mean the absence of pain in the body and trouble in the soul. It is not an unbroken succession of drinking feasts and of revelry, nor the pleasures of sexual love, nor the enjoyment of the fish and other delicacies of a splendid table, which produce a pleasant life : it is sober reasoning, searching out the reasons for every choice and avoidance, and banishing those beliefs through which greatest tumults take possession of the soul. Of all this, the beginning, and the greatest good, is prudence. Wherefore prudence is a more precious thing even than philosophy ; from it grow all the other virtues, for it teaches that we cannot lead a life of pleasure which is not also a life of prudence, honour, and justice ; nor lead a life of prudence, honour, and justice which is not also a life of pleasure. For the virtues have grown into one with a pleasant life, and a pleasant life is inseparable from them.[1]

There can be no question that Epicurus advocated persistently the bringing reason to bear on the choice of pleasure, and that he saw clearly that many pleasures, most exquisite while they lasted, caused more trouble by anxiety, perturbation, and longing than they were worth. He saw too that the pleasure of the flesh, the σάρξ, was but momentary, while the higher pleasures of the mind took in past, present, and future. But whence, upon his theory, he derived his mind or reason, it is by no means easy to say. The scheme, of course, had vast flaws and fallacies ; these however did not trouble the philosopher, so long as it gave him, what he alone cared for, a working hypothesis for the conduct of life. The effort to elaborate a connected and harmonious system he would have condemned as harassing. Though he was an indefatigable and copious writer, he would have said with the Preacher, Much study is a weariness to the flesh. ‘Comparison and reflection,’ he says, ‘are the foe of pleasure. You must be able to throw

---

[1] Diog. Laert., X. 122 f.

yourself wholly into what the moment presents, as if the moment were eternity with no before or after. When another moment comes, treat it in like manner.' But with him mind was but a finer matter, susceptible to more delicate impressions. All things, he said, reviving the atomic theory of Democritus, consist of molecules of matter in constant motion, in various degrees of proximity to each other. What appears to be solid is never really so. Here as elsewhere he is on the track of a great scientific truth. He seems to have been attracted to this cosmical theory of a fortuitous concourse of atoms, by the facility with which it enabled him to eliminate all creative principle, and all intellectual plan, from the world and from life. Somehow these particles got at times, none can know when or how, a slight deflection from the natural perpendicular downward movement, which would keep them in everlasting parallel lines and make structure impossible. Then somehow they are brought into contact and compose bodies, which somehow hold together for a time and somehow get dissolved in time into their original elements. And this is going on through the whole universe. Happy accident everywhere; no order, no plan; nothing that we can profitably reduce to system outside the sphere of our own sensations and the pleasure which they can afford.

Here is another wonderful flash of scientific insight; the same simple process repeating itself in all the worlds. The *unity* of the universe in the principle of its structure and the mode of its existence!

Sensations, Epicurus explained, are produced by infinitely small molecules which every body is continually giving off, molecules that at first are images of the body which sheds them. These molecules, floating abroad in space, strike on the senses and produce perceptions of taste, colour, form, etc., and are thus the cause of the pleasures which the senses enjoy. But these organs of sense were generated by accident.

The eye was not made for seeing; an eye happened somehow to come into existence, and was found useful for sight, and so on with the rest. The mind is but a finer sense, subject to finer and more delicate influences and impressions, but equally getting its pleasure from the impact of those more subtle atoms which belong to what is called the intellectual sphere. The virtue of this cosmical theory to Epicurus was the element of chance which pervaded it; the impossibility of constructing out of it any system which might impose a law or bring external authority to bear on man. He wanted to free man utterly from any influence, cosmical or spiritual, which might interfere with his quiet, serene regulation of his life.

In the same key entirely is his doctrine about the gods. He affirms the existence of the gods. He finds in himself and in man the feeling that there are Beings of a higher nature; accordingly there must be gods. But seeing that the idea of gods and of divine intervention in human affairs was a source of constant distraction and terror to man, he remits the gods to abodes of serene contemplation' and blessedness, where, 'careless of mankind,' they know nothing of the turmoil of creation and of government, where nature is beautiful and bountiful, where storms and plagues never come, and where content with their own tranquil enjoyments

> 'they lie beside their nectar, and the bolts are hurl'd
> Far below them in the valleys, and the clouds are lightly curl'd,
> Round their golden houses, girdled with the gleaming world.'

Here again we have an instance of the wonderful worldly wisdom of Epicurus in the construction of his system. He could not get rid of the idea of the gods; he set himself to neutralise it, and to make it wholly inoperative on the practical life of mankind. Quite in harmony with his doctrine that the senses are the only trustworthy guides, is his notion that the sun and the stars are about the size that they seem; that the sun is somehow lit every morning and extinguished every night, and that the heavenly bodies, instead of being sources of apprehension and terror, are powerless to help or to harm mankind. His whole theory about the outward world is constructed to the moral scale, in such a way as to help man to lead an untroubled and happy life. He bids him take no thought about the gods, about the creation, about the heavenly bodies. They have absolutely nothing to do with man. Take thought for the moment's pleasure, wisely, so as to leave the least aftertaste of pain ; it is your all.[1]

It is marvellous that a doctrine, which denied an order in the creation and a moral element in man, should lay such great hold upon the human heart. But there is nothing in classical history which reveals so strong a bond of fellowship as that which bound Epicurus and his disciples ; after the lapse of generations Eusebius quotes the saying of Numenius, a Pythagorean—'The school of Epicurus resembles a true Commonwealth ; free from civil war, exhibiting a single mind, a single opinion.'[2] True to his central principle Epicurus despised politics. Science was to him a harassing study. He had no desire to meddle with anything which was not a sensible object. Where was there any mathematical line, point, or circle, that he could touch ? Nowhere. Have nothing then to do with these things, they belong to a world of distracting dreams. So with politics. Why should a man who wants only to be happy trouble himself with the needs, the schemes, and the wrangling of knaves or fools. The Epicurean systematically lived out of the world. Like the monk he wished to forget it and to be forgotten by it. The Stoic had a far nobler sense of a man's vocation, and Stoics, especially in Rome, are found constantly in the forefront of public life, among the most active and notable men of their times ; but

---

[1] See the passages collected in Ritter and Preller, *Historia Philosophiæ Græcæ et Romanæ*, Gothæ, 1878, §§ 365, ff.

[2] *Præpar. Evang.*, XIV. 5.

the Epicurean cared only for himself and his company, and let the great world go as it pleased.

The Sect did nothing for the world's elevation and advancement, except produce Lucretius, its one great poet. Lucretius was a passionate Epicurean, and the chief attraction for him of the system lay in the deliverance it brought to men from the distraction and torment inflicted by religion. The religion which he strove to overthrow by his Epicurean philosophy was a degrading superstition, that introduced all kinds of mythological folly and falsehood into the processes of nature, and all kinds of cruel, sensual, magical arts and tricks into the conduct of life. Such a base and slavish superstition his free soul utterly hated, and he hoped by the simple, natural, universal cosmical system of Epicurus to destroy it. Let it be remembered that Epicurus was the first entirely to exclude mythological persons and forces from the government of the natural world.

The system, as we have noticed, laid a very strong hold on men in that stormy, selfish, and miserable time. There is something in the mode of maintenance of that Epicurean company in the Garden, which reminds one strangely of the mode of life of another and far nobler company, who were destined to regenerate the world. The most generous gifts seemed to have passed freely among them ; they did not, as far as we can see, establish community of goods, but they cared with large heart and free hand for Epicurus and for each other. In the gifts which were freely sent, and the genial acknowledgment of Epicurus, we see something which again presents a far off likeness to the history and writings of St. Paul.

What then was the charm of the Sect, and what the secret of its power? Cicero declares that not only Greece and Italy, but the barbarian world around soon felt its influence. Its followers endured persecution, and were often associated in after generations with the Christians, as the mark of scorn and hate. The doctrine was widely adopted at Rome. Atticus, the friend of Cicero, was an Epicurean, and in Virgil and Horace there is very clear evidence of its power. When Christianity appeared it began to die away, but to the last its disciples were enthusiastic in praise of its founder and his work. The satirist Lucian, in the second century, speaks of Epicurus as 'a man truly sacred and prophetic in nature, who alone knew and taught the good and true, and was the liberator of those who companied with him,' and in a passage of unusual earnestness he writes of the blessings the book of the κύριαι δόξαι or 'Articles' of the master brings to those who come to it, 'what peace and tranquillity and freedom it works within them, setting them free from terrors and spectres and portents, from vain hopes and superfluous desires, putting within them truth and understanding, and truly purifying their souls, not by torch and squills, and such idle ceremonials, but by right understanding, and truth and open-mindedness.'[1]

Again, we may ask Wherein lay the secret of the power of Epicureanism? It was due in large measure to the fact that of all the philosophies it offered the easiest and most direct way of rest to man. It asked no intellectual effort; its philosophical system was summed up in a catechism which could be easily learnt and remembered, and its end, pleasure, was one which most men were only too ready to pursue. There was terrible mind and heart weariness in the world of the time; and amidst the shock of contending doctrines and the clash of hostile armies the words of Epicurus sounded like 'Come unto me and rest.' As the quiet cell of the monk to the world-weary soldier of a later age, it had the charm of peace and of freedom from care, and brought with it indifference to the distractions and miseries of the great world's

---

[1] Lucian, *Alexander*, 47.

affairs. Lactantius, a Christian writer of the 4th century, accounts for its attraction thus :—

'It tells the ignorant they need study no literature ; it releases the niggardly from the duties of public beneficence ; it forbids the lounger to serve the State, the sluggard to work, and the coward to fight. The godless are told that the gods are indifferent ; the selfish and malevolent is ordered to give nothing to any one,—because the wise man does everything for his own sake. The recluse hears the praises of solitude ; and the miser learns that life can be supported on water and polenta. The man who hates his wife is presented with a list of the blessings of celibacy ; the parent of a worthless offspring hears how good a thing is childlessness ; the children of impious parents are told that there is no natural obligation upon them. The weak and luxurious are reminded that pain is the worse of all evils ; and the brave man, that the sage is happy even in tortures. Those who are ambitious are bidden to court the sovereign ; and those who shrink from worry are directed to avoid the palace.'[1]

There is truth no doubt in this picture ; just as many foolish and base motives might be suggested with truth as incentives to the monastic vocation in the Middle Ages. But the really strong reason, depend upon it, was a deeper and sounder one ; Epicureanism was the readiest form in which, on the basis of heathenism, men could see a promise—it was no more—of rest to their souls. It reveals, on the other hand, the dignity of man's nature, the grandeur of his moral endowment, the utter inability of mere rest or pleasure to satisfy his heart, to find that Epicureanism, with all its promises, with all its attractions, with all the passionate enthusiasm of its devotees, has always had a brand upon it ; has always been counted by the great world a base and hateful doctrine, while 'Epicure' has gradually settled down as the designation of the most contemptible of mankind.

De Divin. Instit., III. 17.

II.

EPICTETUS AND THE LAST EFFORT OF THE HEATHEN PHILOSOPHY.

II.

EPICTETUS AND THE LAST EFFORT OF THE HEATHEN PHILOSOPHY.

'EPICUREAN and Stoic are twin shoots out of the same stem.' They both, as we have seen, grew out of the new search for happiness that had superseded the old search for truth, which Socrates had pressed so keenly, and for which he had been content to die. The question common to the two schools was, How shall I secure the dignity, honour, and happiness of my own life. The Epicurean answered it in one way, the Stoic in another and a nobler way. Epicurus shut up his disciples to what was on the whole a purely selfish form of philosophical discipline, which recognised the senses as the sole inlet of truth, and pleasure as the chief good. 'Avoid distraction and perturbation,' he said in effect; 'cultivate serenity in kindly intercourse with friends, surround yourself as much as possible with the objects which minister rational and satisfying pleasure, and let the outer world go as it pleases.' The Stoic looked at the matter in quite another light, and his aims and methods we have now to consider.

The Cynic was the rudimental form of the Stoic. Epictetus had constantly the word Cynic on his lips. The original starting point of the two Sects was probably the indifference of Socrates to outward things. At any rate, Cynic and Stoic cultivated the most severe simplicity. In the case of a Diogenes, this took the form of a boorish roughness and coarseness, but Zeno, the founder of the Stoic school—the Sect took its name from the Stoa or Porch where the teachers conducted their instruction—shewed on every occasion, though in less obtrusive forms, his contempt for externals.

The Cynic position, as laid down by Antisthenes, the founder of the Sect, was a very simple one. Nothing is really good but virtue, nothing is really bad but vice; all speculation which does not bear on morals is idle and fantastic; only in moral action is man free, for this is the action of the one thing he can really call his own, the mind. These precepts of the famous Cynic really give the key to the Stoic thought and discipline. The doctrine of virtue as the chief good finds place also in the Epicurean system, for according to Epicurus virtue was the only thing which was pure pleasure, with no flavour of bitterness. But here was the essential difference. The virtue of Epicurus had not anything behind it; the virtue of the Stoic had. Epicurus believed that there was nothing outside a man which had any title to rule or to influence. He destroyed all fear of God, all conception of an order in nature, all idea of duty, except duty to self, in life. Hence it follows that an Epicurean, who had once accepted the creed 'pleasure is the chief good,' had nothing except a mere opinion that virtue was prudent, to keep him from settling into the lees of a sensual life. The Stoic, on the other hand, believed in God, and in a grand order in the world. The Stoic doctrine about God has a certain obscurity which belongs to that inscrutable theme. At bottom no doubt it was thoroughly Pantheistic. The Stoics thought that there must be a power inherent in the world to move it, as the soul moves the body; and pushed home they would confess that *they* themselves were part of the All which this Supreme Spirit made the vehicle of his energy, and that existing beings and things represented only a passing stage in the grand progress. From God all things proceed, and to him they return; and everything that is, fulfils the universal Law. But their language oftentimes seems to distinguish God as a personal, intelligent and righteous Being, above all, beyond all, his works, upholding and ruling them all.

This appears in the great hymn of Cleanthes to Zeus, one of the noblest passages of the earlier Greek Stoicism, which exhibits to us in their highest form a Stoic's thoughts about God.

'Thee it is lawful for all mortals to address. For we are thy offspring, and alone of all living creatures possess a voice which is the image of reason. Therefore I will ever sing thee and celebrate thy power. All this universe rolling round the earth obeys thee, and follows willingly at thy command. Such a minister hast thou in thy invincible hands, the two-edged, flaming, vivid thunderbolt. O King most High, nothing is done without thee, neither in heaven nor on earth, nor in the sea, except what the wicked do in their foolishness. Thou makest order out of disorder, and what is worthless becomes precious in thy sight; for thou hast fitted together good and evil into one, and hast established one law that exists for ever. . . . . Nay but, O Zeus, giver of all things, who dwellest in dark clouds and rulest the thunder, deliver men from their foolishness. Scatter it from their souls, and grant them to obtain wisdom, for by wisdom thou dost rightly govern all things; that being honoured we may repay thee with honour, singing thy works without ceasing, as it is right for us to do. For there is no greater thing than this, either for mortal men or for the Gods, to sing rightly the universal Law.'

Here is something which is at the opposite pole to the doctrine of Epicurus. A righteous power at work in the universe was before the eye of the Stoic; a fortuitous concourse of atoms without reason or law was before the eye of the Epicurean. The latter had nothing but himself to look to or to be bound by; the former, the Stoic, had what he called God. He saw one 'universal Law' pervading and ruling all things and all beings, and that Law, if stern, was righteous, and enjoined virtue on man. To live according to Nature was the Stoic formula. The Epicurean would equally have accepted it. But then his Nature would have been the private particular nature of the individual, with all its faults, flaws, and foibles, its imperious passions and lusts. True, he would do his best, according to the doctrine of his master, to give the higher part of his nature full scope in the conduct of his life. But there would be nothing outside him to help him; nothing above him which could bring to bear any truth on his decisions or moral pressure upon his conduct. To live according to Nature would after all be to do what was right in his own eyes, and it might easily be a very base part of his nature according to which at last he came to live. To the Stoic the word Nature had a much larger and more authoritative meaning. He regarded himself as under a Law that ruled equally men and States, and tides and stars; and the voice of that Law was always sounding in his ears, Virtue is the only good, vice is the only evil, for man. To him Virtue had a sanction, a hold on his conscience and his imagination, which in the case of the rival system it utterly lacked; and accordingly under the Stoic doctrine and discipline we might expect on the whole a very high standard of moral action, and a high tone of moral conduct in the life.

The history of Stoicism justifies the expectation. It contributed altogether the noblest men and the loftiest conduct that we meet with in history, between the martyrdom of Socrates and the preaching of St. Paul. For the Stoic drew from his contemplation of this grand universal Law the conviction that there could be no idlers in the creation. To keep quiet and enjoy was the maxim of Epicurus; the Stoic thought that man was sent here to bestir himself and live. Stoicism contributed its full share of manly upright and fearless characters to the service of humanity. Not that Stoicism was specially favourable to the development of the patriotic passion. Its weakness was that its eye was too constantly bent inwards. The motive of actions was all that it cared about; and to external things it professed itself indifferent. It regarded the multitude as fools, and nursed no small measure of intellectual and spiritual pride. The Stoics formed an aristocracy of wisdom, and a small one; and these features of the system did not much encourage devotion to the public welfare. Their 'apathy,' which they so successfully cultivated, was a defence against evil surroundings, and rather a hindrance than a stimulus to political action, or efforts for reform. Indeed in these days politics amounted simply to 'a battle of kites and crows,' and reform was hopeless. In happier times their idea of the manly life and of the claims of duty might have made them energetic champions of the cause of justice and of liberty; for in evil days they proved themselves able to suffer for this cause with a courage and dignity which have never been surpassed. But public life was, on the whole, a distraction which they avoided; and charity, beneficent thought and work for others, they did not cultivate. Their doctrine about the indifference of outward things made them hard to the appeal of sorrow. 'Who can tell?' they said,—'these evils from which this poor wretch seems to be suffering, may be evils only in appearance; or, if they are real, he should exercise himself to endure.' They had no conception of true benignity in the order of nature. It was all good, they would say, very good, but only to the philosopher, the man who lives according to nature; there is no hope for making things work for good to weaklings and fools. So that all round it was a hard doctrine, and a narrow one; and like the doctrine of Epicurus, it tended to shut man up within himself; though it made him within his narrow circle a much nobler and more useful being. The effort of Stoicism was to make life a fortress, well-armed and guarded; while Epicurus would have made it a garden of delight. The Stoic prided himself on being the soldier of duty, and he had the martial manliness, strength, and dignity in his bearing; he is altogether a more impressive and inspiring figure to look upon than the man who was bent on making pleasure his god.

It is not in Greece that we can see the full form of Stoicism, or estimate its influence on human thought and life. It nursed within it a certain sternness and hardness; it magnified the moral above the intellectual element in Philosophy; it tended more and more as time went on to regard Philosophy as the handmaid of practical conduct; and these were characteristics by no means specially attractive to the bright, acute and mobile Greek, though at the same time the state of the world and the misery of life were driving the later Greeks to the philosophers who could best teach men to endure. There was great intellectual discursiveness in the Greek Stoical School. Chrysippus, who succeeded Cleanthes as the head of the Sect, is said to have written more than any other philosopher; and the Stoic Metaphysics, Psychology, and Cosmology are full of curious interest. They concern themselves with the vexed questions of Philosophy which are in debate in all ages, and are as unsettled still as when Thales first began his quest of philosophical truth. The secret of things is still undiscovered. The 'eureka' of philosopher after philosopher has awakened alternately the hope and the despair of mankind. But the actual philosophizing, the endeavour to discover, is itself a necessary intellectual discipline and is enlarging continually the realm of truth. 'Man is not born,' says Goethe, 'to solve the mystery of existence; but he must nevertheless attempt it, that he may learn how to keep within the limits of the knowable'; and not only that, but that he may continually enlarge the circle of his knowledge, and have clearer light to guide him on his way. But there would be but little profit in studying these speculations in brief, and it will be best to pass them by, especially as it is through its moral theory of life, and its moral influence on man and on society that Stoicism is known to the work-a-day world.

Manifold, however, as was the intellectual activity of the Stoic School in Greece, and able and famous as were many of its teachers, the Stoic type of man and form of life were not Greek at heart, and it is not the Greek who rises before the mind's eye when one talks of Stoicism, and searches into the measure of its influence on mankind. In Greece the Stoic was prophetic; prophetic first of the coming Roman, and then of that which was behind the Roman, Christianity. The Roman type of character from the first was moulded on the Stoic lines. The sternness, the strength, the indomitable endurance of the Roman; his indifference to intellectual speculation or intellectual activity of any sort, his moral dignity, his devotion to duty, and the simplicity of his tastes and habits—which lent a strong tinge to the character of even the degenerate Romans of the Empire—seem to mark out the Roman as the typical Stoic; and accordingly we find that the most famous names and the most pregnant histories in connection with the Stoic doctrine, belong to the Roman world.

It is a common observation that the Romans conquered the Greeks by the sword, while the vanquished overcame their victors by their civilisation, of which Art, Literature, and Philosophy, were the most prominent factors. Through Rome, it is pointed out, Greek civilisation was handed on as a legacy to the Christian world, while at the Renaissance, Greek literature, reintroduced in its original and perfect form, wrought an intellectual revolution in Europe, and

mightily prepared the way for the Reformation. As early
as the days of Scipio Africanus Greek teachers began to
exercise a powerful influence in Rome, and the Stoic philosophy attracted the Roman mind at once. Panætius of
Rhodes, the most eminent Stoic professor of his time, was
the friend and companion of Scipio, and did much to commend Stoicism to the more thoughtful of the ruling class
in the city.   But it must be noted that in Rome Stoicism
somewhat modified its form and changed its dress. The
Roman with his strong sense cared little for the integrity
of the system ; what he wanted was practical help for the
conduct of life, and Roman Stoicism placed the moral part
of the system strongly in the foreground. Of Seneca, for
instance, it has been said, that he should be regarded rather
as a spiritual director than a systematic moralist; his writings
are not dogmatic treatises but moral sermons. Roman
Stoicism was, in fact, the original doctrine largely tempered
by common sense. It was markedly eclectic in its method,
borrowing freely from every school all that seemed profitable for instruction and comfort. Seneca, its most copious
and popular expositor, frequently quotes with approval the
sayings of Epicurus.

This growing tendency of Roman Stoicism to formulate
rules of life, and occupy itself with questions of practical
morals, transformed it more and more into a religion, and
it became the best religion with which, in the decay of the
old beliefs, and before the spread of Christianity, men could
fortify and comfort their hearts. So in the early days of
Imperial Rome the Stoic philosopher became the religious
instructor, the practical adviser, the sick-bed visitor, of the
disciples ; and something like a system of pastoral teaching
and influence became organised on the basis of the Stoical
philosophy among the upper ten thousand of the Roman
world. How thoroughly religious the work of Philosophy

was regarded by the best minds of Rome may be illustrated by a quotation from Seneca's treatise 'On a happy life,' which runs as follows :—

'*Philosophy* is the Art and Law of Life, and it teaches us what to do in all Cases. . . . In Sickness it is as good as a Remedy to us ; for whatsoever eases the Mind, is profitable also to the Body. The *Physician* may prescribe Diet, and Exercise, and accommodate his Rule and Medicine to the Disease ; but 'tis *Philosophy* that must bring us to a contempt of Death, which is the Remedy of all Diseases. In Poverty it gives us Riches, or such a state of Mind, as makes them superfluous to us. It Arms us against all Difficulties. . . . *Philosophy* prompts us to relieve the Prisoner, the Infirm, the Necessitous, the Condemn'd ; to shew the Ignorant their Errors, and rectifie their Affections. It makes us Inspect and Govern our Manners ; it rouses us where we are faint and drowzy ; it binds up what is loose, and humbles in us that which is Contumacious : It delivers the Mind from the Bondage of the Body ; and raises it up to the Contemplation of its Divine Original.' [1]

It is in passages like this that Stoicism seems in a sense prophetic of Christianity.

The main feature of the original Stoic doctrine in its ethical branch was the firm assertion that the mind is the man, and that what happens through the consent of the will is that on which the welfare of the being absolutely depends. The things which are independent of the decisions of the will, which are ordered for a man by a power outside himself,— call it God, or call it fate,—such as health, wealth, comfort, reputation, and all the externals of life, the Stoic taught himself to regard as absolutely indifferent. They made no matter to the man ; through all their vicissitudes he remained untouched and in full possession of the true treasures of his being. How absolutely the Stoic aimed at 'apathy' about the accidents of life, and refused to be moved by them, perhaps the following passage from Epictetus will shew better than any lengthened description :—

'A certain person's son is dead. Answer: the thing is not within

---

[1] Chapter iv., L'Estrange's translation, Lond. 1722, p. 119.

the power of the will; it is not an evil. . . . Cæsar has condemned a person. It is a thing beyond the power of the will, not an evil. The man is afflicted at this. Affliction is a thing that depends on the will; it is an evil. He has borne the condemnation bravely. That is a thing within the power of the will; it is a good. If we train ourselves in this manner we shall make progress. . . . Your son is dead. What has happened? Your son is dead. Nothing more? Nothing. Your ship is lost. What has happened? Your ship is lost. A man has been led to prison. What has happened? He has been led to prison. . . . But Zeus, you say, does not do right in these matters. Why? because he has made you capable of endurance? because he has made you magnanimous? because he has taken from that which befalls you the power of being evils? because it is in your power to be happy while you are suffering what you suffer; because he has opened the door to you, when things do not please you? Man, go out and do not complain.'[1]

This was a very high doctrine indeed—'it is a hard saying, who can hear it,' the disciple of Epictetus might well exclaim, aye, did exclaim—for the teaching had to be considerably toned down to become a working theory of the conduct of life for the Roman world. Epictetus, far more than any Roman Stoic, returned to the ancient Cynic views. He was a Stoic Puritan of the strictest type, and he lived in his life what he taught with his lip; every word with him was sacredly real. This doctrine had to be somewhat modified in actual practice.

The Roman School accordingly discovered that among things which are not good or evil, there are differences of an important kind. There are some which meet a natural want, or conduce to a higher good, or keep the body in health, or leave the mind free for thought, and these things they called 'things to be preferred,' while their contraries were 'things to be avoided'; meanwhile the old term ἀδιάφορα (indifferent) which in the ancient doctrine of the school included them all, was reserved for a much narrower class of things of neutral tint and accidental value. This gave a much larger human interest to the doctrine, and conciliated

<hr>

[1] Bk. III. ch. 8.

many disciples of wealth and position, who might otherwise have been driven away. Seneca was a man of large means and high station; a courtier and the intimate, we will not say the parasite, of tyrants, and in his hands the Stoic doctrine, though its high ideal was maintained, was made more genial and benign than it appeared in the teaching of either Zeno or Epictetus. The figure of Seneca is unquestionably the most familiar, and in a sense the most important, in the Roman Stoic School; and if we knew nothing of him but his writings, we might well accept him as its greatest master. But unfortunately we know too much about his life. We may not select him as the Stoic hero of the decline, because as a man he dishonoured the doctrines which he expounded and defended with so much eloquence and power; but we should be wrong to press on him too hardly, for his lot was cast in evil times, and his part was a peculiarly difficult one. He was rich, cultivated, and famous; in the foremost rank in the foremost city in the world; the friend, the tutor, the counsellor of the Imperial masters of the whole realm of civilisation; it was about as hard for him to live out the Stoic doctrine, as, according to a higher Master than Seneca, it is for a rich man to enter into the Kingdom of God. But still the writer of the apology for the murder of Agrippina by Nero her son, must bear a weight of shame which all his brilliant talent and his lofty ideas and expositions cannot balance, and this forbids our taking him as the typical Stoic in the last great struggle of the heathen Philosophy to bear up against the growing degradation of society. This downward tendency was never so dire as in the age when help was hastening to man from the Eternal King, whom Stoicism dimly discerned behind the veil of visible and sensible existence, and who wears as the most glorious legend on His Crown, 'Mighty to save.' A very homely proverb tells us that it is always darkest before the dawn. Never was heathenism morally so dark, so hopeless, as when God was stretching out His hand to bring to it salvation.

The truly typical Stoic of the first age of the Empire was Epictetus, a man almost as grand as Socrates in moral proportion, as vigorous in moral stamina, though of course unquestionably inferior in intellectual endowment. Epictetus is a figure of unique grandeur in that dissolute and terrible time. A slave of Epaphroditus, a freedman of Nero; lame— it is said that his master broke his leg in wanton frolic— and weak and poor, he maintained through life at Rome, and afterwards, when he was banished by Domitian, at Nico- polis, the noblest and most cheerful independence of circum- stances, the most fearless and loyal devotion to truth, and to the true welfare of all who resorted to him for instruction; and he produced a deeper impression on all who were brought into contact with his teaching, than any philosopher but one whom we meet with in secular history. Men sought his school at Nicopolis from all quarters, and hung upon his words. Like Socrates he wrote nothing. All that we know of him is through his disciples. We learn what an impressive figure he seemed to them, and one of them, Arrian, has preserved and transmitted to us a tolerably full record of his discourses. But, alas! Arrian is not a Plato, and one cannot resist the suspicion that Epictetus would have appeared to us in a much braver form, if we had his own words, or if they had been interpreted to us by a master of Philosophy. Still, the record appears trustworthy as far as it goes, and we must be thankful for what we have. A very strong and impressive individuality looks out upon us through Arrian's discourses of Epictetus, and there is a moral consistency throughout which inspires confidence in the portraiture of the great master which has thus been handed down.

The central principle of the Stoical system of Epictetus

was noble enough and true enough, if men could have certainly known its truth. But, amid the contradictions and wranglings of rival systems and philosophers, what men longed to hear was some clear word of certainty which might carry Heaven's own authority to their consciences and hearts; some word which they would not have to judge but which would judge them, command them, and set them authoritatively about their work. Such a word—a word which had power—was already in the world, and was making its way towards the schools, when Epictetus stated his doctrine. The essence of this doctrine, the supremacy of reason and the kinship of man to God, may be discerned in the following passage:—

'If a man should be able to assent to the doctrine as he ought, that we are all sprung from God in an especial manner, and that God is the father both of men and of gods, I suppose that he would never have any ignoble or mean thoughts about himself. But if Cæsar should adopt you, no one could endure your arrogance; and if you know that you are the son of Zeus, will you not be elated? Yet we do not so; but since these two things are mingled in the generation of man, body in common with the animals, and reason and intelligence in common with the gods, many incline to this kinship which is miserable and mortal; and some few to that other which is divine and happy. The few have no mean or ignoble thoughts about themselves; but with the many, it is quite contrary. For they say, What am I? a poor miserable man, with my wretched bit of flesh. Wretched, indeed; but you possess something better than your bit of flesh. Why then do you neglect that which is better, and why do you attach yourself to the lower?'[1]

Well, this is a very noble principle. You have in you a Divine part, born of God, do not play the beast or slave. But how much does it mean, this doctrine that Zeus is our father? Mr. Capes, in his valuable manual on the Stoical philosophy, speaks of Epictetus as having 'a sense of the Fatherhood of God.'[2] This can only be true in a very partial measure, and the question what the divine Father-

---

[1] Bk. I. ch. 3.　　　　[2] *Stoicism*, Lond. 1880, ch. 12.

hood meant to Epictetus is well worth investigating for a moment, as it will reveal to us the fundamental distinction between the heathen and Christian schools. Epictetus formulated clearly enough the doctrine which was expressed in the hymn of Cleanthes, that we are the offspring of God. He saw plainly that there was that in man which was in the Divine image. So far he was at one with the doctrine of Revelation. He might have read the word, 'Let us make man in our image, after our likeness,' though it is quite clear that he had not. But the knowledge of the doctrine of the Fatherhood is quite different from the sense of the Fatherliness of God. The Jews knew the name, the Chinese knew the name, Epictetus had, as we have seen, a very large and real knowledge of the name. But how much did it mean? That was what man needed sorely to know; and that was never known, that never could be fully known, until One stood upon earth, inspired by such love to man as moved Him to endure a life of sorrow and a death of shame to manifest His love, One who said 'He that hath seen me hath seen the Father.' 'Henceforth ye both know him and have seen him.' It was no new idea to man this indwelling of Deity. Euripides wrote the words

$$\theta\epsilon\grave{o}s \ \gamma\acute{\alpha}\rho \ \tau\iota s \ \acute{\epsilon}\nu \ \acute{\eta}\mu\hat{\iota}\nu.^{1}$$

'Est Deus in nobis,' says Ovid.[2] But what man needed was not the doctrine but the fact of Fatherhood; the Revelation in God of a Father's mind, a Father's care, a Father's love. The Stoic doctrine was an inspiration as far as it went. In natures as profoundly pious and faithful as that of Epictetus, it supplied, there can be no doubt, something very near to the comfort and strength which the Christian derives from the knowledge that God is Love,

---

[1] Quoted by Schol. on Pind. *Nem.* vi. 7.   [2] *Fasti*, vi. 5.

a knowledge revealed in lines of living splendour in the
life and death of the Son of God.

It would be difficult to find in heathen literature anything so much in the Christian key-note of joy in God as
this passage from Epictetus :—

'For if we had understanding, ought we to do anything else both
jointly and severally than to sing hymns and bless the deity, and to
tell of his benefits? Ought we not, when we are digging and ploughing
and eating, to sing this hymn to God? "Great is God who has given
us such implements with which we shall cultivate the earth ; great
is God who has given us hands, the power of swallowing our food, im-
perceptible growth, and the power of breathing while we sleep." This
is what we ought to sing on every occasion, and to sing the greatest
and most divine hymn for giving us the faculty of comprehending
these things and using a proper way. . . . I am a rational creature,
and I ought to praise God; this is my work : I do it, nor will I desert
this post so long as I am allowed to keep it ; and I exhort you to join
in this same song.'[1]

The noble old man had attained, we may think, to a
clearness of understanding or rather vision, which came
very near to the perfect knowledge revealed in the Gospel.
But this knowledge was in Epictetus himself, through the
clearness of his moral sight and his faithfulness to the inward light given to him—' the Light which lighteth every man
that cometh into the world.' He had reached it through
a life-long discipline, such as only he in his times had
courage to endure, but there was nothing in his knowledge
that could become a heritage, a possession forever, to his
fellow men. We must try to grasp the wide distinction
between the knowledge that we are God's offspring which
may be gained by those who in prolonged and devout
meditation ' seek after God if haply they might feel after
him and find him,' and that sure, blessed, inspiring knowledge, not only of the truth of the Fatherhood, but of all
the pity, the tenderness, the help, the guidance, which the

<hr>

[1] Bk. I. ch. 16.

word Father promises to man, and which grows out of the mystery of Redemption—'Hereby perceive we the love of God, because he laid down his life for us.' It was the certainty with which the Gospel spoke, testifying to actual facts as matter of history, which laid such hold upon, and brought such uplifting power to bear on, the world.

On the subject of man's immortality the words of Epictetus are very vague and his knowledge obscure. His doctrine about the Divine spark in man,—'a Divine Spirit hath his seat within us,' writes Seneca—looks strongly in the direction of immortality, and there are passages here and there which seem to imply the hope of a personal conscious existence beyond the tomb. Here is one:—

'Death? Let it come when it chooses, either death of the whole or of a part. Fly, you say. And whither? Can any man eject me out of the world? He cannot. But wherever I go, there is the sun, there is the moon, there are the stars, dreams, omens, and the conversations with Gods.'[1]

But here again is a passage in another and sadder key-note, and this is as a rule the dominant:—

'And if you are not supplied with what is necessary, God gives the signal for retreat, opens the door, and says to you, go. Go whither? To nothing terrible, but to the place from whence you came, to your friends and kinsmen, to the elements; what there was in you of fire, goes to fire; of earth, to earth; of air, to air; of water, to water; no Hades, nor Acheron, nor Cocytus, nor Pyriphlegethon, but all is full of gods and spirits.'[2]

There is nothing here of the inspiring certainty which uplifted the heart even of wretched suffering slaves who had heard the Gospel, and which enabled, not the philosophers, but the poor, sick, ignorant, down-trodden pariahs of society, to cry with a ring of triumphant certainty in their words, 'O death, where is thy sting? O grave, where is thy victory? The sting of death is sin; and the

[1] Bk. III. ch. 24.   [2] Bk. III. ch. 13.

strength of sin is the law. But thanks be to God which giveth us the victory through our Lord Jesus Christ.'

It was the Gospel which taught the workman and the slave to hope, and in so doing re-made human society. And here was the weakness of Stoicism, it had nothing with which it could raise and bless the poor. It could do something for a man of high intelligence and moral energy, though to make him a brave sufferer was about its highest ministry, but it was helpless in face of the great mass of mankind. It had some noble thoughts about a man's duty to his fellows, but how to do this duty it found not. It had nothing to take to them which they could look upon as a gospel, no echo even of the angel-song which heralded the Advent,—'Fear not: for, behold, I bring you good tidings of great joy, which shall be to all people. For unto you is born this day in the City of David a Saviour, which is Christ the Lord.' It was emphatically a doctrine of the upper classes, of the world of culture. The rich, the noble, the learned were called, not the poor. The creed tended to dryness and narrowness, it shut a man up and centred him on self. It had a necessary but fatal tendency to the doctrine of indifference, according to which nothing is worth pursuing, nothing is worth caring about; a belief which impoverishes and in the end contracts the soul.

Epictetus looked coldly on marriage, on the home, on the service of the State. They were all distractions; they multiplied a man's interests and anxieties; Philosophy condemned them. It narrowed a man's nature unspeakably, this hardening process. Cutting off his relations, anxieties, and cares, it cut off his noblest means of culture, and stunted the full development of his life. Christianity multiplies a man's relationships, anxieties, interests, and concerns. Christ's first miracle was at a marriage feast. Industry, commerce, intercourse with and relation to distant peoples, all the play and freedom of secular life, Christianity quickened and consecrated, and it set men at work everywhere helping and blessing their fellow men. It too had its doctrine about Care. Take no 'distracting' thought about food and raiment and the good of this life, for your heavenly Father knoweth that ye have need of all these things. It is not Be careless about them; they are out of the sphere of your will, harden yourself to indifference about them. No. The command is work, toil, give scope to all your energies, multiply your interests and aims, but remember—to free you from distracting thought about them—that your heavenly Father is ruling, and that He cares that you should be clothed and fed. First work— your best, your very best; then trust, and be at peace. This doctrine spread like flame. It keeps the heart warm and glowing; it expands the nature; it multiplies the joys that spring from the full exercise of the powers. This Christian doctrine about Care has played a very large part in the culture of Christendom, and is as full of promise to poor sad souls borne down by their burden, as the Stoic doctrine is depressing and deadening.

A second great flaw in the moral system of the Stoics was its intolerable spiritual pride. The following is a characteristic expression of this on the part of Epictetus :—

'For I wish to be surprised by disease or death when I am looking after nothing else than my own will, that I may be free from perturbation, that I may be free from hindrance, free from compulsion, and in a state of liberty. I wish to be found practising these things that I may be able to say to God, Have I in any respect transgressed thy command? have I in any respect wrongly used the powers which thou gavest me? have I misused my perceptions or my preconceptions? have I ever blamed thee? have I ever found fault with thy administration? I have been sick, because it was thy will, and so have others, but I was content to be sick. I have been poor because it was thy will, but I was content also.'[1]

That could be in no true sense a gospel which presented a man in such an attitude before God and his fellow men. It was the Gospel whose Litany is, 'God be merciful to me a sinner,' which touched man's heart at the depths, and touches it to this day, wherever it is preached throughout the human world.

In conclusion, perhaps the most impressive thing in the discourses of Epictetus, and in the heathen Philosophy of that time, is the note of something like despair which runs through it; not personal despair, but despair of its power to do anything for the world. There is one passage in Epictetus which seems like the last wail of the dying Philosophy, and which may fittingly close this chapter. ' Show me a Stoic,' Epictetus cries :—

'Show me a Stoic if you can. Where or how ? But you can show me an endless number who utter small arguments of the Stoics. For do the same persons repeat the Epicurean opinions any worse ? And the Peripatetic, do they not handle them also with equal accuracy ? Who then is a Stoic ? As we call a statue Phidiac which is fashioned according to the art of Phidias ; so show me a man who is fashioned according to the doctrines which he utters. Show me a man who is sick and happy, in danger and happy, dying and happy, in exile and happy, in disgrace and happy. Show him : I desire, by the gods, to see a Stoic. You cannot show me one fashioned so ; but show me one at least who is forming, who has shown a tendency to be a Stoic. Do me this favour ; do not grudge an old man seeing a sight which I have not seen yet. . . . Let any of you show me a human soul ready to think as God does, and not to blame either God or man, ready not to be disappointed about anything, not to consider himself damaged by anything, not to be angry, not to be envious, not to be jealous ; and why should I not say it direct ? desirous, from a man to become a god, and in this poor mortal body thinking of his fellowship with Zeus. Show me the man. But you cannot.'[2]

And the answer to the despairing cry of the grand old

[1] Bk. III. ch. 5.   [2] Bk. II. ch. 19.

heathen   teacher   comes   from   the   lips   of   the   infant
Church :—

'Therefore being justified by faith, we have peace with God through
our Lord Jesus Christ : by whom also we have access by faith into this
grace wherein we stand, and rejoice in hope of the glory of God. And
not only *so*, but we glory in tribulations also : knowing that tribulation
worketh patience ; and patience experience ; and experience hope : and
hope maketh not ashamed ; because the love of God is shed abroad
in our hearts by the Holy Ghost, which is given unto us.'

III.

MARCUS AURELIUS, AND THE APPROXIMATION OF THE HEATHEN TO THE CHRISTIAN SCHOOLS.

D

III.

MARCUS AURELIUS, AND THE APPROXIMATION OF THE HEATHEN TO THE CHRISTIAN SCHOOLS.

THE most significant feature in the development of the heathen philosophy, as the times drew near the Advent, was its endeavour to supply just the same kind of teaching and influence which Christianity came to offer to the world. Seneca was not so much a philosopher as a preacher of moral sermons; and Philosophy in the Roman era constantly tended to discourse of a moralising kind, imparting wise counsel to the individual man about the varied duties, trials and experiences of life. Its main theme came to be the regulation of life with wisdom and dignity, so as to secure some fair measure of happiness, and of security against distraction and distress.

The Greek philosophers whom the leading Roman families attached to their households in the days of the decline of the Republic and the rise of the Empire, filled something like the place occupied by the domestic chaplain of the great English houses in the last century. Of the almost menial position and treatment which fell to the lot of these chaplains Lord Macaulay gives a graphic picture in his History; this is quite capped, however, by Lucian's description of the treatment of the domestic philosopher in Rome. The Roman noble as a rule kept his philosopher for show, and to give a gloss of culture to his life. Lucian, in one of his bitter satires, pictures him at table, obliged, like the chaplain, to put up with the crumbs of the feast. 'If at any time a pig be cut up, or a venison pasty, you had need have the carver your friend, or you will divide with Prometheus, and nothing but the bones will come to your share.' But probably the chaplain and the philosopher got on the whole as much respect as they deserved. In Rome there was no lack of adventurers who donned the philosopher's cloak, and learnt the mere jargon of the schools, to make a living by attaching themselves to the household of some rich patron; and on such no sympathy need be wasted. Dion Cassius makes Augustus warn Mæcenas against such in the significant words, 'Under the cloak of that profession many knaves bring infinite misfortune on the State as well as on their dupes.' Lucian speaks out more roundly. He charges the professional moralists with being 'greedy of lucre, more passionate than dogs, more cowardly than hares, more lascivious than asses, more thievish than cats, more quarrelsome than cocks.' But there were instances of a very different kind, as, for example, when the younger Cato travelled to Pergamos to persuade the Stoic Athenodorus to enter his household, and entertained him till his death.

More important however than the treatment of these teachers is the place they occupied in the social system, and the function they were expected to fufil. They came to be in Rome a kind of clerical order; limited in number, and moving entirely among the upper ten thousand; but expected to say a phrase in season on the important domestic occasions, and above all to have words of consolation for the dying. There is an amusing tale of one Favorinus who was discoursing to his class, when he heard that the wife of one of his former pupils, a man of wealth and station, had been delivered of a son. He proposed that they should go to congratulate her. So off they went. Introduced to the lady's mother the professor inquired after her health. Then he expressed a hope that she suckled her child; and when the mother answered that she was not strong enough, he preached her a little sermon, nay, it was a long one, on the duty of the mother to her offspring, and denounced roundly the new artificial habits. So we see the kind of change which had come over the spirit of Philosophy, and the ideas and habits of the philosopher. 'If a man is well to do,' says Dion Chrysostom, 'he is too happy to give Philosophy a thought. But let him lose his fortune or his health, he will be the more ready to listen then; let his wife or his son or his brother die, then he will send for the sage to comfort him, and to teach him how to bear so much misfortune.' Especially was he expected at the couch of the dying. In those death scenes of some of the noblest men and women of Rome sacrificed to the jealousies and antipathies of the Imperial tyrants, which Tacitus paints with such graphic power, the figure of the philosopher, comforting and sustaining the martyr in his last hours, is rarely absent; and so common was it that Stoics should frequent the houses of sorrow and the chambers of death, that a rich upstart is pictured by Petronius as directing his servants that 'when his time draws near no ghostly counsels are to vex his peace of mind, and no philosopher is to be admitted to his bed of death.'

Very interesting too are the accounts which have come down to us of the schools of the philosophers, which carried on the culture of society during the generations in which Christianity was winning its way to supremacy. Pericles tells the Athenians in his celebrated funeral oration, that Athens was a sort of school of Greece. His words were prophetic; Athens remained the head quarters of philosophical culture, the chief University city of the Empire, for many hundred years. The philosophical schools continued to furnish instruction under a series of teachers, who seem to have followed each other with wonderful regularity, and with an entire absence of contention—the aged head of the school mostly designating his successor, who would take his place in the chair by universal consent, in a spirit of devotion to a sacred duty not always apparent in the Episcopal successions of the Christian Church. The attendance of students was large; more like that at the mediæval universities, where the students were reckoned by tens of thousands, than the Universities of our more modern days. We hear of one Theophrastus who had 2000 students. And they seem to have been very like the students of these present times. The student type is evidently a very persistent one. Town and gown riots were common, practical jokes on the freshmen were not unknown. The various nations had their clubs, and banquets were kept up with great zeal in honour of the founders of the schools. Serious conflicts seem to have been carried on by the students of rival professors, that is the professors of rival schools, for within the school there was no rivalry. Libanius, a celebrated teacher of the 4th century, taunts his pupils that they were not like others whom he had seen, who had wounds on the head and face and hands, sure evidence of the love they bore their tutors, as great as their love for their parents. 'But you,' he adds, disdainfully, 'what service of this sort on my behalf can any of you point to? what risk or blow encountered, or what bold word or look? Nay far from that you run away to other teachers, taking your fees with you; and so rob one professor while you pay court to another.'

It would be easy to retail pleasant gossip about the school of Athens,[1] but the subject has a graver interest for our present purpose. There was a very lofty tone of moral discipline in the schools, that had something of the elevation

---

[1] See Capes, *University Life in Ancient Athens*, Lond. 1877.

of the teaching of the great masters, which we have noted so conspicuously in Epictetus. Philosophy was aiming at a moral regeneration of society; it saw dimly enough that that was the one thing needful. Its society was a very limited clique in the great world; and its salvation was at root but a pedant's dream. And yet it occupied a very definite and important place in the great scheme of human development. It awakened a keen desire which it could not satisfy, and like the friars of St. Francis at a later age, it created a thirst for a living gospel. It was not at heart antagonistic to Christianity; it cleared and laid bare the field for the sower of the living germs of the truth. Clemens Alexandrinus says that God had three covenants with men, the covenant of the Law, the covenant of Philosophy, and the covenant of the Gospel. And there is deep truth in this; inasmuch as God's ordinance for the heathen world that it should 'seek the Lord, if haply they might feel after him and find him,' was as essential though not so visible a step in His education of the world, as the giving of the Law. The Law in one way, Philosophy in another, laid bare the great want of humanity, a power from heaven to heal, to quicken, and to save. 'What the Law could not do, in that it was weak through the flesh,' God accomplished by the Gospel. And so with equal truth we may say that what the wisdom of the wise could not do, in that it was weak through its inability to lay hold on the will in man, the Gospel accomplished, and redeemed them who were 'under Philosophy,' sighing for the redemption, as well as them who were 'under the Law,' watching and waiting for the salvation of Israel. Philosophy led the world up to the point where it could lead it no longer, and with mute voice invoked the help of a higher hand.

Aulus Gellius paints a very striking portrait of Taurus, a philosopher at Athens in the 2nd century, about the time

of Marcus Aurelius, who seems to have devoted much thought
and care to this pastoral oversight of the lads committed to
his charge.

He was 'not content with formal lectures, but did his best to form
the character of his young friends by personal converse ; chatting with
them at his bedroom door when they had walked home with him from
lecture, travelling with them sometimes in the country, taking long
walks to see them when he heard that they were sick, and whiling
away their weariness with pleasant talk, in which the serious mingled
with the gay. If he asked his pupils to his table, he did not care to
tempt the appetite with costly viands ; but the simple fare of pudding
or of salad was seasoned with Attic salt, and his guests were happier
and wiser when they left him. He had a way of delicately hinting
that a fault might be mended or a bad habit dropped, which served
its end while it spared his hearer's self-respect. Yet Taurus was no
easy-going teacher with a standard easily attained. He liked to tell
his faithful friends the story of Euclides who braved death to hear
Socrates, his friend and guide, when it was penal for one of Megara to
enter Athens ; whereas now-a-days, he said, philosophers must often
wait till their pupils have recovered from the wine-party of the night
before.

'He reproached them also for their want of earnestness and depth ;
told them that they wanted to pick and choose, to gather here a thought
and there a hint,' somewhat as lecturers now-a-days complain that
undergraduates are too practically minded, and read not for the sake
of knowledge but a class.'[1]

This glance at the spirit of the philosophical teachers in
the early generations of the Christian era, is a fit introduction
to the philosophy of Marcus Aurelius, in which we can trace
very clearly indeed the approximation of the heathen to the
Christian Schools. Marcus Aurelius is the conspicuous example of the tendency to those modes of thinking, feeling,
and living, which brought heathenism as near as in its own
strength and wisdom it could come to Christianity. For
however strong may be our desire to do full justice to the
heathen striving, however keen our admiration for the essential nobleness of many a heathen life of that time, however
firm our conviction that this Stoical philosophy, with its lofty

<hr>

[1] *University Life in Ancient Athens*, p. 48 f.

moral aim was not without Divine guidance, we cannot hide from ourselves the conclusion that there was nothing widely quickening in it; it was really, though in a high sense, pedantic; it needed culture to understand and practise it; and after all it was but a limited human gospel. There was the human boundary line about it everywhere, and not only that, but the scholar's boundary line, which left necessarily the great mass of the toiling, suffering poor quite outside its pale. Not that this was intentional. Seneca has some very noble thoughts about our duty to the ignorant and wretched; Epictetus speaks in a still more robust and generous tone; Marcus Aurelius, as we shall see, has almost Christian thought for the great mass of the poor. The philosophers did their utmost, though they never felt, never with their views could feel, that passion for the poor which fired the heart of a Christian apostle. The essential weakness, in the long run and on a large scale, of the philosophers' salvation of society, is that it works from the height downwards and never reaches far; the Christian regeneration works from the depth upwards, and permeates society.

This is the fatal incapacity of the wisdom of the wise to work a reformation; it has no hold on the hearts of men. The philosophers who tried the last grand experiment in the days of the Cæsars made clear the truth for all time; our philosophers in these days are repeating their attempt, and will meet with the same failure.

Marcus Aurelius was the Stoic thinker in whom this more benign and ministrant aspect of Philosophy was most conspicuous, and this makes him the link of connection between the heathen and the Christian schools. The Greek in the days of Pericles had been very well content with his life: it was full of free and joyful activity. The masterpieces of art were continually under his eye; the masterpieces of literature were continually in his ear; the conduct of an empire, which was making the brightest page written till then in the world's history, occupied his understanding; and all the cheerful surroundings of Athens gladdened his life. The Roman of the age of Nero and Domitian was not content with his life. The world had known some ages of miserable strife and sorrow since the bright days of Pericles; and it had woke up to the conviction that on the whole it was a sad world, a prey to grievous and continually increasing ills. Man began to find his own body with its lusts and passions a burden and a curse to him—Persius, the Stoic satirist, has the phrase 'accursed flesh.' The world under the terrible tyranny of the earlier Cæsars had learnt to tremble at its future; everywhere in the individual man and in society at large there was the growing feeling that the world was in evil case. It was redemption, restoration from ruin, life from death, which Christianity brought to it. But no one can read much in the literature of those times without hearing a kind of wailing cry running through all its deeper passages. And Philosophy modified its tone in response. There was a growing recognition in its teachings that man was a being who needed to be helped, strengthened, and comforted; that he was not sufficient to himself, and that his life was not sufficient to satisfy him; that somehow and from some source help must be brought to him, in what was becoming his sore and bitter need. When Seneca in dying begged his physician to bring him a draught of the poison which he had long kept by him in store, it reveals the depth of the distress and need; and accordingly in Seneca and Epictetus we recognise a kind of yearning compassion for the sorrows and the sins of men, quite foreign to the spirit of the earlier Schools. Seneca ate with his slaves, and did his best to lighten their lot, but they were slaves still, and his Stoic phrases must have sounded somewhat hollow in their ears. Epictetus recognised earnestly the sin and the misery around him, and there are some tender passages of compassion in his writings ; but his doctrine that the wise man should find nothing painful in inevitable calamity, took the strength out of his efforts at ministry. His only cure for the sin was Philosophy, and for the sorrow a discipline which would make men indifferent to its pangs. 'The heart of man must something love.' For want of something to love in that invisible sphere into which he was straining his sight, the life of man was growing sad and poor. It was the love of God which would save it.

Marcus Aurelius seems to have been nearer to this truth than any other heathen thinker, and he carried up to the highest point that yearning and aspiration of heathendom which was met and satisfied by the Gospel. He was by no means so deep or so strong a thinker as Epictetus. But two very eventful generations had passed since that most robust and vehement of philosophers had longed passionately, but in vain, to see a true Stoic at Nicopolis. The world on the whole had got sadder and more in need of help; and the hearts of great thinkers had got more pitiful, more disposed to bring a helpful, healing hand to bear, if possible, on the maladies and miseries of society. The Empire too had been in existence for near two centuries. The *pax Romana*, though a very clumsy and brutal parody of the peace of which the fond hearts of prophets and poets had dreamed, had at any rate given men some rest from ceaseless and wasteful wars. And not only that, it had brought distant peoples into intimate relations, and had developed those domestic interests and associations between men, families, and communities, such as a long peace only can generate. Men were searching into their relations with each other, their duties to each other, with the idea to inspire them, that brotherhood and not enmity was the normal relation of mankind. And a state of thought and feeling was created which inevitably found utterance by the lips of the philosophers, and brought to the front those questions, those conditions and needs of society, which Christianity discerned to be fundamental.

Marcus Aurelius, although as a thinker he lacked the force of Epictetus, had some graces of disposition and charms of character which the robuster natures miss. He was one of the purest, gentlest, and most conscientious of men; a perfect martyr to duty, a constant censor of himself, and minister to all around. If he was not born in the purple, he was carefully educated for the throne. Early adopted by the Emperor Antoninus Pius as heir to the Empire, he was trained with the most vigilant care for his high duties, under the eye of the Emperor, a wise and upright ruler, and under the hand of the ablest men in Rome. In truth, perhaps he was a little overtrained. As seems to have been the case with Mr. John Stuart Mill, his nature was somewhat narrowed and cramped by the excessive culture of his intellect, and the consciousness of the vast importance of his dispositions and actions, which was kept constantly before his sight. It is possible to have too much even of conscientiousness. It may be so morbidly active as to destroy the healthy balance and the free play of the powers. Some of Dr. Arnold's 6th form boys went up from Rugby to the Universities staggering beneath a weight of conscious conscientiousness which was a little too heavy for them, and anticipated too soon the weightier burdens of life. So with Marcus Aurelius, there is an almost painful sense of anxiety about the discharge of his duties, which somewhat interfered with the freedom and fulness of his life. Perhaps Fortune shewed a touch of her irony in calling him to a throne. His heart was in the schools. His delight was meditation; but as Emperor Fate called him to a life of constant and most critical action; in which, even in the camp, he played his part with singular wisdom and dignity; though there was always a little too much self-consciousness, a little too much thought how this and that would become a philosopher.

His teachers were numerous and able, and his gratitude to them was warm and profound. But there were too many of them, and they helped to overweight his life. ' From my grandfather Verus,' he says, ' I learned good morals and the government of my temper. From the reputation and remembrance of my father, modesty and a manly character. From my mother piety and beneficence, and abstinence not only from evil deeds but from evil thoughts, and, further, simplicity in my way of living, far removed from the habits of the rich.' Then he goes on to give a long list of his instructors and a very methodical, a too methodical, account of what he learned from each. There was his great grandfather; there was his governor from whom among other things he learned ' endurance of labour, and to want little, and to work with my own hands, and not to meddle with other people's affairs, and not to be ready to listen to slander.'[1] Then follow Diognetus, Bacchius, Tandasis, and Marcianus, who were his chief instructors in Philosophy. Then from Rusticus he learned that his character required improvement and discipline, and many other things, among them, happily, to abstain from fine writing; and he made him acquainted with the writings or rather Memorials of Epictetus. Then follows Apollonius who taught him freedom of will and undeviating steadiness of purpose, and to look to nothing else, not even for a moment, except to reason ; Sextus taught him a benevolent disposition ; Alexander the grammarian to abstain from fault finding. From Fronto he learnt that those who are called Patricians are rather deficient in paternal affection—much as amongst us those who are called Christians are often sadly deficient in Christianity ; then follow Alexander the Platonist, and Catulus, and his brother Severus, with Thrasea, Helvidius, Cato, Dion, and Brutus, from whose lives and recorded words he learned ' the idea of a polity in which there is the same law for all, a polity

<hr>

[1] *Meditations,* I. 1—5.

administered with regard to equal rights and equal freedom of speech, and the idea of a kingly government which respects most of all the freedom of the governed.'   Then Maximus, and last of all his father by adoption, Antoninus Pius, the Master of the Roman world.[1]

This long list of names explains much in Marcus Aurelius. A man who could thus map out his intellectual and moral career and trace each feature to its parent, redistributing among the crowd of teachers the gifts which they had bestowed, must have had in him an almost morbid habit of constant introspection which would interfere in no small measure with the natural unfolding of the character.   It gave him a certain scholastic not to say pedantic habit of thought and action, which makes one think that he would have been a larger, stronger man, and more helpful to his times, if he had studied and moralised a little less, and lived a little more.   But be this as it may, we have in the thoughts of Marcus Aurelius the revelation of a mind singularly honest and capable; largely cultivated; tender and pitiful, pious and devoted to duty.   In many ways he reminds us rather of some great mediæval saint than any man of classical antiquity whose words have come down to us; though through the poverty and uncertainty of his beliefs, and the negative character of his Stoic discipline, we miss utterly the force and the fire with which a Benedict or a Bernard acted on the world.   But in spite of this limitation he seems to carry to a higher point and nearer to the Christian faith the great religious ideas which we have already drawn from the works of Epictetus, and which formed the basis of the teaching of Seneca and the Roman Stoic School.

In the first place, as to his belief in God, which is the fundamental belief of the soul.   There is a yet higher strain in these words of Marcus Aurelius than in those of Epictetus:—

------

[1] *Meditations*, I. 5—14.

'To go from among men, if there are gods, is not a thing to be afraid of, for the gods will not involve thee in evil ; but if indeed they do not exist, or if they have no concern about human affairs, what is it to me to live in a universe devoid of gods or devoid of Providence. But indeed they do exist, and do care for human things ; and they have put all the things in man's power to enable him not to fall into real evils.'[1]

Again :—

' Love the art, poor as it may be, which thou hast learned, and be content with it ; and pass through the rest of life like one who has intrusted to the gods with his whole soul all that he has, making thyself neither the tyrant nor the slave of any man.'[2]

Still higher is the following :—

' Live with the gods. And he does live with the gods who constantly shews to them that his own soul is satisfied with that which is assigned to him, and that it does all that the demon wishes which Zeus hath given to every man for his guardian and guide, a portion of himself.'[3]

And this perhaps crowns the whole :—

' To those who ask where hast thou seen the gods or how dost thou comprehend that they exist, and so worshippest them, I answer in the first place that they may be seen even with the eyes ; in the second place neither have I seen my own soul, and yet I honour it. Thus then with respect to the gods, from what I constantly experience of their power, from this I comprehend that they exist and I venerate them.'[4]

In these passages there is something which in the attitude of the soul, in the belief, in the aspiration, is a clear approximation to the Christian piety, which was kindled and nourished by what it knew of God.

The next point in which there is an approach to the Christian view is the deep conviction which he cherishes of the goodness of the order of the world. Take these words of Epictetus :—' But what says Zeus ? Epictetus, if it were possible I would have made your little body and your little property free and not exposed to hinderance. . . . But since I am not able to do for you what I have mentioned, I have given you a small portion of "us."'[5] This is the underlying

<hr>

[1] *Meditations*, II. 11.   [2] *Ibid.*, IV. 31.   [3] *Ibid.*, V. 27.
[4] *Ibid.*, XII. 29.   [5] Bk. I. ch. 1.

thought of the philosophy of Epictetus. Always there is the haunting shadow—a necessity of things which limits the divine beneficence, and makes this a world in which man must always be on his defence against hostile powers. He breaks out into the most noble and beautiful utterances, not of contentment only but of joy in God, and in all the mercies with which He had crowned his life. But, always, as has been said, there is the haunting shadow; the presence of something around us in life which is evil and hostile, and from which Philosophy is our only shield.

Well, there is the same haunting shadow at times in the thoughts of Marcus Aurelius, at times there are utterances of almost despair, and even references to the 'open door' of suicide. But on the whole Aurelius has the calmest confidence in the goodness of the order of the world. So good indeed he is sure it is, so entirely under the hand of a benignant Deity, that he is confident that all the woes and wrongs of life, and even death itself, cannot be evils, since God allows them to exist within the sphere of His benign and righteous reign.

'Nothing is evil that is according to nature.'[1]

'If the gods have determined about me and about the things which must happen to me, they have determined well; for it is not easy even to imagine a Deity without forethought; and as for doing me harm, why should they have any desire towards that? for what advantage would result from this to them or to the whole, which is the special object of their providence? But if they have not determined about me individually, they have certainly determined about the whole at least, and the things which happen by way of sequence in this general arrangement, I ought to accept with pleasure and be content with them. ... But if however the gods determine about none of the things which concern us, I am able to determine about myself, and I can enquire about that which is useful; and that is useful to every man which is conformable to his own constitution and nature.'[2]

In this conception of the whole as good and under wise and righteous guidance we see very clearly the bending of.

<hr>

[1] *Meditations*, II. 17.   [2] *Ibid.*, VI. 44.

the heathen mind to the truth, which to him was still in all its greatness and glory veiled. 'O Lord, how manifold are thy works! in wisdom hast thou made them all.' 'All thy works shall praise thee, O Lord; and thy saints shall bless thee.'

A third point in which we can trace in Marcus Aurelius the approximation of which we are speaking, is in his conception of his duty to man, and of the true bond of humanity, brotherhood—an idea which had dawned on the mind of cultivated heathendom, mainly through the relations which Rome had established between distant and once alien peoples, but which had become a very vital idea to thinkers like Marcus Aurelius. Take this as a specimen of the way in which he handles the subject :—

'For nothing is so productive of elevation of mind as to be able to examine methodically and truly every object which is presented to thee in life, and always to look at things so as to see at the same time what kind of universe this is, and what kind of use everything performs in it, and what value everything has with reference to the whole, and what with reference to man, who is a citizen of the highest city, of which all other cities are but families.'[1]

This will not fail to recall the words of a yet greater teacher, 'For our citizenship is in heaven.' 'A city which hath foundation, whose builder and maker is God.'

The following seems set in a very noble key :—

'Begin the morning by saying to thyself, I shall meet with the busy-body, the ungrateful, arrogant, deceitful, envious, unsocial. All these things happen to them by reason of their ignorance of what is good and evil. But I who have seen the nature of the good that it is beautiful, and of the bad that it is ugly, and the nature of him that does wrong that it is akin to me, not only of the same blood or seed, but that it participates in the same intelligence and the same portion of the divinity, I can neither be injured by any of them, for no one can fix on me what is ugly, nor can I be angry with my kinsman nor hate him. For we are made for co-operation, like feet, like hands, like eyelids, like the rows of the upper and lower teeth. To act

[1] *Meditations*, III. 11.

E

against one another then is contrary to nature; and it is acting against one another to be vexed and to turn away.'[1]

Again :—

'Consider that a good disposition is invincible, if it be genuine; and not an affected smile or acting a part. For what will the most violent man do to thee, if thou continuest to be of a kind disposition towards him, and if as opportunity offers thou gently admonishest him and calmly correctest his errors at the very time when he is trying to do thee harm, saying, not so, my child; we are constituted by nature for something else : I shall certainly not be injured, but thou art injuring thyself, my child. . . . And thou must do this not as if thou wert lecturing him, nor yet that any bystanders may admire; but either when he is alone. . . .'[2]

Now this is no new doctrine in Philosophy. Socrates lays it down in a noble passage, that the man who does the wrong is the injured person, not the man who suffers it. But here there is a tenderness in the tone, and a delicacy in the mode of rebuke which remind one, more than any other mere heathen utterance, of the words of our Lord.

A passage in the 11th book of the *Meditations* on Schism is in true accord with the doctrine of St. Paul.

Here then we have a body of teaching of very noble tone and very pure and lofty spirit. Nothing in a higher key than these thoughts of Marcus Aurelius has issued from the heathen world. And it is clear that the passages quoted represent his matured convictions at his best moments. They would not however give a faithful picture of Marcus Aurelius as a Stoic philosopher, unless there were added for comparison some passages in which the fatal uncertainty and despondency of all heathen thought appears.

'Shortlived are both the praiser and the praised, and the rememberer and the remembered, and all this in a nook of this part of the world : and not even here do all agree, no, not any one with himself; and

<hr>

[1] *Meditations*, II. 1.   [2] *Ibid.*, XI. 18.

the whole earth too is a point.'[1] 'Such as bathing appears to thee—oil, sweat, dirt, filthy water, all things disgusting—so is every part of life and every thing.'[2] 'Generally wickedness does no harm at all to the universe; and particularly the wickedness of one man does no harm to another. It is only harmful to him who has it in his power to be released from it, as soon as he shall choose.'[3]

About immortality he utters an uncertain sound; but none can study his thoughts without perceiving how frequently his mind was busy with the subject of death. Very noble and confident is this passage :—

'How can it be that the gods after having arranged all things well and benevolently for mankind, have overlooked this alone that some men, and very good men, and men who as we may say, have had most communion with the divinity, and through pious acts and religious observances have been most intimate with the divinity, when they have once died should never exist again, but should be completely extinguished?'[4]

But then we have such sentences as these :—

'About death ; whether it is a dispersion, or a resolution into atoms, or annihilation, it is either extinction or change.'[5] 'That which has died falls not out of the universe. If it stays here it also changes here, and is dissolved into its proper parts, which are elements of the universe and of thyself. And these too change and they murmur not.'[6]

And :—

'What means all this? Thou hast embarked, thou hast made the voyage, get out, thou art come to shore. If indeed to another life, there is no want of gods not even there. But if to a state without sensation, thou wilt cease to be held by pains and pleasures, and to be a slave in the vessel, which is as much inferior as that which serves it is superior; for the one is intelligence and deity, the other is earth and corruption.'[7] 'Near is thy forgetfulness of all things, and near the forgetfulness of thee by all.'[8]

And there is this amid much else on suicide :—

'If men do not permit thee, then get away out of life, yet so as if thou wert suffering no harm. The house is smoky, and I quit it. Why dost thou think that this is any trouble ?'[9]

[1] *Meditations*, VIII. 21. [2] *Ibid.*, VIII. 24. [3] *Ibid.*, VIII. 55.
[4] *Ibid.*, XII. 5. [5] *Ibid.*, VII. 32. [6] *Ibid.*, VIII. 18.
[7] *Ibid.*, III. 3. [8] *Ibid.*, VII. 21. [9] *Ibid.*, V. 29.

These extracts will suffice to shew that the uncertainty of knowledge and the miseries of life sometimes mastered him, and led him to give forth an uncertain sound about the great realities of being with which every man has supremely to do. This wavering doctrine of a solitary thinker, however clear at times his intuitions, and however pure and noble his life, could be no gospel to his fellow sinners and fellow sufferers, from whose doubt and anguish the cry for aid was already rising into the ear of heaven.

But now, in closing, let me quote a few of the very deep and beautiful sayings with which the book of his *Meditations* is gemmed, and in many of which we find a truly wonderful likeness to some of the most notable sayings of the Scriptures.

'Since it is possible that thou mayest depart from life this very moment, regulate every act and thought accordingly.'

'Do not act as if thou wert going to live 10,000 years. Death hangs over thee, while thou livest, while it is in thy power, be good.'

'As physicians always have their instruments and knives ready for cases which suddenly require their skill, so do thou have principles ready for the understanding of things divine and human, and for doing everything, even the smallest, with a recollection of the bond which unites the divine and human to one another. For neither wilt thou do any thing well which pertains to man without at the same time having a reference to things divine, nor the contrary.'

'The art of life is more like the wrestler's art than the dancers, in respect of this, that it should stand ready and firm to meet onsets which are sudden and unexpected.'

'For there is one universe made up of all things, and one God who pervades all things, and one substance, and one law   .   .   and one truth.'

'And who has told thee that the gods do not aid us in things which are in our power. Begin then to pray for such things and thou shalt see. The man prays thus, how shall I have that pleasure? Do then pray thus, how shall I not desire to have it.   .   .   .   Turn thy prayers this way, and see what comes.'

'The voice ought to be plainly written on the forehead,   .   .   .   the good and simple and benevolent shew all these things in the eyes, and there is no mistaking.'

'God sees the minds of all men bared.'

There is a sad dignity about the last words of the book. Speaking to a man surprised by death and who says, I have not finished the five acts, but only three of them, he answers :—

'Thou sayest well, but in life the three acts are the whole drama. For what shall be a complete drama is determined by him who once was the cause of its composition, and now of its dissolution. But thou art the cause of neither. Depart then satisfied, for he also who releases thee is satisfied.'

With these sad but patient words we will bid the most gentle, the most benign, the most conscientious, the most Christian of heathen philosophers farewell.

IV.

WHY COULD NOT THE STOIC REGENERATE SOCIETY?

IV.

WHY COULD NOT THE STOIC REGENERATE SOCIETY?

No earnest and sympathetic student of the ancient pagan philosophies can be blind to the gradual approximation of the heathen to the Christian schools in the age of the Advent. This approximation becomes more marked towards the close of the first, and during the second century, when Christianity had already put forth its regenerating power, mainly but not exclusively in the lowest stratum of Roman society. Seneca exhibits an enormous advance, measured by the moral standard, on Zeno, Cleanthes, and Chrysippus, as well as on Panaetius, by whom the Stoic doctrine was first made popular in Rome. But Epictetus exhibits an advance even on Seneca, and Marcus Aurelius on both. The improvement is not in facility, fecundity, or strictly philosophical power. The later Stoics show no tendency to walk in the steps of Chrysippus, and to put forth many and profound philosophical treatises about all things on earth and in heaven. They were, as we have seen, increasingly disposed to confine themselves to moral reflections and exhortations. They tried, in short, though all unconscious of the magnitude and universality of the need, to supply the kind of pastoral care and oversight, which God was providing, not for the favoured few only, but for the great mass of the poor, the ignorant, and the wretched, in the ministry of the Christian Church.

Their ideas, moreover, on many of the most important

subjects of human knowledge were startlingly like the ideas which the Gospel was about to make the common property of mankind. There is no need to recapitulate the argument of the preceding lectures, or to requote the array of passages in which this approximation to Christian ideas is conspicuous. In some of these passages the likeness to texts of Scripture is, not considerable, but complete. 'If you imitate the gods,' writes Seneca, 'confer benefits even on the unthankful; for the sun rises even on the wicked, and the seas are open to pirates.' 'God sees the minds of all men bared,' says Marcus Aurelius, 'consider thyself to be dead, and to have completed thy life up to the present time, and live according to Nature the remainder which is allowed thee.' So, too, Epictetus, 'When you have shut the doors and made darkness within, remember never to say that you are alone, for you are not; but God is within, and your Dæmon is within, and what need of light have they to see what you are doing. To this God you ought to swear an oath, just as the soldiers do to Cæsar.'

In these passages and in others previously quoted we have a body of very pure and lofty doctrine, that is thoroughly Christian up to a certain point in its ruling ideas;—Man the son of God, and bound therefore to live nobly after the fashion of God, and not after the fashion of the brutes; Man surrounded by God with benedictions, mercies new every morning, faithfulness every night, and bound to bear cheerfully life's burdens and trials and to be ever in a mood not to moan but to praise: Man, too, embraced in the bonds of a universal brotherhood, all men having within them a portion of the divine nature, and therefore in the noblest sense brethren; all men constrained by these cords of love to regard themselves as limbs of the great human body, so that in ministering to their fellow men they are seeking their own, as well as their brothers' good!

We note, further, that this approximation to Christian teaching is distinctly the result of a development. Something passed over, or rather through, the heart of society in that first century, which drew the thinkers in the direction of Christian ideas, and at least prepared the way wondrously for the Gospel. Generation by generation, as the Advent drew near, men devoted themselves more and more to these practical questions concerning personal duty, conduct and destiny, questions which the Gospel would press with irresistible force on human hearts, as the first stage of a regeneration of society through all its spheres. When the Church was already founded, and was quietly winning its way upwards from the lowest stratum of society, where its first work was mainly done, the utterances of the philosophers grow more Christian in tone; their ideas about God, about man, about prayer, about praise, about duty, about the human brotherhood, become saturated with the Christian spirit, until in the last great heathen thinker, Marcus Aurelius, there is the following passage about the relation of one member of the great body of human society to another, which it is hard to believe was not taken bodily from the Epistles of St. Paul:—

'Just as it is with the members in those bodies which are united in one, so it is with rational beings which exist separate, for they have been constituted for one co-operation. And the perception of this will be more apparent to thee, if thou often sayest to thyself that I am a member of the system of rational beings.'[1]

This is clearly the doctrine of the Apostle, 'we are members one of another.'

We call Marcus Aurelius the last great heathen thinker; but it is curious and interesting to note how the pagan Stoic philosophy was revived again in the sixth century in the poem of Boethius, concerning whom it is quite an open question whether he was Christian at all. His

[1] *Meditations*, VII. 13.

'*Consolation of Philosophy*' exercised a very profound influence upon the thought and feeling of nascent Christendom; it furnishes the basis of some of the deepest and most pregnant utterances of our own Alfred the Great, who translated the work and enlarged it with most beautiful and powerful thoughts of his own; and it has lent a strong tincture to the literature of mediæval society. It was the last work dealing with Greek philosophy, prior to the breaking up of the Empire, which stayed the study of the literature of Greece for nearly a thousand years. The last voice which sounded from the old classical civilisation through the thousand years during which Western Christendom was growing to its manhood, was that of this very noble teacher of the Stoic School. Through Boethius, accordingly, Stoicism has become an appreciable factor in the thought of Christendom, and carries on the ancient philosophy into the life of the modern world.

What are we to say to these things,—to this Christianisation, up to a certain point, of heathen philosophy? The first question concerns the true origin of this influence. The point has been very keenly debated, whether this development of heathen philosophy in the Christian direction was not due directly to Christianity. Had not Seneca, Epictetus, and Marcus Aurelius some knowledge of the Gospel; of the truths which it revealed, the duties which it inculcated, and the hopes which it inspired? It has been contended very strenuously that this must have been the case, or such startling repetitions—for they are almost such—of sentences in the Gospels could not have been found in the utterances of the heathen schools. Seneca, it is said, for the likeness is perhaps most conspicuous in his writings, must have seen and heard St. Paul, or studied his Epistles, and hence the striking analogies which may be traced.

It is, however, very doubtful indeed whether any such relation between the Stoics of the Empire and the teaching of Revelation can be established. The temptation is very strong to suspect it; but the more the matter is looked into the less likely does the connection appear. The kind of likeness, if it is to be accounted for in this way, would imply a most thorough study of Revelation, and in that case a much larger proof of indebtedness would appear. The philosophers could not have borrowed a few phrases and a few ideas without borrowing much more. For it is most important to note that these Christian adumbrations do not appear anywhere as intrusive elements in an uncongenial system. They are not like borrowed ornaments stuck on, but are thoroughly welded into the system which they adorn; it is all homogeneous. The whole must have been borrowed, or none, and that the whole was not borrowed appears to be established with absolute certainty by the fact that there is no hint about so vitally important a feature of the Christian scheme as the Resurrection; no recognition in any shape of the great historic facts on which Christianity rested its claim, and from which it drew its power. We must hold it to be impossible that men of such candour and probity as the Stoic teachers could have drawn this precious teaching from the Gospels, without acknowledging the source of their inspiration; and equally impossible that they should have spoken with such bitterness of the Christians, if they had had the faintest suspicion that truths so like their own, and yet so much larger and deeper, were to be found in the Christian books.

These negative considerations seem to be really decisive of the question. That the Stoic owes nothing directly to the Christian, may be regarded as established; and this is further confirmed by the fact that these apparently

Christian utterances can be traced as the legitimate development of the principles of the philosophy, and find foreshinings in the earliest doctrine of the School. That hymn of Cleanthes to Zeus is really in the same key with the doctrine of Epictetus. There is no evidence anywhere that the Stoic writers had ever come across the Christian or Jewish Scriptures, while there are abundant traces in the poets and historians, as well as in the philosophic treatises of the time, of a growth of the thoughts and the sentiments of men towards the Christian view of man's life, and of God.

Upon the supposition, again, that the Stoical philosophy, that is the best thought of the heathen mind, was deeply indebted to the truths of Revelation, it is impossible to account for the fact that some of the very best emperors, including the most Christian thinkers of the Stoic School, were persecutors. Marcus Aurelius speaks in one place with bitterness of the Christians. He is describing the attitude of a man who is ready to live or to die—but, he adds, 'let this readiness come from a man's own judgment, not from mere obstinacy as with the Christians; but considerately and with dignity, and in a way to persuade another, without tragic show.'[1] It is a curious phenomenon, that not brutal emperors only like Nero and Domitian were persecutors, but some of the wisest and ablest down so late as the time of Diocletian; and whatever may be the true account of it, it entirely negatives the notion that they recognised any pure and elevating ideas in Christianity.

It is, however, quite in the natural order of things in such an imperfect world as this, that the best rulers should have been the sternest persecutors, seeing that they knew absolutely nothing of Christianity, and regarded it as a secret and mysterious system which set men resolutely against that political order which in their sight constituted the only

---

[1] *Meditations*, IX. 3.

guarantee for the welfare of human society. The best emperors, we must remember, had the highest conception of what the Empire was to do for the world. In their judgment it offered the one hope of the restoration of the golden Saturnian reign. A spirit by which men were led to question the imperial decrees, to judge them by some unseen, unknown standard, and if they were found wanting, to die rather than obey them, seemed to the rulers the very principle of confusion. It was in their sight simple obstinacy and malignity, because there was nothing within their sight which could explain it. The Romans were the most clement of conquerors, the most tolerant of rulers, just because they found nothing in the world which when once conquered was intolerant of their rule. But a Sect which had an unseen King of whom the Romans knew nothing, but who was obeyed with a fidelity which the Roman scourge and axe could not shake, seemed to them to strike at the very root of the order of society. To them the Empire was the sacred thing: the better the ruler the more sacred was the Empire in his sight. On such a one it appeared all the more incumbent to strangle a Sect which dishonoured the majesty of the Empire, a Sect that set above the head of the State—the '*præsens Jupiter*' of his subjects—a King whom the legions could not reach, and yet who wielded a power over His people which cast that of the emperors quite into the shade.

Strictly parallel with the conduct of some of the wisest and most clement of the emperors, is that of some of the most sagacious and merciful of the Popes. The worst Papal persecutors have not been, as a rule, the worst men who have occupied the Pontifical throne. The worst men did not care enough about the matter. It was the best men, who had the largest idea of the blessing with which the Church was charged for the world, who were most impatient of any heresies which threatened to intercept it.

The Roman Church has never cared very deeply about the intellectual element in heresy. Men might think very much as they pleased in the matter of head knowledge, if they possessed an obedient heart, and were ready on all critical occasions to submit to the authority of the Church. A certain filial state of mind was what the Church chiefly desired in her children, a moral submission to her influence rather than an intellectual consent to her creeds; and it was the disobedience in heretics which her best rulers resented; and that chiefly because of the ruin which they believed the disobedience would work for them and for the world. Therefore from very love to the souls of men, though in blind unbelief in the power of the truth to conquer in free conflict with error, did they set themselves to stamp out heresy in the blood of the heretics; and it was just the best rulers, who cared most for truth and for souls, who were most open to the temptation, and have earned for themselves in history the evil name of persecutors.

As it was in the Church, so was it to a great extent in the Empire. The Romans did not care very much what men credited, so long as they believed in the empire, and believed in its mission to rule society. But the men who did not believe that, and had quite other notions of the well-being of society, for which they were willing cheerfully to die, the Empire instinctively laid under its ban. Such men it could not afford to tolerate, but must at any cost put them down. And it was just the men who believed most thoroughly in the Roman mission to rule the world, that is, the best and most successful administrators, who were least disposed to tolerate that mutiny in the camp which called itself Christianity. So Marcus Aurelius, among others, became a persecutor, and this from his very anxiety that no 'obstinacy,' as it seemed to him, should rob the world of the blessing with which both the Stoic teaching and the Roman Empire were charged for mankind. The fact of the persecution is, however, convincing evidence that no direct influence came forth from the Gospel to the Stoic schools.

But while there was no direct influence it is very far from certain that there was not a considerable indirect influence, the real source of which the heathen mind was not able to trace, but which told very strongly on the tone of heathen thought. It is probable that the effect produced by the Jews in the Empire was more considerable than is generally supposed. The Romans hated them, and their satirists scoffed at them, but that shews that they were observed; and in the great influx into Rome of Oriental men and women, and Oriental thoughts and beliefs, some knowledge of the great truths which the Jewish Scriptures taught must have filtered into the Roman world. There would be no direct acquaintance with or study of the Scriptures; but the certainty of knowledge to which the Jews had attained about the great matters in constant debate among the philosophers, as well as the comparative moral purity and elevation of the Jewish personal and domestic life, must have exercised some influence in the circles which surrounded their settlements: while the feeling that certainty was attainable at any rate about the law of duty and that Philosophy was not worth much if it was not operative on the life, a feeling which was growing stronger generation by generation in the Roman schools, may have derived some little nourishment from this spring.

When Christianity arose, the likelihood of such an influence would be immensely increased. The Jews made proselytes no doubt, and numerous ones; but on the whole they lived apart. The Christians made converts by the myriad, in all classes of society, and had no desire to isolate themselves. Theirs was emphatically a missionary faith. The moment

a man was converted to Christianity he sought to convert
his neighbours, and in every way strove to make known
his beliefs. The Christians were everywhere; in the army,
in the imperial household, and above all among the slaves,
who were then in close contact with the higher classes of
society. Seneca associated with his slaves and had them
to his table; and the fact that there was this new life, full
of power, joy, hope, stirring in so many hearts and kindling
in so many eyes, must have lent something to the atmosphere of the times which the philosophers drank in—something vital, something stimulating, something hopeful, which
acted strongly, though they did not understand its nature and
springs, on their ideas and on their lives. Moral elements
may be in the air, and infuse a power into the hearts and
lives of men, the source of which, the exact character of
which, they cannot trace. So we may be sure that the
Christian certainty, the Christian joy and hope, and above
all the Christian charity, vitalised the atmosphere of the
Roman world during those first two centuries of the Empire;
and had something, and not a little, to do with that firmer
assurance, that stronger hope, that warmer and more universal love, which characterised the teaching of the heathen
Schools, in the generations in which Christianity was winning
its way to the hegemony of the civilised world.

We have traced then a very clear advance in the tone
and temper of these heathen Schools; resulting in a certain
approximation to the teaching of Christianity about God,
and about the nature, duties and destinies of man. It has
been established too that this advance cannot be traced
directly to Christianity itself; it is not a theft from the higher
system, but an independent evolution in the philosophical
Schools, a natural and necessary progress. The thought will
immediately occur, how would it have been had this develop-

ment been left to itself? Philosophy was evidently working towards the ideas which Christianity found so powerful to influence mankind. Would not Philosophy if left alone have at last evolved these ideas, and have undertaken and accomplished from its own basis the regeneration of society?

Before the attempt is made to answer that question, we must try to dispose of a preliminary consideration, which is not always set in its proper light. Some think that this advance of Philosophy in the Christian direction makes Philosophy the co-ordinate of the Gospel; so that they ought to be regarded as two rival powers, sharing between them the homage of the world. On the contrary, the truth is that this remarkable development which has been traced, makes Philosophy what the Law was to the Jews—the schoolmaster to bring men to Christ. It gives some colour to that notion of Clemens Alexandrinus that God had three covenants with men, the Legal, the Philosophic and the Christian. What does 'the fulness of the time' mean; the time when man was ready for the Gospel, was pining for the Gospel, and when a Gospel might be preached with a hope of blessed success? Does it not mean that man must advance a certain stage along the road of development, socially, intellectually and morally, before he could fully appreciate the teachings of the Gospel, before the appetite was awakened which the Gospel only could satisfy? This progress in Philosophy was precisely the awakening of the appetite. It is quite in the harmony of the ways of God, that man in his appointed 'feeling after God if haply he might find Him' should be led to those thoughts about God, those longings for clearer light, for purer, nobler life, which alone could be satisfied by Revelation; should in fact come by his own effort under Divine guidance to the point where he could advance no further, where God met him with the Gospel, and led him into a higher, larger, and more fruitful sphere.

It must be remembered, and it is essential to the true understanding of our subject, that the regeneration of society began quite out of the province of the philosophers. That a regeneration was accomplished, and that it was accomplished by Christianity, is unquestionable. The only point is, Was not Philosophy in a fair way of carrying out the task when it was interrupted by Christianity. The philosophers were working in the higher social region: Christianity began at the other end of the scale. Born among a despised and hated people, it everywhere won converts among the humblest classes of society. This was not exclusively the case; scholars, Rabbis, captains, senators, Areopagites, men of all positions and degrees of culture joined the movement; but the great mass of the disciples came from the ranks of the poor—'For you see your calling, brethren, how that not many wise men after the flesh, not many mighty, not many noble are called.'

Soon, in all the chief cities of the Roman world, there was gathered a band of Christian disciples who lived in the closest brotherly fellowship, who ministered to each other freely of their substance, who allowed no bitter poverty to exist among their members, who were pledged by the most sacred and binding of all possible constraints to industry, honesty, purity, and self-renouncing service to mankind. Were there sick, they tended them; were there hungry, they fed them; were there wronged, they righted them; plague had no terrors for them when suffering called them to minister, pain had no menace when duty called them to endure. In face of the ills and woes of life they were 'always rejoicing'; the slow decay and wasting of the body, which so saddened the heathen, they watched with exultation; they had, not composure, but songs of triumph as they stood face to face with inevitable death. As a rule uncultured; poor, ignorant, common-place working men and

women ; artisans, soldiers, fishermen, beggars and slaves; they
had yet learnt and could live this pure and lofty life. Industry,
home life, brotherly fellowship, piety, worship, were all regener-
ated by them, and there was about them and their community,
their Church, a glow of life which was contagious. Their
doctrine, their practice, caught like flame from home to home,
from village to village, from city to city, from land to land ;
and everywhere with the same results. Society was new-
born wherever their Gospel penetrated, and began living a
new life with a vigour, a joy, a hope, an onward upward
pressure, which for ages had been utterly unknown in the
heathen world. Philosophy went on its way among the
higher classes ; but it laid absolutely no hold on men at
large. The reformation which it wrought in a few elect
spirits, failed utterly to spread downwards to the mass of
mankind. The poor were not touched by it ; society was
not helped by it ; its noblest men, and they grew fewer and
fewer generation by generation, bewailed bitterly the universal
indifference. The Schools dwindled into a mere University
system of culture ; Christianity developed into a religion for
the civilised world.

And the question is What is the reason of the difference ?
Is it largely a matter of accident, or was Christianity merely
a higher system of Philosophy, working from the same basis
but with greater advantages, to results which the continually
advancing ideas of the philosophers, had they been let alone,
would equally have achieved ?

Let us understand that it was not new ideas, which, as
introduced by Christianity, wrought the result. New ideas
it had in abundance, but new ideas were not the secret of
its power. The essential matter in the Gospel was that it
was the history of a Life. It was a tale of fact that all
could understand, that all could believe, that all could love.
It differed fundamentally from Philosophy, because it appealed

not to culture but to life. And wherever life was fullest and strongest, wherever hearts beat quickest, wherever hands worked hardest, wherever pain smote deepest, wherever tears fell fastest, there it found the audience that best understood it, and with which it knew that it had most to do. And why? Because its message was not a doctrine how to live, but a record of how a Man *had* lived, a Man who, the Christians believed and the world has come to believe, could lay upon His words and works the emphasis of Incarnate God. The testimony was that this Life of piety, purity, charity, and unselfish devotion to the service of man, had been lived perfectly in our world by the Son of God, who made the world, and who had died to reveal God's righteousness and God's tenderness to wretched sinners, and to commend His life as an ensample, not hopeless of attainment, to every human heart. The Christians lived as brethren because this Son of God had called them brethren; they wrought and suffered, they mastered passion and mortified lust, and faced death with a lofty joy, because the Lord had not only left them His example, but was working in them and enabling them to fulfil His commandment and to gladden His heart. It was the spell of substantial facts, living facts, which the Gospel laid on them, the spell of a personal loyalty to a personal Lord; and those who have not mastered the difference between a philosopher's speculations about life, and the actual record of a life which, in all that makes life holy and beautiful, transcended the philosopher's most pure and lofty dreams, have not understood yet the rudiments of the reason why the Stoic could not, while Christianity could and did, re-generate society.

Christ alone among all great religious teachers felt that the tale of His Life and Death would be the Gospel for the world. Not what He taught merely, but what He was and what

He did, was the Gospel; and therefore, because it belonged to the region of life, it came with such vital impact to the heart of mankind. Everywhere, as if a fresh shock from some vital battery had struck them, men began, when its message reached them, to live: and everywhere within the sphere of the Church's influence there was light, love, energy, and hope. And the fundamental reason was that the Church could tell the eager wistful world, not what man thought about God, which knowledge must be always as limited and variable as man's understanding, but what God thought about man, said to man, did for man, and was doing and would do for man through eternity. Speculations about God, about life, about duty, about destiny, must always be utterly without form and substance, mere mists in cloudland, to the great mass of un-cultivated men. When the world for the first time heard with faith, not what God might be supposed to think, feel, and pur-pose; but what God had thought, said, and done in our world, then began upon earth that vital movement which has issued in the regeneration of human society.

The fatal defect in Philosophy was that it could never get men fairly out of their own shadow. The philosopher was always necessarily the centre to his world; all hung on his own thoughts, feelings, convictions, and powers, and man can never 'Sink into himself and rise redeemed.' The religion of which the individual man is the centre can never lay hold on men, because what man needs most profoundly is to escape from himself; yet not to escape only, but to escape from and yet possess himself. Escape of one kind was always easy to the philosopher. As we have seen, the noblest of them, Marcus Aurelius and Epictetus, as well as the most accom-plished of them, Seneca, always kept in view the resource of suicide. But what gospel could 'escape by suicide' be to the masses, when the very wisest and loftiest minds, by lifelong meditation, could rise no nearer to certainty than a 'perhaps' as to what was beyond ?   Men wanted to lose themselves and yet keep themselves; and Philosophy could not help them; those only had mastered the secret who buried their lower baser self when through Christ they died to sin, and who found a new and higher self in God: 'I live, yet not I, but Christ liveth in me; and the life which I now live in the flesh I live by the faith of the Son of God, who loved me, and gave himself for me.'

The subject before us is not, however, why the Gospel could, but why the Stoic could not, regenerate society.   The utter want of clear certainty in the doctrine was fatal to any deep or wide-spread religious influence upon men.   We do right to take at the very highest possible value the work which the philosophers accomplished for the moral and intellectual development of man.   It was an important, not to say essential, element in the preparation of humanity for the coming of Christ.   It is a mistake to sneer at the Alexandrian school of Christian thought.   Many crudities, many absurdities, we may find in the pages of its chief doctors, but the attempt it made was a noble one.   Its endeavour was, not to blend Christianity with the highest results of human thought, and so make a new amalgam which should neither be Christianity nor Philosophy but a mingling of both; but rather to find room in the Christian scheme and in the Christian life for truths and modes of experience as old as the creation and as wide-spread as humanity, and so to enlarge the dogma of Christianity as to make it intellectually, as it was spiritually, the religion of the world.   But men wanted not to guess, or to think, but to know, the truths on which they were to build their Sion.   A system of truth which could never rise higher than the speculations of a human brain, might be an admirable *culture*, but could never be a *religion* to mankind.   The best of the Stoics talked indifferently about the gods and about God; now about dissolution into the elements, and then again about conscious existence after death; sometimes, though feebly, about sin, and sometimes about the force that is working through all, saint and sinner alike, the great harmony of life; here about tender pity for the poor, the maimed, the wretched, there about all calamities being things indifferent, which a man should steel himself to reckon no calamities at all: on one occasion about gladness in all the gifts of Providence, and on another about stern and persistent defiance of Fate. And the uncertainty lay in the organ; it was inherent in the philosopher's method; in the nature of things there was no possibility that if it had been left to work with the stage all to itself, it could have spoken a clear word of certainty to men about the unseen verities.

Philosophy was entirely powerless to combine, confederate, and command men. There was no Power above them all which commanded the assent of their understandings, and which spoke with authority alike about truth and about life. They were scattered stars in the sky, with no visible order and no particular function in relation to the great mass of mankind. The doctrine of Christ came like the sun, and then everyone felt that he lived in an orderly and divinely governed world. The philosophers devoted themselves with honest intention to minister to human want and pain, and to be at hand with a seasonable word on all the great occasions of life. But all depended on the individual thinkers; there was no authority above them to commit this ministry as a charge to them, and to raise up in each generation a kindred band. There was nothing in Philosophy which could create a new organ of ministry, and sustain it as it worked in the world in an ever-widening circle, in concert with the ever-widening perception of human need. The philosophers rose and taught and passed away, each, as it were, at his own will. In the Church men found an institution which could be depended upon for the supply of that service for which the world was pining, and which had become an imperative need of mankind. There was that in Christianity which called forth, constrained, and inspired the service, and which assured to the world age after age successive and ever-increasing companies of teachers and ministers. Christianity sent these out generation by generation with a vigour which was never paralysed for a moment, even in the darkest days of ignorance and wretchedness, days in which the philosopher utterly vanished; and this was because that vigour was fed from a perennial celestial spring.

Through all the ages there was a unity in the Christian teaching, and in the Christian service, because these were not dependent on the ever-varying thoughts and impulses of man, but on the Word and the Will of One who remained ' the same yesterday, and to-day, and for ever,' and who had the power to call forth men to be His messengers and ministers according to His righteous and unerring will. There is abundant play of individual thought and individual character under the Christian system. The sects of Christians have been more numerous than the sects of the philosophers. But the Christians have had the conviction that above all the sects there is the Truth which changes not and fails not, and which is ever working on the sects, correcting their error, enlarging their narrowness, and leading them into fuller knowledge and nobler life; and it is hardly possible to estimate the influence that this conviction about the absolute eternal Truth possessed by all the Christian Schools, has exercised on man in the moral, intellectual, and political spheres.

The Christians, moreover, threw themselves into this ministry with consuming passion. There was no passion in Philosophy, nothing to inspire passion. But the Church was aglow with ardour. A host of eager, enthusiastic ministers started forth when the love of Christ had laid its constraint on their spirits, and threw themselves with the instinct of conquerors on the sin, the vice, the wretchedness of the world. Round the disciples hope breathed wherever they moved: around the philosophers the lassitude of indifference or the paralysis of despair.

Very deeply connected with the helplessness of Philosophy to meet the profounder needs, and satisfy the imperious cravings of mankind, was its teaching, or want of teaching, about sin. Stoicism as we have seen was a doctrine of self-gratulation, and the Stoic was a Pharisee at heart. The world needed beyond everything to be convinced of sin, righteousness, and judgment: and only when the conviction of sin was brought into its heart, with the promise of deliverance, did it begin to look up and live. The most terrible vices were rampant in the society in which Epictetus, Seneca, and Marcus Aurelius moved; but they pass them lightly by. When Paul 'reasoned of righteousness, temperance, and judgment to come, Felix trembled.' So the world trembled before the Christian preachers, as it never trembled, and never could tremble, before the Stoics, and that fear was the beginning of its regeneration. For through the world a message ran, which was never heard in the Stoic Schools, 'Behold the Lamb of God which taketh away the sin of the world.' That message wrought conviction of sin, it proclaimed forgiveness of sin, it promised victory over sin— and from that hour the struggle of man against the evil which was destroying him, acquired the sanctity and intensity of a crusade. And then, from the Gospel of the forgiveness of sin, sprang forth the passion of the Divine Love.

Here we touch the last, the deepest reason why Philosophy could never be a religion to man, nor exercise a regenerating power on society. Its gospel was essentially a loveless gospel. It is love which kindles the eye, fires the blood, and strains the energies to their highest tension

The world which had listened coldly to the philosophers, with no stirring of a pulse of passion or of hope, started literally into new life when this gospel was preached to it:—— 'The love of Christ constraineth us: because we thus judge, that if one died for all, then did all die: and that he died for all, that they which live should not henceforth live unto themselves, but unto him which died for them, and rose again.'

V.

THE MONASTIC SYSTEM, AND ITS RELATION TO THE LIFE OF THE CHURCH.

V.

THE MONASTIC SYSTEM, AND ITS RELATION TO THE LIFE OF THE CHURCH.

WHEN Epictetus urged his disciples to set before them some man of supreme excellence, and to imagine themselves always in his presence, had he quite forgotten how bitterly he had complained that no true Stoic could be found, no man in whom he could discern the realisation of his ideal? But even while Epictetus was teaching, myriads of his fellow men had found One whom they could at once worship with the profoundest reverence, and love with the most passionate devotion; One who had laid hold on all which they believed to be the higher elements of their nature, and who drew them by a resistless spell into the path of self-abnegation, self-devotion and ministry to mankind, which He had trodden Himself to the last extremity of shame and death. The great mass of mankind, the ignorant, the poor, the enslaved— shut out inevitably, not in any wise by the jealousy of the philosophers, but by the very nature of things, from the wisdom of the Schools—had found, or, as St. Paul says, had been found by, a Being who stirred and swayed them with a force and absoluteness till then unknown; and who inspired them with a love so passionate and absorbing that poverty, bonds, wounds and death were no longer terrible, but beautiful and glorious, if they might but express the depth of their devotion to their Saviour, and translate them more swiftly to His sphere.

This passionate personal love to Christ is a feature of the Christian life of the early centuries which no wise student of their history will underrate. In the earlier Christian ages, it is not too much to say that Christendom was fairly drunk with the new wine of the Spirit. A new power from heaven had fallen upon men and filled them with rapture. Nothing is more notable, in the comparison of the Christian and the Pagan literatures of the first and second centuries, than the tone of exhilaration which breathes through the one, and the sadness, the hopelessness which characterise the other. This, probably, quite as much as the *'non eloquimur magna, sed vivimus,'* explains the power which Christianity wielded from the first over the mass of mankind. And this love to Christ manifested itself in forms of imitation often very wildly extravagant, but not altogether marvellous to those who know to its depths the passion of human love. The stigmata of St. Francis, whatever may be the truth of that marvellously attested phenomenon, are really but the culmination of what the higher class of monastics—and these are the men to be studied—were pining and panting after through all the monastic ages. To imitate Christ in the form of His life, while they drank inwardly its inspiration, was their highest thought and hope. And it was inevitable, surely, that the Christian life should, in the most earnest, take the form of a studious outward reproduction under the constraint of an absorbing passion, before the world could rise to the comprehension (partly through this experiment,) of the inner meaning of the life of Jesus, and the true character of its influence on mankind. To live as He lived, poor, homeless, way-faring, and apart from domestic cares and joys, was the ideal of the Christian life which the first ages cherished. The poverty of Christ, His simple trust, like that of the birds and the lilies, His homeless lot, His virgin life, were all made the objects of eager and passionate imitation.

In all this there was much that to some may savour of fanaticism, but the truth is that we must make up our minds to a large measure of pure fanaticism in all, save one, of the great movements which have strongly influenced the course of human affairs. All save one. Christ was no fanatic. He gladdened alike marriage festivals, cottage homes, and mourners by new-made graves; and we are tempted to think that the larger spirit of Christ's teaching might have taught the early saints a nobler lesson than that which they drew from the study of some outward forms of the life of the Lord. We must however be largely tolerant of fanaticism if we wish to scan with a sympathetic eye the page of human history. Such is the weakness, the want of balance in our nature, and such is the proneness of society to be moved, not by what appeals calmly and solidly to its reason, but by what strikes strongly its imagination or touches its heart, that no great principle ever gets thoroughly wrought into the texture of human beliefs, and becomes a constant factor in the life of the race, without the agency of a strong fanaticism in those who first forced it on the attention of mankind.

The fanaticism dies out, as all excess dies out, in confusion and shame, but not until it has done its work, and compelled men to recognise and reverence what was of vital worth in the schemes of the man or the school thus brought into prominence. Society works into its own life the life that was in them, and lets the foam and the fury die away. Monachism was a strong fanaticism; and so too was scholarship at the Revival of Learning; the worship of the letter of the Bible at the Puritan era was a strong fanaticism: the Total Abstinence movement is a fanaticism now. When we approach the study of the influence of the religious life on Christendom, we must accept the fanaticism as inevitable, we must understand that it is as much the condition of getting certain great moral ideas into the heart of Christian society, as the fever heat around a healing wound is the condition of its cure. We may smile, if we will, at the fanatics, and give thanks, if we will, that we are not as one of them: though the smug contentment of modern society with its posture and its achievements makes some fanaticisms look very lofty and noble indeed.

Furthermore—and this is a truth important to the understanding of the influence of the monk on mediæval life—we must be prepared, with a nature like ours and in a world like this, for great drawbacks in the very noblest work, much more in that which is only partially noble. Look at even our almsgiving; the saddest thing to a generous heart is the question which will force itself on us, whether the harm that we do by it does not more than balance the good. All great social movements seem to have blessing in one hand and bane in the other, and we are happy if we can rest in the conviction that on the whole, after the balance is struck, the cause of progress gains. Terribly slowly, we say sometimes in our weak impatience, the kingdom of light and truth advances. The great influences which act on each generation do so much to hinder as well as so much to help, that we must be thankful if we see, as thank Heaven we do see, age by age a slight advance, a slow lifting up of human society; doubly happy if we can trace it day by day in our own individual lives.

There is so much weakness, so much perverseness, so much foolishness in every one of us, that we should be prepared for a very large infusion of the same sad elements in every great institution which has wrought strongly on the development of the world. Take despotism; take aristocracy; take democracy; take commerce, nay take our present idol constitutional monarchy, which of them is charged with clear unmingled blessing to . man ? So the religious life, as the monastic profession got to be called, had, without any doubt, very much baseness mingled with its nobleness, and many degrading destructive influences to set against those which have helped to beat down selfishness, gluttony, impurity, and brutality in man. We may be quite sure that an institution which stretched its vital influence on Europe through a thousand years, and gave to the world such men as Benedict, Columba, Gregory, Bede, Boniface, Anselm, Bernard and Francis—all of them passionately devoted to their vocation—had on the whole a balance of blessing to its account. It will of course be understood that though it is the purpose of this chapter to set forth something of the good the monks wrought for Christendom, it would be possible, were that the matter in hand, to say, not as much, but very much, on the opposite side.

Nay, more, we are wont to criticise from the lofty height of our advanced civilisation, from the vantage ground of our admirably wise and noble social habits and actions, the austere excesses of these fanatical champions of purity and self-devotion. Well! when we look round on some of the features of our own age, when we survey the vices and follies of any age, we may find something that does not amuse or amaze, but rather impresses and stimulates us, as we see Benedict rolling himself in thorns to quench the fever of his blood; or Bernard trying, not how much, but how little, he could eat in his lonely cell; or Francis stripping himself to one coarse cloak of serge, as he went forth to tend the plague-stricken and wretched, as hungry, as poor, as homeless as his Lord!

What would the Middle Ages have been without their Saints? As the saintly image was distinctly monastic from the fourth century to the thirteenth, this is equivalent to the question, What would the Middle Ages have been without their hermits, monks, and nuns? St. Louis, in the thirteenth century, marks the dawning of a new era. The great saintly figure of that time is a king and a layman. It is the age of the birth of a vernacular literature in the Western European kingdoms; it is the age of popular movements which bring the great third estate on to the arena of political action; it is the age in which the West reaps fully the social and commercial fruit of the Crusades. It is deeply significant that in such an age one of the ablest and busiest monarchs in Christendom won a reputation for saintliness, which few Churchmen can rival. It is prophetic of that sanctification of secular life, that passing forth of the 'religious' idea into a wider world, which was the real meaning of the Reformation, and of all the most vital movements in the Church during the last three centuries. The influence of the Saint during the ages of which we write (and every monk and nun was saintly to the secular herd), was the influence of the Church in its most intense and concentrated form. And it reacted on the Church most mightily, and continually nourished its power to influence and rule society. We must not confound the influence of the Church with the whole influence of the Gospel—that is, of the ideas and powers which Christ brought visibly to bear on mankind. That was a much larger matter, and must be sought equally in the development of the social life and political institutions of the nations which inherited, thanks largely to the monastics, the Christian traditions and polity of Rome. The 'religious life' was, as it were, the electric jar into which all the most vital forces of the Church were gathered, and whence they discharged themselves on society. And the Church represents incomparably the most powerful of the many influences which were moulding the life of Europe during the earlier Middle Ages.

The formation of Christian society was the great problem of Providence during all those ages. Alas! it is the great problem still. To form a Christian community or communities in limited areas within the bosom of the wider society, named in contrast the world, has too easily satisfied our conception of what is to be desired and aimed at for the accomplishment of the Divine purpose. This was not however the aim—if we read history rightly—of the Divine workman through the Middle Age. The formation of Christian society is quite another and a larger matter. A society which should be Christian in its very foundations, and in which the ideas of Christianity should be recognised in all the relations of men and all the duties of life—this is what we must understand by Christian society. It is a society of which the law of God as revealed in Christ is recognised as the basis, and in which men acknowledge that their rights and duties must be referred to a supreme standard in the will of God. And no student of history can fail to see that the recognition of the Christian basis and constitution of society was characteristic of the Western European nations during their formative ages— that is from the fifth century when the seed of the Teutonic nationalities began to be sown in the fertile, because disintegrated, soil of the decaying Roman Empire, to the thirteenth, when these nationalities assume their full form and enter on their manly career.

These national communities were Christian societies because they confessed Christ. It is easy to understand that those who have only glanced at the troubled surface of mediæval life, and have heard or read of its wild doings, its sanguinary strifes, its cruel tyrannies, may be tempted to exclaim, This confession of Christ seems to have been a very low, poor, carnal confession, scarcely worthy of the name. And surely they would be right. But I imagine that this is precisely what the angels are thinking about ours. I know not any

Christian society upon earth which does more than strive in a very feeble and trembling fashion to order its life after the Christian law. Envy, hatred, malice, littleness, selfishness, worldliness, sins against which we are always witnessing and from which we are always striving, with but partial success, to free ourselves, may seem to the unseen watchers as grossly carnal as the strong, bold evils of mediaeval society seem to us. None can hope to understand the Middle Age who cannot see that the effort to be Christian was the key to its vital development. And, therefore, without forgetting that the breath of the Divine Spirit is abroad in the very air around us, and streams in upon us by a thousand channels of nature and of life, we are justified in affirming that the Church, which held the Christian standards and cherished the Christian ideals, was the most powerful visible agent at work on the nations of Western Europe during the Middle Ages. In truth, the history of the Church, up to the time of the development of a national life and a national literature in those Western nations—which dates from about the thirteenth century—is in the largest sense the history of mediaeval society.

The influence of the monastic principle on the world at large, including Asiatic, Jewish, Oriental, and Western monachism, forms an important chapter wherever comparative religion is scientifically studied. Altogether the most vital and fruitful portion of the subject concerns the influence of the Benedictine rule on the development of Western Europe.

We must not stay to enquire, where was the original home of ascetism. It is certain that in the far East monachism of the most pronounced type had run its course ages before it was heard of in the Christian Church. It seems, however, inevitable that some such institution as the monastic should have arisen in Christendom. It was in a measure necessary that that form of the Christian life should be tried thoroughly and on a large scale; it was necessary that it should be tried and should fail, though in failing it was to leave noble legacies of influence to Christian society. Idolaters of the *word* of Scripture—and the word is certain to be idolised before it is apprehended with full intelligence—find sentences there which the severest ascetic discipline seems alone to satisfy. Hegel says that nowhere are there to be found such revolutionary utterances as in the Gospels. Hegel is right, but let no red revolutionist think that either their letter or their spirit will help him. The first thing he will find, if he reads the New Testament honestly, is that it lays the axe to the root of his arrogance, his impatience, his self-will, and his idea that Society can be a God to itself. All fruitful revolution begins from within. Some of the sentences of the New Testament are, however, startling enough—

'Jesus said unto him, If thou wouldest be perfect, go, sell that thou hast, and give to the poor, and thou shalt have treasure in heaven; and come, follow me' (Matt. xix. 21).

'And he said unto all, If any man would come after me, let him deny himself, and take up his cross daily, and follow me. For whosoever would save his life shall lose it; but whosoever shall lose his life for my sake, the same shall save it' (Luke ix. 23, 24).

'If any man cometh unto me, and hateth not his father and mother, and wife, and children, and brethren, and sisters, yea, and his own life also, he cannot be my disciple' (Luke xiv. 26).

'And as they went in the way, a certain man said unto him, I will follow thee whithersoever thou goest. And Jesus said unto him, The foxes have holes, and the birds of the heaven have nests; but the Son of man hath not where to lay his head. And he said unto another, Follow me. But he said, Lord, suffer me first to go and bury my father. But he said unto him, Leave the dead to bury their own dead: but go thou and publish abroad the kingdom of God. And another also said, I will follow thee, Lord; but suffer me to first bid them farewell that are at my house. But Jesus said unto him, No man, having put his hand to the plough, and looking back, is fit for the kingdom of God' (Luke ix. 57-62).

Nor are these vague words. They are sustained to their uttermost literal meaning by the life of the Lord. We are familiar with their purport; alas! so familiar that we can hardly realise the startling emphasis with which they would fall on the unaccustomed but eager ears, which were listening in those days to the word of Eternal Life. Men believed profoundly that those words were spoken on earth by the Lord of everlasting glory, and they were taught by inspired lips that His life was the Light of the world. Was it not most natural, and indeed inevitable, that those on whom the power of the higher life descended should take these words in what seemed to be their simplest sense, and try what would come of an honest endeavour to work them out as literally in practice?

The first Christian ascetics were like men dazzled by the splendours of the invisible world that had burst suddenly upon their sight. The higher and eternal interests of their being seemed so transcendent that the present was eclipsed and vanished. The world became a prison, and all that they asked of earth was a lonely wilderness, wherein they might feel themselves free to think only of heaven. They sought a gymnasium for spiritual exercises. Just as the athletes submitted themselves to a special discipline that they might contend successfully in the arena, so, they thought, the spiritual faculties needed to be drawn forth and strained to their highest tension by some special culture, which should be quite other than, and apart from, the common duties and burdens of life.

There is an important sense, surely, in which the ascetic was right. We are here to train the highest part of us for lofty service; to detach it from its bondage to the world and the flesh, and to stretch its powers to their full strain, by exercising them constantly and strenuously in their appropriate sphere. But that perfect school of discipline is just what God has provided for us in the scene of our daily callings, the world of our daily interests, and the home of our daily loves. 'Our America is here,' in the body, in the world, 'or nowhere.'[1] Here the training of our highest faculties is to be perfected, here the crown of our spiritual manhood is to be won. The monastic idea had its root in a schism, schism in that which God made one: the noblest and completest unity, the image of His own. Man is one. Not through an interior schism of body, mind, and spirit, is man to attain to his highest, but by an inner harmony, drawing his trinity of powers into closer and holier union by their exercise in the appointed field of human culture and work—the world.

Monachism, rooted in schism, had always a strangely divided influence upon man. Noble strength and terrible weakness, splendid achievement and disastrous failure, pure inspiration and foul degradation, are curiously mingled in its history. Its strength has always been that it is, on the whole, the higher part in man which it has cultivated, and that it has kept, on the whole, before the eyes of men in rough and stormy centuries the purity, the self-denial, the love of nature and of art, the intellectual culture, and the mercy and charity, by which communities are blessed and saved. Its essential vice has been that it is an artificial state, and that which is unnatural and out of harmony with the being of man, never fails to bring after it in the long run a retribution, which proves in the end that God's law in the ordering of human life is right.

The root of the monastic institution was this notion of an ἄσκησις, the idea that the soul, as well as the body, needed some special gymnastic culture and discipline. In the earlier days of the institution this discipline was carried on in connection with the ordinary scenes and activities of life. But after a while, partly through the growing sadness and degradation of secular society, but chiefly, we may be sure, through the growing fascination of the career itself, the ascetic as-

<hr>

[1] *Wilhelm Meister*, Bk. VII. ch. 3.

pirants found that they could not bear the presence of their fellow men, and betook themselves to remote places, the wilder the better, where they could more freely carry on what they mistook for the culture of their souls. The ascetic then became an Anchorite, one who retreats from the world, or an Eremite, one who lives in the desert, and there, far from the sobering influence of his fellows, he gave himself up to austerities and subtleties of self-torment which fill us alternately with amazement, pity and disgust. There were wide districts of the East, especially the Egyptian and Syrian deserts, which in the fourth century literally swarmed with hermits. They burrowed in the hill-sides, like rabbits in a warren, and studiously lowered the pitch of their lives, as far as food and shelter were concerned, to the level of the brutes.

The next step in the development of the monastic system was the association of these isolated anchorites in communities, for the purposes of fellowship and strength. How the transition was accomplished it is not easy to trace. Much, no doubt, was due to the influence of powerful and celebrated men like Anthony and Pachomius, who drew, by the magnet of their attraction, crowds of anchorites to their neighbourhood over whom it became necessary to establish some kind of rule. The need of organisation had become imperative. That ascetic spirit which had been floating in a vaporous form about the Oriental Church, must condense, take shape, and enter the congress of life. The Eremites became Cœnobites, men living in common, under a common rule, with a common head: and then the development of the monastic institution fairly began. The organisation of the scattered solitaries was attended by an immense increase of numbers. We may accept Jerome's authority for the vast concourse which attended a congregation of an order in the fifth century, without trusting too implicitly to the numeration of even so distinguished a father of the Church. In truth, a competent judge of numbers on a great scale is rare even at the present day. But there were enough of them swarming about the deserts and established about the cities of Egypt, to revive in another form the ancient sneer, that in Egypt it was far easier to meet with a god than with a man.

In judging of this Oriental asceticism we must take account of the manners and habits of the Eastern peoples, and of their climate which renders shelter and any but the simplest food needless; we must remind ourselves of the kind of world from which the monks came out, and must recognise the fact that these fanatics did really have heavenly aspirations, and that they did honestly desire to live a spiritual life detached from all earthly trammels, and masters of appetite, affection and lust. However amply we may recognise these special features of the position, it seems hard to speak of Eastern monachism with the respect that so powerful and popular an institution deserves. The Oriental monks appear, as a class, to have been filthy and prurient. Constantly fighting against a certain class of temptations, they kept them constantly and engrossingly before their sight. Save in one respect, as we shall presently see, they ministered but little to the culture and progress of mankind. Simeon Stylites, *facile princeps* of Oriental ascetics, on his single pillar where he lived for 37 years and where he finally died, is no lovely figure—spending as he did his days in countless prostrations, and lifting himself, as he said, every few years nearer to heaven—by raising the height of his pillar!

It is true there is no lack of flowers of rare and exquisite grace scattered over this monkish waste. Touches of beautiful affection, acts of heroic courage and constancy, begem what were else a dismal history. The monks of the Thebaid were, at any rate, not afraid of the worst which the world could inflict on them. Athanasius found in them the most constant and courageous champions of the truth of the Incarnation; and it was mainly by their help that he won the greatest and most pregnant of doctrinal victories.

Still, on the whole, it is a dark, sad history.

The asceticism of the Eastern Church is distinctly inhuman: the taint of manichæism runs through it and poisons its springs: a bitter hatred to the body, as the organ of the flesh, was its ruling principle, and it tended to gross and foolish excesses, helpful neither to earth nor to heaven. Before, however, we leave it to study the far nobler monachism of the West, which mingled itself in very vital contact with the development of the secular society by which it was surrounded, we must in fairness pause to weigh one consideration, which may tell in favour of even this comparatively low form of the religious life.

Look, for example, more narrowly for a moment at this very Simeon Stylites. As matter of fact his age did reverence him profoundly, and he wielded a very powerful influence over men. Very foolish of the age to be influenced by such extravagant absurdities, we may say. Most surely. very foolish, it might have kept its reverence for nobler things. Perhaps the republican enthusiasm for the rant of the demagogue, and the evangelical worship of the popular preacher are parallel absurdities in ours. If, however, we are to understand history we must take each age as we find it, and study with respect and sympathy those elements in it which were found at the time to be of power. We may be sure that if any great movement seems to us to be absurd or extravagant, those who come after us will find much that may be called by the same names in the doings of our own days.

Here, in this Oriental asceticism, we see rising in the world a new kind of power, at which it is worth one's while to look a little closely. This Simeon, by his austerities and his constant contemplation of the unseen, won such in-fluence in the world that multitudes flocked around his pillar, and bishops, archbishops, even emperors, listened to his words with reverence, as if to a special organ of the voice of God. The life which he lived would not have been possible for any man unless sustained by intense conviction: and that life manifested at any rate remarkable power of self-denial, shaming by its simplicity and purity the world's glaring vices, gluttony, dishonesty, and lust. Fantastic as it was, it occupied itself evidently with unseen eternal things, and in this way did actually bring down to earth influence out of the invisible world. The power which these ascetics were winning was one before which the forces of the world trembled: in some way or another, men in a lonely wilder-ness had won an authority before which monarchs quivered on their thrones. These men were absolutely incorruptible in an age when every one had his price, and though they constantly erred in their judgments, they had respect in these judgments—everybody knew it—to truth and righteous-ness. They made their influence felt on the side of mercy, gentleness, and charity; they were always against the op-pressor and on the side of the poor.

Here then was a new power, which, when organised and developed in the more rational and manly West, had in it the germs of a very lofty and potent influence on the develop-ment of society. In the East, however, it was soon, like the East itself, exhausted and doomed to decay. Self-enfolded nothing can live. And age by age this Eastern monachism grew more boneless and bloodless; and now probably the dullest and dirtiest sloths that are slinking about Christendom, are these monks of the Eastern Church.

The monachism of the West looked out of itself and lived. There is a clear, bold, working aspect about it from the first.

We may best express the diverse characteristics of the two systems by observing that, war with the body out of hatred and revenge was the key to Oriental asceticism; war with the body for the sake of its subjugation and use, was the key to the monachism of the West. The monasticism of the extravagant and unsavoury monks of the Thebaid, though not without grand and noble passages, was one thing; the monasticism of the rule of St. Benedict among the vigorous, laborious, and progressive Western peoples was another. Eastern Christianity died with its monachism, perhaps died of it: Western Christianity lived through its ascetism, perhaps lived by it: and it has laid up in the inner cells of its life that vital force which will one day restore the mother lands of the Gospel to the visible kingdom of the Lord.

How the system got introduced into the Western empire, and how it grew in its infancy we know not. Possibly the great Athanasius brought it to Rome. The monks were his fearless and devoted supporters, and he was at Rome in A.D. 340, with some monks in his train. All great things, however, spring, like the corn, 'man knoweth not how,' and only as it grew did it reveal its wonderful power. It is highly characteristic of the practical and sober genius of the West, especially of Rome in her imperial days, both pagan and Papal, that at first it was received with hostility. At the funeral of Blesilla, a young Roman nun, supposed to have died of excessive fasting, the Roman populace was for throwing 'these detestable monks' into the river. Monachism needed to be baptised with a new spirit before it could root itself deeply in the West. But from the first it was noted that in the West communion was the leading idea, not isolation. No doubt here also, as in the East, the hermit's cell was the core of the institution, but in the West the tendency was markedly towards organisation: and even before the time of Benedict, the leading Western monasteries, especially in the south of

France, were exercising a very powerful influence on the culture and life of their times. They were opposed to over-rigid fasting, and recognised that in the hardier climates of the North-west men need more food than in the sunny South. 'Much eating,' they said, 'is gormandising among the Greeks, but natural among the Gauls.' The truth is that fasting is absolutely useless and senseless, except in so far as it clears the brain and heart for their higher work. Some men it invigorates, others it sickens and depresses. Let each study honestly the habit of his own nature, and observe the discipline which is best for his intellectual and spiritual powers. There is no doubt, however, that in the Middle Ages people ate enormously too much, and let us thank the monk who reminded his age how little a man could live upon, and who did something thereby to form the habit of moderation which on the whole reigns benignly in these modern days.

Until the beginning of the sixth century the monasteries of the West were isolated, and each did what was right in its own eyes. Not a few grew rich and wanton, and the danger was that in the general decay of everything in the empire, in the dark days which were at once the deathbed of the Roman and the cradle of the modern world, the monastic institution would be swept away with the wreck. Then arose Benedict of Nursia (c. 480—c. 542), and by his celebrated rule settled the character of Western monachism for all time. Like other great leaders he had the eye to see the special character of the facts with which he set himself to deal. He gave a per-manent form to what was already the instinctive tendency of the monachism of the West; he interpreted to itself the spirit which was abroad in society around him, and gave it wider and freer range.

Benedict was born of a noble family at Nursia, a descendant of the Anician house, and early devoted himself to the solitary life in its austerest form, at Subiaco, in the Roman Campagna.

There he acquired immense influence; was chosen abbot of a monastery; attempted a reformation; was nearly poisoned, and fled back to his solitude. Men gathered rapidly around him; 12 monasteries of 12 monks each were founded near his cavern; again he was in peril from poison, and again, after thirty-five years at Subiaco, he took up his pilgrim-staff to depart. He now settled himself at Monte Cassino, near the head waters of the Liris, amid scenes of singular and gloomy grandeur, and there he founded the monastery which was destined to be a mighty factor in the development of the Christian world. There he thought out and published the celebrated rule which bears his name, which simply crystallised into clear form and order the ideas which were floating in the powerful and practical minds of the founders of monachism in the West. For powerful they were, as well as practical. We do not need M. de Montalembert's brilliant rhetoric to teach us that the cloister was, on the whole, no shelter for the weaklings of society, men easily dashed and bruised by the rough world around them, and safer in a cell than in a battle-field or on a throne. The great monks bear full comparison with the greatest soldiers, statesmen, and kings. We may lament or condemn the form of life which they elected, and see clearly whitherward it tends. But we must bear in mind that it was for ages the chosen field of action of some of the very strongest, ablest men, and the noblest, purest women whom God sent forth into the world, and we may be sure that a high and noble inspiration was at the heart of a movement which occupied such splendid energies, and left such marks on the higher development of mankind. There can be no doubt that the rule included a vast crowd of weak, dreamy *fainéant* devotees; but, on the other hand, it would be hard to find, in any other sphere of human activity during the Middle Ages, a grander company of clear, strong, firm, and far-sighted men. We are bound to believe in this life as one which had a specific rightness of adaptation in its times, or its secret will remain veiled.

Benedict drew up and promulgated a rule of monastic living, which may be regarded as the complete expression of the Western mind with respect to the nature and the aims of the religious life, for it met with immediate and almost universal acceptance, and has dominated the monastic world for 1300 years. The rule spread with marvellous rapidity through Europe. Placidus carried it to Sicily, Maurus to France, Augustine probably to England; and towards the close of the eighth century it was so general as to cause Charlemagne to inquire whether any other rule existed throughout the vast dominions which he had subjected to his sway.

It is well known to the most casual students of monastic history that the three foremost ideas in the rule are self-abnegation, obedience, and labour. Perhaps, next to the novitiate, which will be touched on presently, the great distinctive feature of the Benedictine as compared with the Oriental rules, is the importance attached to manual and agricultural labour. Incidentally this became a matter of large importance to Europe, and it reveals the clear, practical direction of the institution from the first. Not that it was a new thing in monastic history. Even the most self-enfolded of the Oriental monks had some notion of a duty to scratch the ground about his cell, and raise the herbs he needed for his food—that is, if he was so far from the Oriental idea of perfection as to prefer salads to grass. But it never assumed in the Eastern system anything like the dignity and importance which from the first it attained to in the West.

St. Benedict and his followers went to work with the axe and spade, and cleared the wilderness where they were resolved to settle. Order, culture, fertility, the land smiling under tillage, the wilderness and the solitary place made glad, the desert rejoicing and blooming as the rose—these were the fruits of the institution which delighted them; the outward and visible symbols of the inner culture, the clearing of the moral wilderness, and the rearing of the flowers of patience, hope and charity on the bosom of the desert within. The following is a passage on labour from the rule of St. Benedict :—

'Laziness is the enemy of the soul, and consequently the brothers should, at fixed times, occupy themselves in manual labour; at other times, in holy reading. We think that these should be thus regulated. From Easter to the month of October, after the first prime, they should work, nearly to the fourth hour, at whatever may be necessary : from the fourth hour, about to the sixth, they shall apply themselves to reading. After the sixth hour, on leaving the table, they shall repose quietly in their beds; or if any one wishes to read, let him read, but in such a manner as not to disturb others : and let nones be said at the middle of the eighth hour. Let them work till vespers at whatever there may be to do; and if the poverty of the place, necessity, or the harvest keep them constantly employed, let them not mind that, for they are truly monks if they live by manual labour, as our fathers and the Apostles did ; but let everything be done with moderation, for the sake of the weak.'[1]

The proportion here ordained is about two or three hours for reading, and seven for manual labour. And at a time when a great part of the culture of the Roman world was carried on by slaves, this rule of St. Benedict was the resurrection of industry, free industry, for the want of which mainly the Empire was dying, nay, was dead. '*Latifundia perdidere Italiam*,' said one well able to judge.[2]   Great farms, cultivated by slaves, while their wealthy owners rioted in luxury in the city, ruined the Empire ; and would have ruined humanity but that monk and barbarian, German barbarian, wrought together to save it. Wrought together. Great forces never work alone. While the monk was restoring labour to its Divine dignity—'My Father worketh hitherto, and I also work'—German freemen were pouring into the

<hr>

[1] *Reg. S. Benedicti*, c. 48.   [2] Plin. *Hist. Nat.* XVIII. 7.

Empire, and seizing all its most fruitful provinces, to make them homes of industry once more. The conquering barbarians became the free cultivators of the fair fields of Britain, Gaul, and Italy, and the land broke forth into singing under the tillage of their sinewy hands.

The monks of St. Benedict had begun the restoration within the bosom of the Empire; and they still continued in the Teutonic era to render to agriculture a service which is too little recognised, and which made their rule as helpful to the industry of the German, as it had been to the Roman world. They constantly brought lands into cultivation which nothing but pious labour could have reclaimed and subdued.

We wander among the graceful and splendid ruins of the great Benedictine and Cistercian houses, with which in time our country and Europe generally were begemmed; and we are prone to indulge in a sarcastic reflection on the keen appreciation of natural charms which the choice of the sites exhibits. The taunt is somewhat thread-bare, but we meet with it still even among those who ought to know the truth. Tintern, Bolton, Fountains, and Melrose, are familiar names to most of us. They are the fairest scenes even in this fair land. The great abbeys abroad occupy mainly kindred sites. They seem to claim the softest valleys, the greenest pastures, the most fruitful hill slopes, the most teeming rivers, as their own. These gardens of Europe are the monastic eulogies. Fountains Abbey stands in a Yorkshire valley, of which one is tempted to complain that it is too exquisite, too suggestive of luxurious plenty, security, and repose. But turn to the picture which the valley presented to the first monks who invaded it, in search of a dreary wilderness, where they might be sure of finding hardship, hunger and toil. They came out from the rich abbey of St. Mary's at York to live a simpler and purer life, and they settled in the valley where in time they reared their splendid fane, because they found there a dismal marsh and a thick forest, with no clearing big enough to grow them even a few sheaves of corn. Half their number died in the first winter from famine and marsh fever; the rest held on, and the result of their pious labour we enjoy to-day.

If we search the records of the settlement of Benedict at Subiaco or Monte Cassino; of Columbanus at Luxeuil or Bobbio: of his chief disciple at St. Gall; of Abelard at the Paraclete, and Bernard at Clairvaulx, we find substantially the same history. These scenes which seem so fit to be the homes of a soft and indolent quietude, were chosen because of their wild and desolate sternness; and they were tamed to their present beauty by the strenuous toil of husbandmen, the like of whom no other history reveals. These men believed that each fen which they drained, each copse which they cleared, each acre which they brought under the ploughshare, was an acceptable offering of pious hands and hearts to God. At least this belief animated the leaders; the mass of the followers at any rate caught the habit, and to catch a good habit is something for the great mass of men in such a world as this. It would be idle, of course, to contend that this was the constant character of monastic labour throughout the Middle Ages. Monasteries grew fearfully rich, and, like the secular lords around them, cultivated vast estates by the labour of a peasantry bound to the soil. But the primal *motif* never wholly failed them; agriculture was always a main concern with the great religious communities; and the quasi-consecration of all that belonged to them secured for their lands some share of immunity from the horrors and devastations of war; though the protection was more imperfect than is generally supposed. Something of the noble motive to labour which inspired the first founders, continued to animate their relation to their labourers and dependents, and a long book would be needed fully to set forth the debt which European agriculture owes to the monks of the Middle Age.

In connection with the self-abnegation and obedience demanded by the Benedictine rule, it is to be noted that the founder introduced a most important feature—the perpetuity of the vow. Before his time the monastic vow had remained under the control of the man who made it. He was simply a layman who chose to do certain things, and when he was tired he might depart and do what else he pleased. St. Benedict established the perpetuity of the vow under the most solemn and awful obligations, while at the same time he provided a long and severe novitiate. Here is the ordinance about the vow :—

'Let him who is to be received promise in the oratory before God and His saints the perpetuity of his stay, the reformation of his manners, and obedience. . . . Let a deed be made of this promise in the name of the saints whose relics are deposited there, and in presence of the Abbot. Let him write this deed with his own hand, or, if he cannot write, let another at his request, write it for him, and let the novice put a cross to it, and with his own hand deposit the deed upon the altar.'[1]

From Benedict's time 'Once a monk, always a monk,' became the law; and it is easy to see how immensely this perpetuity of the vow increased the power of the system as an influence on European society. The novice being received at length and with difficulty into the brotherhood, made it his supreme concern to offer up, in every possible form, the sacrifice of himself. How absolute was this self-abnegation, this suicide of the will, appears in many passages of the Rule. Here is one forbidding the possession of individual property :—

'It is especially necessary to extirpate from the monastery, and unto the very root, the vice of anyone daring to give or receive anything

<hr>

[1] *Reg. S. Benedicti,* c. 58.

without the order of the Abbot, nor may he have anything of his own peculiar property, not a book, nor tablets, nor a pen, nor anything whatsoever; for it is not permitted them even to have their body and their will under their own power.'[1]

The obedience which the monk was to render to his abbot was of the most abject and unquestioning kind. It was pure, passive, lifeless obedience, yet we have to remember that it was by an act of high and deliberate volition, under circumstances that secured its perfect freedom, that the man made himself a slave. When the choice was once made, slave was the title he gloried in, and servile punishments for breaches of rule were willingly and even joyfully endured. Nothing can be more suicidal in the long run than this idea of self-surrender, but it is important to understand how earnestly Benedict sought to secure that it should be voluntary. He balanced the demand for absolute obedience by the length and the careful training of the novitiate.

So extraordinary is this feature of unreasoning self-surrender on the part of the monastic votary, that inquiry has naturally been made into the question of its origin. Here is the view of M. Guizot :—

'Together with labour St. Bernard prescribes passive obedience of the monks to their superiors : a rule less new, and which prevailed also among the monks of the East, but which he laid down in a much more express manner, and more vigorously developing its consequences. It is impossible, in studying the history of European civilisation, not to be astonished at the part which is there played by this idea, and not curiously to seek its origin. Of a surety, Europe received it neither from Greece, Ancient Rome, the Germans, nor from Christianity, properly so called. It began to appear under the Roman Empire, and arose out of the worship of the Imperial majesty.'[2]

A deeper source may however be found for the feeling which made this self-abnegation possible, if we connect it

---

[1] *Reg. S. Benedicti*, c. 33.
[2] Guizot, *History of Civilisation*, Eng. Trans., II. 77.

with the same enthusiastic personal devotion to the Lord, which, as we saw at the beginning of this chapter, goes far to explain the monastic life at large. The abbot was to the monk as Christ. It is to this root that the submission must be referred, rather than to the servile habits of Imperial Rome. That entire obedience to the Father's will, which is so conspicuous a feature in the life and discourses of the Lord, the monks delighted to imitate in their submission to the man whom Christ had set over them—who was to them as a present God. Men pined, amidst the confusion and darkness of their intellectual sphere, in an age when the constructive instinct was strong, for visible tangible manifestations of unseen spiritual powers. The Abbot was this to the monk, the Pope became this to the Catholic world. In both spheres the submission was abject and destructive; though ennobled for a time by the vision of some more awful form behind both Abbot and Pope. But it was simply idolatrous—the endeavour to grasp within some form which could come within the cognisance of the understanding, the substance of the unseen but ever-present Lord. Self-denial is one thing. A man may deny himself in the free exercise of his loftiest faculty, and realise an inner freedom of the personal will and fulness of personal life in the effort. But the real aim of the monastic discipline was to leave a man no self to deny. There was its essential weakness. The Buddhist is the only monk who grasps the whole meaning of the institution, and dares to set clearly before himself the idea which is behind every high form of the ascetic life. It is a perpetual draining of the springs of the personal being: it strikes a death-blow at that which makes man worth redeeming, in the hope of making his redemption more complete. Could it have run its course unchecked, unmastered by other and yet higher human forces, it would have killed at the very root the development of society, by leaving for development nothing but machines.

Having glanced thus at some of the main features in the Benedictine rule, we may now take a rapid survey of the whole field of mediæval monachism, by considering:—

I. The part which the monks played in relation to the visible body, the Church.

II. Their relation to the inward and outward life of men—the human affections, interests, and duties.

III. The service which they rendered incidentally to the culture of Christendom, and the unfolding of the life of secular society.

I. In regard to the relation of the monastic communities to the Church at large, we must note that the monks at first were simply laymen. The process by which, almost in spite of themselves, they became not clerics only, but the elect of the clerical order, it may be interesting briefly to trace. Primarily the monastic instinct tended to seclusion from the world, and from all offices of natural, political, or ecclesiastical duty. For many generations the monks, as a class, retained their lay character; and the most earnest of them kept themselves rigidly aloof from the offices and services of the Church. They were, in fact, taught to put on the same level the call to ministerial duty and the temptations of the flesh. The warning is conveyed in a curious passage from Cassian :—

‘It is the ancient advice of the fathers, advice which endures, . . . that a monk at any cost must fly bishops and women : for neither women nor bishops allow a monk who has once become familiar with them, to rest in peace in his cell, nor to fix his eyes on pure and celestial doctrine, contemplating holy things.’[1]

The ascetic would, indeed, be likely to hold himself superior to ordinances of all sorts. He worshipped in an inner

----

[1] *De Cœnob. Instit.*, XI. 17.

sanctuary, and his priesthood refused the imposition of earthly hands. To him, Church officers and offices would appear in the light of worldly tempters and distractions, drawing him away from the rapt contemplation of things spiritual and divine. Still, from the first, complications, sometimes of a serious kind, arose. Monks of a certain class, covetous of power, pressed into the priesthood, and able monks were coveted and sometimes caught with guile by scheming bishops, and of this curious tales may be read in the literature of the times. On the whole, the lay character was for a while successfully maintained, though it was a hard matter to escape the bishop's crook, which tended terribly to become a claw.

The fifth century was an age in which the episcopal order consolidated and extended its power. The records of that epoch are full of legislation which had for its direct object the subjection of the monks, both in the establishment and the conduct of their monasteries, to episcopal control. Monachism was at that time establishing itself in the West with little method or uniformity, and naturally, having no *point d'appui*, the monks in the various districts fell under episcopal sway. But as they became organised as Benedictines, and increased in influence, power and wealth, the monks bore with growing impatience the supervision of an official whose grade in holiness they regarded as lower than their own. Material considerations, too, soon complicated the matter. The monasteries gathered treasure; the bishops of the fifth, sixth and seventh centuries were greedy of revenue for their sees. The monks, as the ecclesiastical legislation amply proves, suffered grievous spoliation, and even violence at their hands. The parochial clergy had already utterly lost their independence, and were held in servile, and often brutal subjection. But the monks fought hard for freedom. They had a standing ground of their own, which the clergy lacked, and they offered an organised and sometimes armed resistance. The struggle lasted with more or less vehemence through three centuries, and terminated at last in favour of the monks, by the intervention of the Papal See, from which in those ages many deliverances sprang.

While the monks were battling with the bishops for independence, a great change was passing over their relations to the Church. As they felt their power, honour, and authority increase, they lost something of the primal ascetic inspiration, and began to aspire to official functions. The way would be opened by practical demands which would constantly make themselves felt. A numerous company of monks, settled at a distance from the church where the ordinances and sacraments were celebrated, would be in some perplexity: partly from distance, and partly from the feeling of superiority to the common mass of the faithful, they would strive to get what came to be called a chapel consecrated in their monastery. in which, at intervals, a priest might officiate. But this intrusion of a ghostly man, of an inferior order of ghostliness, would cause some soreness in the monastery, especially as the jealousy between the clergy and the monks increased. Then they would naturally seek to have one of their own order consecrated as their priest, to minister to them in holy things. And thus it actually befell. But this would introduce a distinction, an inequality where equality was fundamental: and so it came about that the whole body of the monks began to aspire to the clerical office, and gradually, by the force of the virtues which, whatever we may think of them, were most honoured in those times, they made their way into the front rank of the ministers of the Church. It is impossible to fix the dates of the various steps of the transition. Early in the seventh century, Boniface IV. proclaimed them *plus quam idonei*, 'more than fit' for the clerical office, and from that time we may regard them as on the high way to supreme clerical power, which they finally achieved by the sheer weight of their intellectual and spiritual superiority to the priesthood, in those points which struck the imagination of that rough but idolatrous age.

A notable era in the development of Western monachism is marked by the career of Boniface (c. 685-754), the great Anglo-Saxon missionary to Germany, and one of the ablest and most far-sighted statesmen of the eighth century. He had the eye to discern and comprehend the bearings of two rising powers which were destined to play a prominent part in European history. He saw that the true cure for the miseries of the Merovingian kingdom was the assumption of the regal power by Pepin, the founder of the Carolingian Empire, and he attached himself with zeal to the fortunes of that powerful family. At the same time he saw that a principle of order, not of the purest or most perfect kind—Boniface knew that full sadly—but still powerful, practical, and full of promise for the future, was to be found in the extension of the dominion of the Papal See; and he lent the whole weight of his remark-able character and influence to strengthen and enlarge the rising authority of the Popes, which had still in it some original spiritual force and life. It was in devout submission to Rome that he carried on his missionary labours; the bishoprics which he founded, after the fashion of his own see of Mainz, were placed solemnly under Papal control, and it was as the representative of Pope Zachary that he anointed Pepin king. In fact, Boniface was the leading statesman in Northern Europe during the whole of that era of transition, and the institutions which he mainly helped to found were destined to a mighty success.

The career of Boniface had in many remarkable ways a powerful influence on monasticism, as his copious correspond-ence reveals, and in founding the monastery of Fulda in 744 he placed it directly under Papal protection. Thenceforth the monks began to see in the Papacy the power which would uphold them against the tyranny both of the bishops and of the secular lords. From that time the monks and the Roman See begin to draw together in closer relations, and in the end the whole army of the monks, during the palmy days of the institution, became the army of the Papal Church.

Without the monks the work of the Church would probably have been impossible. For good or for evil they served her with singular fidelity, and were as a body her devoted champions. Celibates—after the manner of all standing armies—they were at the disposal of the Church, to maintain her pretensions, to fight her battles, and to carry out her plans. The extension to all the *personel* of the Church of the monastic principle of celibacy threw into her hands a power of enormous magnitude. It kept the whole spiritual force of Christendom under one head, and ready, as it were, at the single word of command. Terrible as were the evils of Church pretensions and claims, and of the wrongs and outrages perpetrated in the most sacred Name, it was doubtless better for humanity at large that the particular form of Christ's kingdom represented by the mediæval Church should be wrought out to the fullest possible perfection. The Church completed her organisation by adopting the principle of the monastic orders, and could always count on them for consistent and effective service.

Hence it follows that our estimate of the value of the influence of the monks in mediæval society will largely depend on the value we attach to the influence of Rome. A very noble idea was at the root of the devotion of the monks to the Papal chair. It was in the conviction that the Roman See represented the unity of Christendom, that they vowed themselves to its service ; they would realise through Rome the visible kingdom of the Lord.

It must, however, be remembered that the idea of the unity of Christendom took different forms in the early Christian and mediæval centuries. We must not suppose that the one form in which this unity presented itself was the kind of theocracy that floated before the vision of Gregory VII., Innocent III., or Boniface VIII. Churchmen were, indeed, slow to entertain the idea of a united Christendom under the rule of a priest. That Christianity was the World-Religion was a fixed idea, and the Roman rule naturally suggested a World-Empire as its outward form. At the conversion of Constantine a temporal prince had actually stepped into the headship of the Church-State, which was regarded as a kind of vicegerency of Christ in the world. The position which Constantine assumed, and which the Church continued to recognise—Gregory the Great wrote to Maurice as to his master, and Leo bent before Charlemagne as he crowned him at Rome—made the emperor the unquestioned head of Christendom. The conception of a complete Christian State, a visible political body of which the emperor under Christ should be the head, and of which the Church should be the inspiring soul—the conception of 'the Holy Roman Empire'—is the key to the aim and effort of Christendom through much of the mediæval period. How passionately a great layman could cling to this idea, the *De Monarchiâ* of Dante reveals, and at one time the imperial power had no stronger support than the ablest minds of the Church. But the dream was but a dream. Not in that form could a kingdom of Christ be realised in the world. If we contrast Dante's dream of the Empire with its history under all but the ablest rulers—nay, under the ablest, for the splendid reign of Frederick Barbarossa is among the saddest of all—we shall see that the Empire, complicated as it was with German politics, was palpably unequal to its mission, and that there was ample room for the pretensions of the purely spiritual power to grow.

On the wreck, therefore, of the temporal unity of Christendom arose the idea of the imperial power of the Church. The steps by which the Roman See, aided by the monastic institution, attained its supremacy we cannot even in outline trace. A terrible history of usurpation, fraud and shameless forgery may be gathered from the records of Church history. 'Janus' parades them in one startling chapter, dealing too tenderly with Nicholas I., who laid the foundation on which Hildebrand built the empire of the Church.[1] But forgery does not explain a power which was wielded with such tremendous force for ages, and which M. Comte—who considers that the positive philosophy, 'being as free from monotheistic as from polytheistic or fetish belief,' is singularly able to form a calm judgment—regards as '*formant jusqu'ici le chef d'œuvre politique de la sagesse humaine.*' There must have been a great preparation in the public mind of Europe for the usurpation; there must have been a sense that the advancing power would fill a vacant throne, and restore a lapsed idea; and this must be fairly taken into the account, when we would estimate the procedure of the Papacy in these times. It is easy to detect a steady growth of pretension and power, from the days when Gregory the Great wrote humbly to Maurice and worse than humbly to Phocas, to the day when Boniface VIII. issued the bull, *Ausculta, fili;* or when seizing a sword he declared, 'It is I who am Cæsar; it is I who am Emperor; it is I who will defend the rights of the Empire.' This was however the first stage of the decline. When the emissary of Philip le Bel struck the old man with his mailed hand, he marked an era in the history of the Church. Philip le Bel, one of the most unbeautiful figures

<hr>

[1] *The Pope and the Council,* ch. 3.

in history, was yet a national monarch with a nation behind him; and with the rise of the national spirit the Papacy began to decay. The death of Boniface was followed speedily by the seventy years' Captivity; then came the councils of Constance and Basle, and then things ripened rapidly for the Reformation.

On the whole the growth of the institution up to the fourteenth century was continuous and sure, but even in the period of its highest power, as will be shown on a later page, Christendom was at all times ready to turn from the Papacy to any influence which seemed to present higher claims to a Divine sanction. A man like St. Bernard, for example, was, as we shall see, recognised as an authority far beyond and above that of any occupant of the Papal chair.

The Roman Church during the period of its supremacy was just a rude battery of force, the main direction of which was Christian, acting on a state of society too hard and gross to be influenced by more subtle and spiritual means. The Gospel, sheltered within this citadel, strove to stir the sluggish spirit of the times, and to bear such witness as was possible against the more crying evils that were desolating society, and in favour of justice, temperance, and charity, as graces still dear to God and blessed for man. One thing the Church did accomplish, though at such a moral cost as makes it difficult to strike the balance between loss and gain; she wrought the facts and truths of Christianity into the very texture of the intellectual, social and political life of humanity, and impressed that Christian character on our civilisation which is its distinguishing glory, and which, once inwrought, abides for all time. On the whole, the things which were of *supreme* importance were in the custody of the Church, and despite Mr. Lecky's able argument, we must conclude that though the ages of her sway were little fruitful in the highest Christian sense, they were the parents of a great future: they were ages in which ideas and habits of action were being worked into the very heart of European society, which will Christianise humanity to the end of time. The monastic orders, mighty helpers in this great work, share fully in whatever glory or whatever shame attaches to the rule of the Roman Church throughout the Middle Age.

II. The relation of the monks to the inward and outward life of men—to the human affections, interests and duties. In this connection it will be sufficient to refer to the missionary work of the monasteries, and to the influence on society of the virtues they chiefly cultivated.

One great and unquestioned service rendered by the monk to Christian society was in his capacity of missionary to the Teutonic settlers, within the limits of the Empire and beyond, who were destined to grow into the European nations of the West. There was that in the monastic life, its simplicity, its purity, its severe abstinence and contempt for pain and death, which had a strong attraction for the imaginative but somewhat brutal barbarians who settled within the Empire, and for the still ruder tribes who dwelt beyond. To these the monastic orders furnished, generation after generation, the most courageous, devoted, and successful missionaries, and their influence was enormous on the manners and morals of the barbarian peoples. Their success in this work largely depended on the fact that they were the only men who could travel about Europe in safety. The old *Pax Romana*, which had been an indispensable condition of the rapid spread of Christianity, was broken up. The Empire had gone to wreck, and a new cycle of storm and strife had opened, in which the monks seemed, as it were, born to be the ministering spirits.

The monastic profession made a kind of ark, where the truth and power of Christianity could take shelter; and the monks themselves were the men who had the power and courage to bear it through the world. The monk as a rule was safe among the rudest barbarians and amid the shock of war. He was as safe as a holy Christian woman is safe in these days in visiting the haunts of impurity and crime, and for the same reason. He could move where he would, securely, and, moreover, he was everywhere at home. A hut of boughs, a bit of bread, a spring of water—he had all he wanted. He found, too, brethren to shelter and help him. His monk's dress was a ready passport to every monastic establishment, to every eremite's cell. Here was a great brotherhood spread all over the European world, whose watchwords were purity, abstinence and toil. The monks did not live up to these watchwords (do we live up to ours?) but they tried their best;—it was their ideal at which they aimed. They were ever on the watch to support and strengthen each other. They kept up a close intercourse by letters; they were brethren, corresponding as brethren though subjects of hostile states, and the effect of this constant effort of a widespread and powerful community in favour of the Christian virtues was incalculable. England was one of the countries in which in the seventh and eighth centuries the monastic institution took the deepest root and exercised the widest influence; and the intercourse of the great conventual establishments in England during the Heptarchy, the unity of the monkish fraternity and of their regulations and offices, did more than any one political movement to consolidate the realm of England, and to make the several States one Nation under Egbert's and our great Alfred's hand. It may incidentally be noticed that many of our towns in Western Europe grew up around the religious houses. A very able and learned writer, who has studied the subject deeply, estimated that three-eighths of the towns of France owe their existence to monasteries.

It may be asked, had not Europe to pay a terrible price for the advantages she gained through the labours of the monks?   Was not the principle underlying monachism one that in its essence was really destructive of social life?   Were not many of the dearest and most sacred interests of society trampled in the dust by the celibate?   Could they have fully wrought out their will would they not have made life a purgatory and the world a waste?   There is this side of the question to be looked at, and the truth which underlies the charge is fatal to the monastic life as a permanent and universal Christian institution, but by no means conclusive against it as a thing of virtue and use in its own times.   Looking at the domestic affections, it is easy to pronounce stern judgment on a system which wrought in tender hearts such an unnatural hardness as we find sometimes cultivated under the ascetic rule.   There are, however, some startling words in the Gospels about a man 'hating father and mother' for the sake of Christ.   We have seen that the ascetic tried to lift himself into the sphere of Divine experience, through a partial and often mistaken outward imitation of the Lord, and this may explain the attitude of monachism towards this side of human nature.   There is however another point of view.   It may fairly be urged that some such isolation and sublimation of the domestic affections was essential to the realisation, after the struggles and self-mortifications of ages, of that purity, delicacy and spiritual beauty, which in modern life lend a holy charm to the perfection of wedded and kindred love. In other words, so ensnaring, so debasing, had been, in the ancient world, the influence of the flesh on the domestic and social relations, that men under the overpowering attraction of the new spiritual life felt compelled to cut themselves off completely from this lower sphere.   The separation, however, was really preparatory to a lasting union—to that blending of the spiritual life with the natural, which should redeem and purify those very affections that at one time it seemed to oppose and threaten to destroy. Plato, too, had dreamed this dream of the sublimation of all earthly relationships, and he, too, like the monks, believed that it was the condition of a heavenly rather than an earthly world. He says of his form of the spiritual republic: ''Αλλ', . . . ἐν οὐρανῷ ἴσως παράδειγμα ἀνάκειται τῷ βουλομένῳ ὁρᾷν καὶ ὁρῶντι ἑαυτὸν κατοικίζειν.' The new power which had entered into the world with Christianity had, like the Baptist, to draw itself off to the desert, and nurse itself there, before it could enter the circle of life, and rule the whole sphere as lord. And ages are but as days in this great history. For ten centuries the spiritual element in the Church, as far as man could detach it, passed through this narrow, stern, but intense discipline—there is eternity before humanity in which to reap its fruit.

It is noteworthy, too, that, though monachism might seem to bring a most potent battery to bear against everything by which secular society could increase and prosper, society yet increased and prospered mightily. One grand feature of the social influence of the monks, to which M. Comte does full justice in his critique on the Middle Age, is the career which they opened to power of every kind. ' La carrière ouverte aux talents,' was the gospel of the French Revolution, according to Mr. Carlyle. As regards the secular sphere, he is quite right. But ' the career ' had always been open in the monastic. One of the noblest features of our English society and one main source of its stability, is the access which is open to men of high capacity, through the law and the legislature, to the peerage and the highest offices of the State. What that element of our life does for England, the monastic orders did for Europe during the formative ages of its history. The religious profession was absolutely free to every one; prince and peasant were equal in the cell; birth was nothing, capacity was all. The poorest, if he had power, might scale the highest throne in the world. And thus there was, in an age when the caste organisation of society was peculiarly hard and rigid, a constant ascent of fresh blood and strong brain power from the lowest stratum to the highest, whereby to an extent which is not always appreciated by historians, a most powerful influence for good was exercised over the great world's affairs. Again, in an age of supreme monastic influence, even when the greatest of monks wielded imperial power in Europe, woman rose to a position of dignity, and developed a power and beauty of character, which we cannot refuse to connect largely with the elevating and purifying influence of monastic life and thought, on the thought and the life of society. The monks did more to help society upwards by the spirit which they breathed, than to crush it downwards by the maxims which they promulgated. Their theory would have destroyed the civilisation which they themselves helped mightily to consolidate and raise.

Nothing, too, can be a greater mistake than to suppose than this stern repression of the natural affections issued necessarily in hardness and poverty of nature. Sternly as they strove to indurate themselves *quoad* world and natural affection, the monks often lived in their monasteries lives full of human gentleness and tenderness, and in their best days not without some pure gaiety and gladness of heart. *Simplicitas, benignitas, hilaritas,* were no idle words upon their lips. Some of the most tender and passionate effusions which have come down to us from the records of the past are contained in monastic chronicles and correspondence. Though there is something sweet in those tender and apparently satisfying friendships of the cloister, they are unnaturally strained and therefore in the long run weakening; nor can it be doubted, that from that side sore temptations pressed them, and a flood of evil at length broke in. But the reason why this hardening process did not harden, but left men with sensitive hearts and vivid affections, is not far to seek. The love which they denied their kindred was not wasted, they spent it with passionate fervour on the Saints and on the Lord.

It has been said of Christianity that it is deficient in stimulus to the patriotic virtues. It individualises men, and places each one under such tremendous pressure, that the State vanishes, the individual and his individual belongings are all. We have already seen, however, that before the Advent this individualising process had been in full play. The patriotic sentiment in Greece had been greatly weakened by the cosmopolitan empire of Alexander. The philosophical ideas both of Zeno and Epicurus, as we have noted, are remarkable for the earnestness with which they deal with individual interests, and let the grander range of the elder philosophy pass out of sight. To bear up the man against the ills of life was their main problem; and it stated itself yet more strongly in the stoical philosophy of Rome. Christianity, cultivating the individual, and making him, at the same time, the conscious citizen of a wider, even a celestial commonwealth, left him to deal with his mundane duties in the new spirit which it inspired. The result, as a matter of fact, was that the mundane suffered at first some harm and loss. The monks seemed to carry to an extreme the isolating tendency; country, kindred, were nothing to them; but, on the other hand, they acknowledged a spiritual brotherhood that was all in all. The world was immensely richer for this idea of spiritual fellowship, and as M. Ozanam points out and as we have already in another connection explained, in the break-up of the Empire, this universal monastic brotherhood was a strong *nexus* of society, and helped to keep the unity of Christendom before the minds of men.

III. The service which the monks rendered incidentally to the culture of Christendom, and the unfolding of the life of secular society.

There is a preliminary question which forces itself here on the attention, and which has been a good deal discussed of late years. Did not Europe, it is asked, greatly suffer from the withdrawal of such a vast army of capable men from her fields of secular activity and toil? It is a question that had claimed an answer in an earlier age. The Emperor Maurice found that the army was seriously affected by the withdrawal of those who desired to devote themselves to religion. He was for taking strong steps to check it. Gregory the Great wrote to him: 'The armies of my sovereign will be strengthened against their enemies, in proportion as the armies of God, whose warfare is by prayer, are increased.'[1] And Gregory was right. Industry draws strength from the spirit of man as well as from his sinews. Those who put new life and hope into humanity are preparing for the fields the noblest tillage. Population, agriculture, industry, grew mightily through the monastic ages; and nothing was lost but, in the long run, much gained by the anti-secular action and influence of the Church. Our own Alfred understood the matter thoroughly. 'These are the materials,' he writes, 'of a king's work, and his tools to govern with, that he should have prayer-men, and army-men, and work-men. What! thou knowest that without these tools no monarch can show his skill.'

One of the most fruitful works done by these 'prayer-

---

[1] *Epistol.*, II. 62.

men ' for society was their care for education and for literature and art. On this subject there is the less need to speak because on the whole it is fairly recognised. Those who have not looked into the matter, would be amazed at the vast apparatus for literary work and for the instruction of children, and that not for ecclesiastical purposes only, which was maintained by all the great Benedictine houses. They had their outlying schools and preaching stations in the most obscure villages, as the Methodists distribute their local preachers in these days. In truth a fair picture of a day's work at such monasteries as Corby under Paschasius, Fulda under Rabanus, or Glastonbury under Dunstan, would reveal an earnest, loving, and energetic activity in the work of the world's culture, which would have put the work of our leading Universities fifty years ago, to an open shame. Taking even the darkest of all dark ages, the tenth century, which Baronius says, 'for its sterility of every excellence may be denominated iron; for its luxuriant growth of vice leaden; and for its dearth of writers dark,' a diligent study of its records would reveal, that the decay of learning and scholarly zeal was the fruit of war and political misery; while it is as full as any age of the noble devotion of the harried and miserable monks to literature, and of their sorrow over its inevitable decline. Their lamentation, when their houses were laid in ruins, was over their books as well as their relics, and many a touching story might be narrated of the cost at which even the fragments which survived were saved. The question, too, has to be considered, if we would understand the times, how far very much of this literary work, especially the wearisome task of transcription, would have been possible except under the constraint to labour which the monastic law brought to bear on man. The poor transcriber of St. Gall who scratched on the margin of his MS. '*Libro completo Saltat scriptor pede læto,*' was only one of a vast army of devoted workers for the intellectual good of mankind. Nothing but their conception of the virtue of monastic obedience could have borne them through the wearying toil. We owe them a bitter grudge for the treasures they destroyed. Many a copy of the lost books of Livy or the lost plays of Menander was obliterated, no doubt, for the sake of some wretched saintly biography; but we accept this as the inevitable counterpoise to the grand literary service which they rendered to the world. Not for themselves, but for us they did minister. They laboured; we have entered into their labours. It was a monk, a monk of monks, a pure and lofty spirit, the beloved and honoured Bede, who wrote our first history, and brought the civilising influence of literature to bear on our land. It was a monk, Benedict Biscop, who brought back from Rome plans of churches and dresses and vessels, which started our fathers on their path of industrial and artistic development; it was in monasteries that the master-pieces of ancient literature, as far as they were preserved, were studied with passionate ardour, and the course of intellectual development was commenced which Shakespeare, Milton, and Newton crowned. One is surprised to find how much time the famous Boniface, greatest of all missionary monks, spent in correcting the themes of English girls in the nunneries! The monks, too, were the chroniclers of mediæval society. Why? Distinctly because they were able to grasp, as no other men were able to grasp, the idea of God's interest in human history, because they saw that man's history in its wholeness was a Divine work. Each little chronicle of an obscure monastery must weave itself in with the history of the Creation, the Deluge, and the Advent of the Lord. We may almost say that here, in the monastic cell, was nourished the germ of our great modern achievement, the philosophy of history. This is a tempting theme; how the beginnings of secular art, science, and literature rose from the monastic root, but there is no space for further details.

Very deeply, also, the literature which the monks loved and fostered touched the heart and lightened the burdens of the great mass of the poor. Monkish and saintly biographies—there are some 25,000 of them in the Bollandist Collection—are full of grotesque images and childish miracles. But with all their fantastic supernaturalism, their puerile superstition, their trivial and unnatural incidents, at the heart's core of them they were sound enough; purity, loyalty to truth, and above all charity were the graces which they celebrated, and the victory of meekness, modesty, truth and mercy, over brutality and ferocity, was always their theme. We must remember that this was the age of the childhood of Christian society. Our children's books still are full, and long may they be full, of the most miraculous triumphs in the long run of the good·boy or girl over the bad one: and all the agencies of nature are freely laid under contribution to secure the victory. These lives of the saints, the literature of the poor, were the nursery books of Europe, and they helped mightily to keep some thought of what Heaven loved and cared for, alive in the popular heart.

Here, then, is a vast body of most invaluable service rendered to the intellectual, the moral, and the political progress of society. We can hardly believe that any purely secular combination of men to build, and work, and write, on the best patterns; to multiply manuscripts; and to rebuke injustice, brutality, and war, could have endured for a generation. The monks did what they did in the secular, because they felt they were doing an appointed work in the spiritual sphere; bringing according to their lights, the power of Christ's Gospel to bear on men.

In conclusion, it would be wrong to be unmindful of the

fearful picture of corruption, of the tales of unutterable abominations and horrors, which might be drawn from authentic monastic history. A life of such high tension, kept at full pitch so long, inevitably, when the tension relaxed, sunk into dark, sad depths. Great spiritual movements are powerful for a time only. Very noble, beautiful, heroic, in many respects, this one was, while the red blood of its youth was in it; very pallid, foul, and base it became when it dragged on a dull mechanical existence after its work in the world was done. To judge it aright we must look at it in its prime: in the light of its aims, aspirations, and hopes. It would be easy to show what dragged monachism to the dust; it is more profitable to consider what enabled it, in spite of this constant human proneness to corruption, to regenerate itself so often, and to endure so long.

On the whole, we must say, to sum up the matter, that nothing in the long run and on a large scale succeeds in God's world but God's law. Extremes on either hand are ultimately fatal. In the beginning God made them male and female, body and soul, man and the world. All rebellion against His institution is in the end futile and ruinous. No doubt it would have been a blessed thing if the monks had had an open eye for this world as well as for the world to come. Men, however, as a rule, see but one thing thoroughly at a time. Any great principle which has entered largely into the life of humanity, has held for generations and even ages, almost exclusive possession of some considerable section of society. Hence the march of humanity has been a march *en zigzag*. Whenever any one masterful principle has possessed the world and bent it powerfully in one direction, there has never failed to appear some equally important principle which has seized society in time and turned it in the other, and thus, the world swaying now in one direction, now in another, but ever onward, a clear progress through the ages has been gained.

VI.

ST. BERNARD, THE MONASTIC SAINT.

VI.

ST. BERNARD, THE MONASTIC SAINT.
1091-1153.

THE point now reached is one that affords an opportunity
for a glance backwards and forwards over the ground already
traversed and that which lies before us. In the age preceding
the Advent, the philosophic schools had devoted increasing
attention to practical questions of the conduct of life, and
during the first Christian centuries the most earnest thinkers
among the Stoics, by their attention to pressing personal and
moral problems, had approximated in certain respects to the
Gospel. As soon as Christianity was established it began to
carry out that fundamental regeneration of society at which
the Stoics had aimed. Christian ideas now clothe themselves,
in successive ages, in different institutions which attempt one
after the other to maintain the body of Christian truth and
influence against the many opposing tendencies of the times.
From the fifth century onwards the monastic system gathered
in to itself the best life of Christendom, and strove to effect
the salvation of society. Later on in the Middle Ages, behind
the monks appears the structure of the mediæval Church, in
which the Popes stand forth as the organs of the thought and
influence of the whole clerical world. Then the Papacy grows
magnificent and wanton, rich in possession and prerogative,
but poor in honour and love. Behind it, in the hour of its
chief splendour, rise up to sustain it the Mendicant Orders.

Little dreamed Innocent III., as he walked that evening on the terrace of the Lateran Palace, when Francis of Assisi with his tattered troop of disciples drew near, that the men were before him who should restore the faith of Christendom for a while in the ideas which the Papacy was dishonouring, and by renewing the springs of its life, secure for it a new lease of power. When these fail there is nothing behind to serve as a fresh support, at least nothing 'of this building.' The next great movement, the herald of the Reformation, will open with John Wyclif, and a fresh reading of the word of the Gospel, and with a new baptism of the Spirit of the Lord.

Four conspicuous men of the saintly order left their impress deeply on the life of Europe during the Middle Age—St. Bernard, St. Thomas of Canterbury, St. Francis, and St. Louis. Each was typical of a certain aspect of the saintly character, and from the point of view thus indicated they are dealt with in the following pages.

The two greatest of the saints were St. Bernard and St. Francis, and the greatest of the pair was St. Francis. He was a creator; the rule which he founded had a new idea in the heart of it, and his Mendicant Order, in ways which it would be very interesting to trace, led on in a direct line to the Reformation. St. Bernard created nothing, but his career and his vital influence on his times, were perhaps the greatest moral forces which through the whole Middle Age of Christendom were brought to bear on men. He carried to the highest point of perfection and of power that monastic idea, which was a great constructive force in Christendom for centuries, but whose function ended with his life. Bernard entered the world frequently, in fact the world had need of him and could not get on without him; but he always entered it sorrowfully, and as matter of dire necessity, longing the while with a passionate desire for the quiet cell and the holy duties of his beloved Clairvaulx. He was the greatest of the great monks and the last of them. When he died an age died with him, and the old monachism lay buried in his grave. Monachism as an institution lived on ; the monks as great landlords and scholars rendered noble service to agriculture and learning, but the Cœnobite as a vital power in Christian society was last incarnate in St. Bernard.

If St. Bernard ends an age, St. Francis opens one. Bernard gathered up the whole strength and nobleness of the popular opinion of his times, and used it to serve his times. But he was really a man of the past. Like Pompeius, he rooted his life in an old and perishing order of things. Francis, like Cæsar, was the pioneer of a new order; when he died he left behind him a new ecclesiastical world. The friars of St. Francis would now play the chief part on the stage of the Church till the era of the Reformation, opened in England by John Wyclif. If the passionate desire of the monk was to get *out of* the world, that of the friar was to get *into* the world, and to mix freely with men. Wherever the throng was thickest, there was his work ; he mingled with the people and lived by persuading them. By bringing the Gospel into intimate contact with the daily life and busy occupations of mankind, St. Francis leads on to St. Louis, in whom the saintly character and life passed out into the secular sphere, while on the other hand the teaching of the Franciscan school formed the true link of connection between the Middle Ages and the sixteenth century.

Between St. Bernard and St. Francis, a very remarkable man, who earned as a saint an almost unique reputation, played a leading part on the theatre of European history. St. Thomas of Canterbury, better known to us as Becket, was almost worshipped as saint and martyr for generations after his death. But he was after all but an ecclesiastical saint. He sought and he used the saintly character, quite honestly no doubt, but very visibly, as an instrument of ecclesiastical power over men. Becket lived in the world of popes, bishops, kings, barons and statesmen, as a man of the world, whose business lay in the midst of the political and ecclesiastical activities of his time. He was more at home fighting the battle of the Church against Henry II. than playing the saint at Pontigny. The battle of his life to maintain the privileges of the hierarchy, and to secure the independence of the *imperium* of the Church from any secular control, was as purely a worldly battle as the struggle of Henry to maintain his throne. It was power which Becket was fighting for, the power of the priesthood, the power of the Church; though he had, no doubt, a very high purpose of using that power for the protection of the oppressed and for what he deemed the best interests of mankind. The uppermost thought in Becket's mind throughout his stormy primacy was the influence of an Order, the triumph of which as an Order would have been just as fatal to the true welfare and progress of society on the one hand, as, on the other, the unchecked dominance of the most absolute secular tyranny.

St. Bernard was the monastic saint. His monk's cell was dearer to him than any spot on earth; his deepest desire, his most fervent prayer, was that he might be left there alone with God, far from the haunts of men and the turmoils of the great world, to train his soul in Christian knowledge and holiness, and help his brethren around him in the path to heaven. That cell was a storehouse of spiritual force with which, again and again, he shook the civilised world. He had no longing for the power; he greatly dreaded the constant stormy excitement in which it enveloped him; though we can hardly question that a man with such a remarkable capacity for command felt a throb of satisfaction when he saw the pope, the emperor, kings, prelates, and all the host of Christendom, like clay under his hand to be moulded by his will.

The true spring of the incomparable power which he wielded was his noble simplicity, purity and unselfishness. He embodied more than any man of his day the Christian idea, as it was then understood, and men believed that through Bernard it was Christ that was ruling their hearts. He mistook, as we all in our measure mistake, the counsel and spirit of the Master to whose service he gave himself with passionate devotion. He did not understand, it was hard for such a man in those days to understand, that the great world with all its temptations and snares is the divinely appointed training school of man's spirit; and that the proscription of any faculty or element in our wonderfully compacted nature avenges itself in the end with unfailing retribution. No scheme which would re-make man's nature on a simpler and more one-sided plan, has in it the elements of more than a momentary success. Men we are, men we must be: with passions and appetites as well as convictions and sympathies: with a spirit which can believe, with an intellect which can question, and with a flesh that can desire its own satisfaction. Not in the proscription of any, but in the harmony of the whole, lies the true dignity of our nature and the true happiness of our lives. We are able to understand this better in our day, because Bernard and men like Bernard tried so thoroughly the ascetic scheme of life in their own. Bernard was the saint pure and simple. His ecclesiastical influence was enormous, his political influence was enormous; but they were, if we may so say, the mere accidents of his saintship. The true core of his influence was spiritual: his one great aim in his intercourse with men was to make them more pure, more just, more merciful, more peaceful. Even the Crusade was preached by him in the hope of bringing in more swiftly the peaceful and blessed Divine reign.

Quis custodiet ipsos custodes? Who shall guard the guards, who shall rule the rulers? was the question which forced itself on the most thoughtful and provident minds in heathen society. Through all the epochs of the great Oriental despotisms, in the time of Alexander and the Macedonian kingdoms, and finally and signally in imperial Rome, men felt the need of some fixed principle or superior power behind and above the human potentate; some overlord, whose righteous decree, remaining constant through the ages, should bring a strong constraint to bear on the caprices and passions of the rulers of mankind. One of the characteristic differences between heathen and Christian society, lay in the recognition in the latter of such a superior power, such an overlord of all the lordships of the earth, who held the sovereign direction of the affairs of the great world. It is impossible to understand the development of Christendom, unless we take note of the enormous influence which this sense of a living authority on high, exerted on the heart and the conscience of mankind. In the heathen States a Nero or a Commodus was the 'præsens Jupiter,' and he seemed to the anxious eyes and hearts that watched him practically omnipotent to work out his malignant will. In Christendom, though there might be a tyrant on the throne, he was not felt to be the supreme arbiter for the time of human destinies. Men saw an authority above him, able to set him bounds and to maintain, through all the wreck which he made around him, the order and progress of society. There can be no question that the sense of this overlordship of the King of kings, did exercise a strong controlling and regulating influence, both on the conduct of rulers, and still more on those thoughts of men about the duties of superiors and the rights of inferiors, from which the enlightened public opinion of modern times has been in great measure evolved. In these days monarchs, statesmen, bishops, magistrates, all who are in authority, and whose acts may be a great blessing or a great bane to mankind, proceed under strong but benign constraint: they are ruled in ruling, to an extent they little dream, by the public judgment of their fellow men. We may call this the growth of the Christian conscience of society; some speak of it as the consolidated experience of the past generations of mankind: and this is true of the body of it, though the soul of it comes from above, and descends to us through this idea of a supreme Lord of monarchs and masters, which has been one of the most powerful forces that have moulded and developed Christian society.

We shall quite mistake the matter if we imagine that Christendom, throughout the Middle Age, was content to seek this authoritative supervision in such an institution as the Roman Church. If the Christian world had been able continuously to trust and to obey the Roman See, nine-tenths of the struggle and anguish which have attended its development might have been spared. The chronic distress of mediæval society arose, from its intense conviction that there was such superior divine authority, joined with the difficulty it found in discerning and bringing it to bear. It was essentially an ideal thing, this kingdom which ruled the kingdoms. No one knew what was its organ, and how its power was exercised. And yet men believed profoundly that it was real, the greatest of all realities; and that it did through all manner of channels make its influence felt in the world. The Papal See offered itself as its earthly regent. The Roman Church had indeed immense advantages in its organisation, its continuity, and its host of zealous servants in every land of Europe devoted to the will of its head. One of the points of deepest interest in mediæval history is, however, to be found in the struggle of Christendom *not* to be made an earthly empire under the supreme sway of the ' vicar of Christ ' at Rome.

The effort to discover something nobler, purer, diviner, than the rule which Rome could offer, constitutes the real drama of the epoch. Rome seemed to offer what Christendom wanted, a symbol of unity and an authoritative head; and yet men moved uneasily under the paternal authority of the Papacy. Not in the Reformation epoch alone, but through the whole Middle Age, the resolution of Christian Europe not to put herself under the hand of Rome, is the key to the most momentous passages in European annals. The Pope conquered at Canossa; and the emperor shivered in his shirt in the snow. But it was a fatal victory. It made the lay mind understand that the paternal rule was a stern tyranny, and there was always suppressed, and often open, war between the secular mind and the Church from that day until the Reformation. When Bernard lashed the vices and corruptions of Innocent or Eugenius, when Catherine of Sienna laid bare the iniquities of the hierarchy in her days, when Petrarch uttered his tremendous anathema against the Papal Court in the celebrated sonnet :—

> Fountain of woe, harbour of endless ire,
> Thou school of error, shrine of heresies !
> Once Rome, now Babylon, the world's disease,

the mind of Europe went with them. Christian men saw the corruption and pollution and groaned over it; and yet if this higher authority were not there, Where was it ? and so this question kept Europe in unrest for at least five hundred years. Whenever a man of eminent holiness and fervour, like Bernard, arose, Europe turned from Rome to him as flowers turn to the sun. The Papacy for a time was nothing, the saint was all. Why ? Because he seemed to waiting hearts to realise the hope which long had mocked them; to wield a pure and righteous authority, which looked like some fair earthly image of that of the unseen King: and as he moved about the world an incarnate conscience of Christian society, everywhere observed with the deepest veneration and served with the most passionate devotion, he seemed to them to reveal the longed-for principle of unity. Christendom became then, for a time, one great household of faith, whose abbot, or father was a man of holy heavenly spirit, the law of whose rule was the celestial wisdom, the sceptre of whose sway was the divine love. A man like Bernard, in his unselfishness, his lofty indifference to ease or pain, his high idea of the virtue, the purity, the nobleness becoming a Christian profession, and in his incomparable influence over men, seemed to supply to Christendom that for which it had long been pining, but which the Roman Church, in spite of the honest efforts of its best rulers, could not in the nature of things afford. In Bernard men saw a true paternal authority, a head of the great family, whose headship, like the kingdom of God, was not in word but in power; a father whom they could with their whole hearts obey, honour, and love.

It is probable that Bernard wielded the strongest personal influence over his fellow men that was ever exercised by a man in this world. There was a certain magnetic force about him which was resistless, but, at the same time, to admit that he possessed this unique individual power, is far from implying that he was the greatest man of the Middle Age. On the contrary, even in his own days, Peter Abelard was a man of far higher genius, though the fair unfolding of the noble germs with which his nature was richly charged, was sadly marred by his selfishness and vain-glorious pride; while, in the next age, a greater man was St. Francis with his new and far-reaching ideas. We may depend upon it that a man must have a certain strain of commonness in him, who is so universally popular and successful as was Bernard. The men whom the world worships in their lifetime are neither its prophets nor its pioneers. Bernard, however, in his times and for his times was a man of altogether matchless force, and made it felt, in a way which has no parallel before or since, over the whole Christian world.

No attempt need here be made to recount the mere outward events of Bernard's life, but it may just be noted that he was born at Fontaines in Burgundy in 1091. He entered the monastery of Citeaux in 1113. He was sent out in 1115, young as he was, at the head of twelve monks to found a new monastery in the waste. In 1130 he conducted, we may say single-handed, the struggle which placed Innocent II. in the Papal Chair. In 1140 he entered the lists with Peter Abelard, the leader of an intellectual movement, destined in time to undermine the system of authority which Bernard so strenuously upheld. In 1145 he preached the second Crusade. In 1147, six years before his death in 1153, he was in the South, and extinguished for the time the nascent heresy in Provence, a district two hundred years in advance of the rest of Europe in point of culture and free thought. Bernard was contemporary with Henry I. of England, Louis VI. and VII. of France, Henry V., Lothair II., Conrad III. of the Empire, and Popes Innocent II. and Eugenius III., and he is altogether the most prominent figure in Christendom between the two greatest Papacies of the Middle Age, that of Gregory VII. which closed in 1085, and that of Innocent III. which opened in 1198. The Papal Empire was founded by Hildebrand at the close of the eleventh century. It attained to the height of its power under Innocent III., who was reigning in the year 1200. In the year 1300 Boniface

VIII., the last of the great Imperial Popes, held with great pomp and splendour the Universal Jubilee, and from that hour the Papacy began visibly and rapidly to decay.

There are five great acts in the drama of Bernard's life. His sweeping with him every member of his family, the married and the unmarried alike, into the monastic profession ; the campaign, we can call it nothing else, by which he seated Innocent II. in the Papal Chair ; his struggle with the great free-thinker Abelard and his signal conquest ; his preaching the second Crusade ; his battle with the heretics in Provence, shortly before his death. The intervals were filled up by attention to everything above average importance which took place in Christendom, by incessant correspondence, some of it of remarkable power, with all sorts of men and women, and on all sorts of themes. Nothing indeed came amiss to him, from the squabbles of Yorkshire monks to the struggle for the Papacy, from ruling the conduct of counts, kings and popes to contentions about some unhappy pigs [1]—all was within the scope of his interest. It is more than possible that his greatest achievement in point of difficulty was his first ; and to that, that we may understand the man Bernard himself, we will now proceed.

Towards the close of the eleventh century there was a knightly household living in the Castle of Fontaines in Burgundy. The province is the richest, the most splendid, the most joyous, the most vital of all the regions of France. The men are like its wines, full of colour and fire. It is the country of great orators ; Bernard and Bossuet were born in Burgundy, and many a masterful spirit beside. Fontaines was the home of a very noble, but by no means rare, specimen of the feudal household of the times. Tesselin was at the head of it ; a man who strove hard in a stormy time to be the knight of Christ ; fighting with such con-

<hr>

[1] See for the incident. Morison's *Life of St. Bernard*, Lond. 1863, p. 492.

spicuous courage in all the wars in which he was bound to serve, that it is said that whenever he followed his Duke to the battle, victory continually attended him; but one who was also resolved as firmly, to do justly, to love mercy, and to walk humbly with his God. Bernard came of a noble line, but that was absolutely of no account in this matter of saintship. The Roman Church did at any rate keep open, through the ages in which the caste organisation of society was peculiarly hard and stern, a career of splendid possibilities of distinction and influence to the capable among the poorest of the poor; and the value of that to the development of Christian society it would be hard for us to rate. At the same time, through Hildebrand's victorious struggle to impose celibacy on the clergy, the Roman priesthood never became a caste, as it has become in the Eastern Church, to the degradation of the priest and the impoverishment of society. The wife of Tesselin, the mother of Bernard, Alith or Aletta, ruled the household in Christian love, and, as we might be sure about the mother of Bernard, she was one whose life helps us to understand how in that twelfth century, among rude soldiers who had not lost the eye for nobleness, purity, and grace, the worship of woman arose. Six sons and one daughter were born to her, whom William of St. Thierry says she nursed herself, and in infancy devoted to God.

Bernard was educated in the school of Chatillon. Space will not allow of any notice of his boyhood, but he was unquestionably both following the inherited instinct and fulfilling his boyhood's passionate dream, when in his twentieth year in a wayside church, he fell on his knees and with a torrent of tears gave himself to God. In that age this meant monastic vows, for the age of the saintly layman, St. Louis, had yet to dawn. But Bernard was not a man to move alone. The young monk must begin at

once his work of persuading and ruling men, and began it
where it was hardest, in his own country and in his father's
house. His uncle and two of his younger brothers yielded
at once. Guy, the eldest, was married and had children ;
and he fought hard against the spell. At last he promised
that, if his wife would consent, he would yield. 'She will
either consent or die,' said Bernard. But she did neither,
and Guy was in sore distress. He offered, so strong was
Bernard's power, to give up house and lands, and to till the
soil as a peasant, if his home might remain unbroken.
But Bernard knew no middle course. The absoluteness
which marked him through life was already developed.
Then heaven seemed to help him. The young wife fell into
a grievous infirmity, and the scales dropped from her eyes.
She cried that she was kicking against the pricks, sent for
Bernard, and yielded herself unreservedly into his hands.
Gerard, the second son, was a gay and gallant soldier : a
man of rare fascination, as we may gather from the wonderful sermon which Bernard, after long years of monastic
fellowship, sobbed out over his grave. He took a light
view of the matter, and tried to laugh off Bernard's claim.
Bernard is said to have fixed a finger on his side, and
warned him quietly. 'A day will come and soon, when a
lance shall pierce thee here, and make a way to thy
heart for the counsels of salvation which thou despisest.'
Gerard, struck shortly after by a lance-head in battle, cried,
'I turn monk, monk of Citeaux.' The youngest son, Nivard,
was now alone with the old man in his almost childless
home. Guy said to the lad as the brothers took their last
farewell of their domain, 'See my brother, the whole of
our inheritance will devolve on thee.' 'Heaven to thee, and
earth to me ; that's no fair division,' said the lad, and
promptly followed in the same steps. The old forsaken
father, the last of the line, soon joined the band at Clair-

vaulx, and died in Bernard's arms. Many whom the young novice won round him were married. He had a nunnery built for the wives at Juilly, in the diocese of Langres; the wife of Guy became the first abbess; and there, after a worldly career among the noblest in France, Hombeline, the only sister, found rest at last.

They all betook themselves to Citeaux. It had been founded fifteen years before, by some monks who were weary of the luxury and splendour of Cluny, in a savage wilderness near Chalons, and was then under the rule of Stephen Harding, an Englishman, whose discipline was the austerest in France. These first Cistercian monks rose at two in the morning, and they took their only meal at two in the afternoon, after twelve hours of prayer and work. Meat, fish, butter, and eggs were absolutely forbidden, and milk was a rare luxury. Their garments were of the coarsest wool, and their house of the severest simplicity. There, one day in the year 1113, the iron hammer which hung at the lonely gate of the monastery sounded, and a large number of men entered the cloister, which was hardly ever visited except by some traveller who had been benighted in the forest. Thirty persons entered, and coming to Stephen begged to be admitted as novices. There were among them men of middle age who had shone in the councils of princes, and who had hitherto worn nothing but the furred mantle and the steel hauberk which they now came to exchange for the cowl of St. Benedict. The greater part of them were men of noble features and deportment, and well might they be, for they were of the noblest houses in Burgundy. The whole troop was led by a young man of about twenty-three years of age, and of exceeding beauty. He was rather tall in stature, his neck was long and delicate and his whole frame very thin, like that of a man in weak health. His hair was of a light colour, and his complexion was fair, but with all its paleness there was a virgin bloom spread over his cheek. His face was such as had attracted the looks of several high-born ladies, but an angelic purity and a dove-like simplicity shone forth in his eyes, which shewed at once the serene chasteness of his soul. This man was he who was afterwards St. Bernard, and he now came to be the disciple of Stephen, bringing with him four brothers and a number of young noblemen to fill the empty cells of the novices of Citeaux.

Bernard, intense in everything, plunged into the austerities with a kind of rapture. Harding, an able as well as holy man, saw the promise of a great future in the young Bernard, and young as he was, twenty-four, sent him forth as the abbot of twelve monks whom he despatched to seek out some wild waste spot, where they could found a new monastery attached to the Cistercian rule. They found the 'valley of wormwood,' near La Ferté, desolate and rugged in aspect. There they built their modest home, making it as the 'Clara Vallis,' celebrated through the wide world. There the austerities were renewed, if possible with fresh vigour, and Bernard's health utterly gave way. His frame fell into a state of collapse. 'Wholly absorbed in the spirit, seeing he saw not, hearing he heard not, tasting he tasted not, scarcely anything by any of the senses of his body did he perceive.' His life was in peril. His friend, William of Champeaux, bishop of Chalons, got an order from Harding that Bernard should place himself under his direction for a year. He had a cottage built for him and put him under the charge of an attendant, who was to see that he had proper food. The attendant miserably mismanaged it. William of St. Thierry, his friend and biographer, visited him in his hut. He was horrified at the disgusting coarseness of the food and the brutality of the attendant. He asked Bernard how he fared in his new mode of life. 'Excellently well,' he replied in his own noble manner, 'I, who have hitherto ruled over rational beings, am now given over by a great judgment of God to obey an irrational beast.' But he never complained. He had been taking coagulated blood, thinking it to be butter, and oil, thinking it to be water. 'Water,' says poor Bernard, simply, 'is the only thing that is pleasant to me, for it cools the fever of my throat.'

He struggled through, though he remained always a sickly, wan and weary man, able however to gather up his strength for any demand which the interests of Christendom made upon him, and to enter into every conflict with a vigour which entirely prostrated every foe. He had juster views of asceticism before he died. There is a passage in his book *de Consideratione*, that runs thus, and it is a valuable testimony from such lips, 'Temperance is not only in cutting off superfluities, but in admitting necessities.' Much solace and inspiration he found in the beauty and splendour of the world around him; indeed the monks may be said almost to have kept alive in the human heart the love of nature through the stormy Middle Age. 'Trust to one who has had experience,' writes Bernard, 'you will find something far greater in the woods than you will in books. Stones and trees will teach you that which you will never learn from masters.'[1] And we are told that he said that 'whatever strength he had in the Scriptures, he gained chiefly in meditating and praying in the woods and fields: and that his masters in this matter had been oaks and beeches.'[2] There can be no shadow of a question that Bernard's whole heart was in the monastic life. No ambitious dream could win his love from it; and later, when he was the most famous man in Europe and passed through it more than once in triumphal progress, he ever, like the dove to the ark, returned to his quiet cell as the true home of his spirit and place of his

---

[1] *Epist.* 106.   [2] *Vita S. Bern.*, auctore Guillelmo, I. 4.

rest. He remained at Clairvaulx, praying, preaching, and carrying on an almost universal correspondence, with perhaps only two brief absences, probably on monastic business, until 1130, when the scandal of the Papal schism drew him forth. But his fame spread far and wide, and his letters won for him growing influence and honour, and prepared the way for that splendid conflict and triumph to the history of which we will now proceed.

Early in 1130 Pope Honorius II. died. A great scandal attended the election of his successor. One party nominated Gregory, Cardinal of St. Angelo, who took the name of Innocent II. The other, the most numerous but the most mercenary, elected Peter Leonis, the rich grandson of a Jewish usurer, who took the name of Anacletus II. There was fighting in Rome, and St. Peter's was stormed and spoiled. Innocent fled to France and was warmly received: Anacletus was most powerful in Italy. The French clergy were strongly on Innocent's side, and it would appear purely on moral grounds. The French king and the secular authorities were in suspense. Henry I. of England was adverse. Lothair of the Empire, though disposed to recognise him, thought it a grand opportunity to renew the struggle about Investitures, in which his predecessor had been signally defeated. The French king, Louis le Gros, with whom the first duty of decision lay, assembled a council at Étampes, to discuss the question. Bernard's aid was earnestly sought. Hesitating and trembling, but comforted on his way by a vision, he attended the council. No sooner was he in presence than the whole council enthusiastically resolved to leave the decision to Bernard—'the business which concerned God, should be entrusted,' they said, 'to the man of God.' He accepted the task, examined the proofs, weighed the evidence, and solemnly declared Innocent the head of the Christian world. There can be no doubt that the moral weight was entirely in Innocent's scale, and having settled the question of right decisively, Bernard threw himself with intense, resistless force into his cause. The whole French Church and nation he carried with him by acclamation. Henry I. of England, a stern and able man, strongly influenced moreover by the prelates of his realm in favour of Anacletus, endeavoured to make head against his rival. Bernard brought his battery to bear upon him. He went to visit him, and pressed him long in vain. But like all other men, Henry went down utterly at last. The final shock is characteristic:—'Are you afraid of incurring sin if you acknowledge Innocent? Bethink you how to answer for your *other* sins to God, that one I will take and account for.' Then Bernard, allowing himself no breathing time, threw himself on Lothair. He and Innocent went to Liège. The Emperor thought that the opportunity had come to revise the decision about Investitures. Innocent and the Roman Churchmen trembled; they were absolutely in their enemy's power; Bernard alone trembled not. He spoke to the Emperor, that was all. He had nothing but the power of what he firmly believed to be the word of God, and it was sharper than a two-edged sword in his hands. The Emperor too fell before him, the Investiture question was dropped, and Lothair, taking the bridle of Innocent's white palfrey, meekly conducted him through the streets of Liège.

The most difficult task was however still to come. Anacletus was strong in Italy, and Bernard was resolved to seat his Pope in the Pontiff's Chair at Rome. The cities of Italy were first attacked by letters. Genoa, Milan, Pisa, were admonished and threatened, and again Bernard's words were all-powerful. Step by step, from city to city, he conducts his Pope in triumph. At Milan, the whole population, nobles and people, streamed out as far as the seventh milestone to meet him: they thronged around him and plucked fragments or single hairs from his mantle, and prostrated themselves before him to beg his blessing. A transport of enthusiasm swept round him and bore him on his triumphal way. The events here described occupied about three years, and the chief acts of the drama were separated by considerable intervals, but there was no break of the continuity of Bernard's influence. From first to last he swept everything in Europe before him, and at length, with the Emperor on the one hand and the Pope on the other, he entered Rome in triumph and seated Innocent with his own hand on the Papal throne.

This healing of the Papal schism was perhaps the most signal triumph of Bernard's life. And those who are able to picture before the mind's eye the Europe of that epoch, and to comprehend the impossibility of any purely political combinations as comprehensive as this, will see in that triumphal progress perhaps the grandest instance of the resistless force of this one human spirit, who gathered up, not the deepest thoughts, but the purest practical aims and the wisest practical judgments of the time, into the cells of that battery of vital force, by whose shock he moved the Christian world.

In the course of this struggle, the greatest of Bernard's life, a striking episode occurred, which perhaps reveals better than any other single incident in his life the marvellous power which he wielded over men. William Count of Poitiers, the father of that formidable Eleanor, wife of Louis VII. of France, and afterwards of our Henry II., had adopted the cause of Anacletus and driven Innocent's bishop William from the See. The Papal legate in Aquitaine resolved to trample out the opposition at once. Only Bernard could do it, and Bernard, sick and weary, was dragged to Poitiers. He sent for the Count, and the Count came. He argued with all his force in vain. The Count was at last persuaded to give up Anacletus, but flatly refused to have anything to do with William, his bishop. Bernard broke off the useless discussion, and entered a church to perform mass, leaving the Count outside the church door as an excommunicated person. When he had consecrated the Host, he came forth with flaming eyes and countenance of fire, bearing the Host before him, and sternly reproached the Count for his contempt of the Divine command. Then fixing his terrible eyes upon him, for Bernard was terrible at such moments, he said—'Your Judge is here, at whose name every knee shall bow whether in heaven, on earth, or in hell. Your Judge is here, into whose hands your soul will fall. Will you spurn him also? Will you despise him as you have his servants?' The Count fell senseless to the ground. They raised him; he again fell prostrate, foaming at the mouth. When he came to himself he meekly gave the bishop the kiss of peace, and led him back to his church amid general joy.

Only a word can be said on Bernard's proceedings in regard to the heretics of the South of France.

Provence and Languedoc were in the twelfth century very markedly in advance of the rest of Europe north of the Alps. Southern France was to Europe in the twelfth century very much what Alexandria was in the first to the Roman world. It was the meeting point of Oriental and Western influences and the theatre of an immense fermentation of thought. Oriental Manichæan heresy was there, and there too was pure Scriptural Christianity. It is a tempting subject, the life of Languedoc in the twelfth century, but it must be passed by. Enough, that heresies were fermenting there which had a strong tincture of the Reformation, though this, owing largely to the nobly conservative influence of men like Bernard and Francis, was still centuries away. The advisers of the Court of Rome were growing seriously anxious about Languedoc and perplexed as to its action, till at last they were driven to turn to their unfailing champion the Abbot of Clairvaulx. Bernard accompanied the Papal legate, and, as usual, all opposition went down before him. Wondrous stories are told of what was called the miraculous power of his works, and the hardly less miraculous power of his words. He completely prostrated the heretics; but, as has been well remarked, as soon as Bernard's back was turned they seem to have got up again and gone on very much in the old way!

It is time that we glanced at Bernard's relation to the great intellectual movement of his times, and surveyed the lists in which the strongest champion of orthodoxy, and the most brilliant and adventurous free-thinker of Christendom, fought *à outrance*, with the result that the free-thinker for the time was vanquished.

There are two classes of men in every age. The great majority, who are 'of their times,' who believe the beliefs, are occupied with the interests, and busy in the work, that belong to their own epoch. There is always too a small minority, in whom the ideas and the hopes of the coming age are budding, in whom the future is beginning to shape itself, who are partly out of touch with their own age, and speak to it what seems a strange language; and who are accordingly accounted to be troublers of the peace of Israel, perhaps emissaries from the great enemy of souls. Their lot in their own age is mostly distrust and obloquy, a life of disappointment and sorrow, and perhaps a broken heart. In the twelfth century Bernard stands as the representative of the first class. He carried up to their highest completeness the ideas, the aims, and the hopes of his contemporaries. He lived their idea of the perfect life. He was the popular man in a word: and though the popular man is never the highest, he was perhaps the greatest, noblest, and most powerful popular man that has ever lived.

The type of the second class in the age of St. Bernard was Peter Abelard. As the representative intellectual man

of the era, he was the leader of a movement which shook
to the foundations, not indeed the faith which Bernard
cherished in his heart, but the whole system of things
which Bernard upheld as the temple of that faith. The
movement embodied in Abelard was purely intellectual. He
had no programme, he proposed no reform, he simply de-
signed to enquire; to search by the light of reason for what
was behind those forms of thought and modes of action,
consecrated by the tradition of ages, which such men as
Bernard rested upon with unquestioning confidence. Abelard
was a Breton, and like Bernard the son of a nobleman of
splendid prowess and fame. Although the eldest son, he
resigned at twenty all the honours and prospects of his position,
that he might devote himself to learning; not, we remark,
to embrace, like Bernard, the contemplative life of the cloister,
but to attend the schools, dispute, and take part as a knight-
errant of Philosophy in all the intellectual tournaments of
his time. The stirring outburst of life which that twelfth
century witnessed, was nowhere more conspicuous than in
the intellectual sphere. The schools of great teachers were
thronged; the lecture room where metaphysical subjects were
discussed with intense eagerness was rising as the rival in
attraction to the monastic cell. Abelard was a man of
literally exuberant intellectual power, full of the Celtic
brilliance and fire. He was vain, arrogant, used to conquest
and loving it for its own sake; hardy to excess in reviewing
the most assured beliefs and habits of his times. I think
he made it more difficult than it need have been for his age
to understand him, as is often the way with heretics, and
he did much to provoke that bitter hostility which hunted
him to his grave. Heavy were his burdens and sorrows.
It is touching to find the greatest thinker in Christendom, one in his way as good a Christian as St. Bernard,
meditating a flight to the infidels, 'where' he says, 'I

may live at peace the Christian life among the enemies of Christ.' [1]

We must remember that Abelard had no desire to be, and no idea that he was, other than orthodox ; and his belief was that all that he was doing was not against the truth but for the truth ; a view of things which theologians would do well to remember, when they take in hand the crushing of heretics. Abelard's intellect was unquestionably sceptical, but he had no consciousness that he was a sceptic. His appeal to Rome at the Council of Sens is conclusive on this point. But he had the genius of enquiry. Bernard had the genius of belief. The 'why' and the 'how' were supreme questions in the mind of the one ; to the mind of the other they seemed dangerous and paralysing suggestions of the great troubler of the peace of souls. But what the world owes, nay what the Church owes, to these men that have the genius of enquiry, is a history which has yet to be writ. Abelard had hold of the method which alone could plant belief on sure and lasting foundations, while Bernard's ground of assurance was already trembling beneath men's feet. Though the life of Abelard seemed a wreck, his relation to his age was deeper and more fruitful than St. Bernard's. Bernard was the last of the Fathers. His quiet rest on the authority of the Church would be possible to great souls like his no more. His life ends an intellectual era ; Abelard's begins one. The one crowns a past ; the other quickens a future. From the time of Abelard even the great monks will be schoolmen, and will handle the weapons with which he fought his battle, with consummate mastery in defence of their orders and the system of the Church. But they will be costly victories. The monkish schoolmen will but build their own sepulchres. The Reformation, and much more than the Reformation, much that is beyond us still, began to be from the days of Peter Abelard.

[1] *Historia Calamitatum*, c. 12.

It is not possible to dwell in detail on Abelard's teaching; it is a subject by itself, and a noble one. Much of his doctrine we should call in these days reasonable Christianity; while on such subjects as 'prayer,' 'sin,' 'the true Christian life,' and 'the offerings which are acceptable to God,' he seems to come near the very heart of the truth. Bernard dreaded Abelard and that spirit of free enquiry which he represented, far more than he dreaded his actual heresies. He had that instinctive fear which the theologian in all ages feels for what he calls 'rationalism.' Bernard saw with vague dread a spirit rising and spreading which was beyond his mastery; which was fed from springs and which aimed at objects, which were altogether beyond his sphere.

The point of view adopted by Abelard is sufficiently indicated by the following words of his:— .

'It happened that I first of all applied myself to discuss the basis of our faith, by the aid of analogies drawn from human reason, and composed a treatise on the 'Divine Unity and Trinity,' for my pupils, who wanted and asked for human and philosophical reasons, and such as could be understood rather than merely spoken.'[1]

This discussing the basis of faith is naturally intolerable to Bernard who writes as follows:—

'We have fallen upon evil times. Masters we have with itching ears. The scholars shun the truth and turn them to fables. . . . We have Peter Abelard disputing with boys, conversing with women. . . . He does not approach alone, as Moses did, to the darkness in which God was, but advances attended by a crowd of his disciples. In the streets and thoroughfares the Catholic faith is discussed. Men dispute over the child-bearing of the Virgin; the sacrament of the altar; the incomprehensible mystery of the Trinity.'[2]

Bernard was quietly keeping Lent with his usual austerity at Clairvaulx, when William of St. Thierry wrote to him in great distress of mind, beseeching him to take this new spirit in hand. The answer is quite characteristic of Bernard. When he had finished his Lent exercises, he said, he would

<hr>

[1] *Hist. Cal.*, c. 9.   [2] *Epist.* 332.

take it up. He did so, and was filled with dread. He remonstrated with Abelard in vain. Then he wrote against him with his usual vehemence. Abelard challenged him to a public disputation at Sens. Bernard shrank from it. 'I am but a boy,' he writes, 'and he a man of war from his youth.'[1] But in the interests of the faith he determined to enter the arena. Abelard appeared with a troop of disciples; Bernard with two quiet monks. There was intense excitement and eager expectation; but to the amazement of all, Abelard declined the contest and appealed to Rome. Again Bernard was master. Before the nameless something which he bore with him, the foremost intellect of the age went down. Bernard got him condemned and branded as a heretic. There is no need to quote the bitter, abusive words with which the saint assails the sinner, the champion of orthodoxy the heretic. Alas! they remain the same through all the Christian ages, and we may read them in the theological literature of the last few years unchanged.

Abelard's stormy life was near to its bourne. On his way to Rome to prosecute his appeal he rested at Cluny. The then Abbot of Cluny, Peter the Venerable, the good man of those days, pitying tenderly the crushed and broken-spirited scholar, tempted him to remain among them and end his days. There he spent a few quiet and comparatively happy years. Peter reconciled him with Bernard and with Rome. He bears noble testimony to his studious diligence, his piety, humility, and gentleness, and with this beautiful prayer, which he wrote for Heloise and sent to her as his last gift, Abelard fades out of sight :—

'Thou hast joined us, O Lord, and hast set us apart when it pleased Thee, and as it pleased Thee. Now, O Lord, that which Thou hast begun in mercy, do Thou in mercy perfect, and those whom Thou hast severed in the world, do Thou join for ever unto Thyself in heaven. O Lord our

[1] *Epist.* 189.

hope, our portion, our expectation, our consolation, who art blessed for ever, Amen!

'Farewell in Christ, thou spouse of Christ! In Christ farewell! in Christ live! Amen!'[1]

So the dogmatist fell upon the thinker and crushed him. The process repeats itself through all the Christian ages, though perhaps it is the turn of the thinker to fall upon the dogmatist now. But thought, crushed, like grass swiftly springs again. The five thousand poor, hungry, ragged scholars who streamed from city to city after Abelard, thirsting to drink of the new intellectual spring, and to arm themselves with the weapons of the new learning, scattered broadcast through Europe the quickened intellectual germs, and commenced a movement which ten thousand Bernards could never stay. Slowly but surely, as dawn flashes into day, thought conquers. There is sore conflict: the old order of things groans and shudders: men's hearts fail them for fear; but in the end always a nobler, truer, freer and more blessed order is born.

The position of the champions of the old order has also its dignity and power. What did orthodoxy represent to Bernard; what made him its passionate defender? It represented not only what he believed to be God's everlasting word of truth, but the tradition of twelve centuries of heroic struggle and suffering: it was the rock on which he and his fellow men were standing, and on which alone he believed they could live and work. There is but one thing more sacred than the established order, and that is the germ of the order which is to succeed, and that germ is with the thinkers. It always goes hard with the assailants of the orthodox order which the Bernards defend, and it ought to go hard with them. Let not any man put his hand lightly to the task of shaking the most assured beliefs

<hr>

[1] Abelard, *Epist.* 5.

of his fellow men. Who shall measure the anguish of the travail through which the new order is born? No sympathy is due to those who whimper over the sufferings entailed by the opening up new paths for men. The pioneers must expect to suffer, but they ought to persist and to conquer. No man who dares not suffer for men, is fit either to lead or to reign. There is no justification for the senseless antagonism which is raised in these days between faith and science, reason and revelation, religion and culture, Hellenism and Hebraism—call them how we will. The two are as needful to each other as the right hand and the left, nay, as the man and the woman in the order of human society. It is the shameful putting asunder of that which God has joined, that is the fatal spring of all the most bitter miseries which afflict the world. The life which is kindled by faith quickens and moves men: the thought which is lit by reason rules them and guides. The Bernards inspire and energise the great community; the Abelards light it to its tasks, widen its horizon, open its paths of progress, and lift higher and yet higher through the ages the standard of its aims and hopes. What we need is the blending of the influence which they severally represent. Neither the faith without the reason nor the reason without the faith, but the two in concert and concord, conspiring, breathing together, like loyal helpmeets, having learnt that their internecine strife is shame and confusion, will one day bring back to earth the Saturnian reign.

One other great enterprise St. Bernard was destined to accomplish before his work was done; he was to preach the second Crusade. The Crusades were perhaps the most purely ideal enterprises ever undertaken by man. None can understand the movement who has no eye for the great vision which was behind and beyond it, the fair realm of Christ governed from Jerusalem in peace and splendour, Christendom nobly reconstituted with the Holy City for its centre, and the Prince of Peace for its King! This is what the Crusade meant to the noblest spirits that embraced it, nay, one could shew that this is what it meant to the poor peasant, who followed his lord to what seemed to him a holy and glorious enterprise, and who left his bones to bleach in the waste. We have no imagination to picture the joy that thrilled through the great heart of Europe, when it was told in every city and hamlet, that on July 15th, 1099, Godfrey of Bouillon, the stainless hero of the Crusade, had stepped from his wooden tower on to the walls of Jerusalem, and fulfilled the passionate dream of the Christian world. The vision had not faded, the dream had not vanished, in Bernard's days; bitter but still not hopeless disappointment was gnawing the heart of Europe when Bernard, with a voice which rang through Christendom and stirred it as it has never been stirred before or since, preached a new, final, triumphant Crusade. It was this vision which fired his passion, and made all men plastic in his hands. It was this vision, too, which kindled the imagination of a yet loftier spirit than Bernard, the last great dreamer who dreamed the dream of the Crusade—Columbus. The spring of the lofty enthusiasm of Columbus, the key too to the enormous and seemingly avaricious demands on which he insisted with the sovereigns, was the hope that he might win such wealth as would enable him to lead a mighty army to Jerusalem, and establish there, as regent of the King of Kings, the last great empire, that 'fifth monarchy,' which in fulfilment of the blessed and glorious visions of the poets and prophets, the Lord had promised to set up.

The Crusaders embarked on a purely ideal enterprise,

and the wrath of man was to accomplish it. They took the sword to establish the peaceful kingdom, and by the sword they terribly perished. It is a sad, sad history. Still though it miserably failed, and broke many a noble heart, there is hardly a movement which has helped to create our modern civilisation which did not spring from it, and few secular events in the world's history have offered more powerful and practical ministries to the onward and upward progress of mankind. The breaking down of the feudal tyrannies, the emancipation of the serfs, the rise of the commons, the growth of the maritime towns, the progress of navigation, the establishment of banks, the development of trade, and the splendid revival of art and literature, all either sprang out of, or were mightily stimulated by, that most purely ideal of all great human enterprises, the Crusade.

How Bernard preached it, the burning enthusiasm at Vézelay and Chartres, the storm of passionate crusading fervour which he evoked in the indifferent or hostile Rhine provinces, till, as he wrote, the cities and castles were empty and hardly one man to seven women were left,[1] the way in which he set all Germany in flame, and compelled the emperor by the sheer force of his eloquence to assume the Cross; how the vast Christian hosts swept on the East like a resistless avalanche, only to be broken and die; how a shattered fragment of the crusading armies struggled back again, and bowed all Europe in shame and sorrow to the dust; all this is known to the most casual student of history.

Bernard's heart was well nigh broken by the failure of his hope. From that time, though he continued his manifold activity, he set himself to die. One other entirely noble witness he was to bear before his work was done. This was his manly and most Christian protest against

<hr>

[1] *Epist.* 247.

the persecution of the Jews, upon which he wrote as
follows :—

'Does not the Church triumph more fully over the Jews by convincing
and convicting them from day to day, than if she, once and for ever, were
to slay them all by the edge of the sword? . . . For if the Church
did not hope that they which doubt will one day believe, it would be vain
and superfluous to pray for them ; but on the contrary she piously
believes that the Lord is gracious towards him who returns good for evil
and love for hatred.'[1]

Bernard's work was done. His old friends and comrades
were dropping on every hand. Suger, the Abbot of St.
Denis, next to himself the most venerated ecclesiastic in
France and his much loved friend, died in 1151. Then in
1152 Count Theobald of Champagne, and in 1153 Eugenius
the Pope, his pupil, his child in the faith, fell asleep. He
felt that his hour was at hand. The prayer of his monks
was ceaseless and importunate. 'But why do you thus
detain a miserable man?' he cried. 'You are the stronger,
you prevail against me; spare me, spare me, and let me
depart.' A gradual failing of the brain came on; that brain
which had influenced every great event and movement in
Christendom in his times. Public affairs ceased to interest
him. 'Marvel not,' he said, when they tried to rouse him,
'for I am no longer of this world.' Looking round on his
weeping brethren, he exclaimed, 'I am in a strait betwixt
two, having a desire to depart and to be with Christ, which
is far better; nevertheless the love of my children urgeth
me to remain here below.' Then raising his dove-like eyes
to heaven he said, 'But the Lord's will be done.' A
moment, a sob, and it was done. Bernard was for ever
with his friends and 'with the Lord.'

[1] Epist. 365.

VII.

ST. THOMAS OF CANTERBURY; THE SAINT AS ECCLESIASTICAL STATESMAN.

VII.

ST. THOMAS OF CANTERBURY; THE SAINT AS ECCLESIASTICAL STATESMAN.

c. 1118—1170.

IT is said by the great Teacher 'He that loveth his life shall lose it,' and 'he that loseth his life for my sake shall find it.' It is true of happiness, of power, of whatsoever outward good is desired by man. He who seeks happiness will lose it : he who is content to lose it in strenuous duty will find it. He who seeks power will grasp but the phantom of it ; he who loses all thought of power in unselfish service of others, will find it to his own honour and with the benediction of his fellow men. Bernard, having no dream of power, caring nothing for power, lost himself in a passionate desire to grow into his Saviour's likeness, and became the most powerful man in Europe : Becket, of whom we have now to speak, known among the saints as St. Thomas of Canterbury, aiming at power by saintship, lost it, became a fugitive and an exile, and died at last by brutal violence, while the power became manifest only round his grave.

St. Thomas of Canterbury was a saint of an entirely different type from either St. Bernard or St. Francis. With him saintliness was distinctly cultivated and employed as an instrument of ecclesiastical power. Ecclesiastical saint is the term that most truly describes him.

Becket was by nature a statesman; one of the ablest whom we meet with in English history. First, a secular statesman of remarkable resource and insight; then, when the archbishopric was forced on him, an ecclesiastical statesman of splendid vigour, intensity and devotion to the cause of the Church. His saintliness was part—an indispensable part—of his equipment for his work. This does not mean that Becket merely played the saint. He appears to have been, on the whole, a thorough and upright man, incapable of sustaining the hypocrite's part through life; but his saintliness did not grow, as in the case of St. Bernard, St. Francis and St. Louis, out of the depths of his nature, it was not a part of his very life. It was rather a habit put on as the proper dress of the position of lofty power and dignity to which he found himself exalted; it was worn by him, we need not doubt, with entire sincerity, but always with a certain ostentation, and a latent consciousness of its great influence over men. The value of Becket's testimony to this influence of the saintly life on Christendom is that of a man who found that he could not get on without it; that if he was to carry on a stern conflict with the secular power of his day, and guard and extend the prerogative of the Church, he must rely mainly, not on his conspicuous personal genius for command and his high endowments, but on the love and veneration which saintliness might win for him.

Very beautiful, very touching, in a rude coarse age, is this reverence for the man who was believed to be up in the heights and nearer to God than his fellows. Men rough, brutal, hard and grasping, bent with a humble child-like submissiveness to a fellow mortal, if they believed that he had more to do than themselves with Heaven. Great multitudes in Christendom would care more for a hair of St. Bernard's cloak, than for the favour of its secular imperial head, and this simply because they believed him to be a better man, a holier man than themselves; one through whom their rude lives might catch a gleam of the sunlight and a breath of the air of the higher world.

Becket, accordingly, not at all a saintly man by nature but rather a courtier and a captain, paid the deepest reverence to the saintly idea, when, as he entered on what he foresaw would be a stormy Primacy, he devoted himself with unmeasured intensity to the exercises and austerities of the ascetic life. Most people know the tales which were current about him—the hair shirt swarming with vermin: the coarse food; the water rendered nauseous by fennel: the nights passed in prayer with intervals of flagellation. We are told that his sleepy chaplain, Robert of Merton, would be roused to scourge him, and when his weary hands could not lay on hard enough, the Archbishop would roll on the floor, in his sackcloth, and pass the remainder of the night with the boards for his bed, and a stone for his pillow. We cannot believe that all this was acting in Becket. The worst austerity, the coarse sackcloth over his whole body and limbs, was not discovered till after his death. There was a certain thoroughness running through his whole career —his Chancellorship, his embassies, his wars, as well as his Primacy—which proclaims him at least no hypocrite; at the same time there was a certain ostentation about it which a little profanes its sanctity, and makes it a thing for us to look into and measure, rather than a thing which looks into and measures us. Becket in fact saw and seized the true springs of a Churchman's power when he made himself a saint. It was for power he did it, but we need not doubt that he honestly endeavoured to make himself as good a saint as possible.

The Romish idea of the living presence of Christ with His Church, in the person and in the judgments of the Chief Bishop of Christendom, was hardly condensed into form in the twelfth Century. It was floating in a nebulous state in the atmosphere of mediæval society, and it touched with something of its unearthly lustre every minister and ordinance of the Church. Then the Church was the ruling idea, now it is the Pope. Men trembled before churchmen because of the Higher Presence that was supposed to be in them: and there was a constant struggle between the reverence which the priest challenged as the organ of Christ, and the hatred and contempt which the actual priest, as a person, constantly awakened. So long as reverence for the Church remained a sentiment pervading in a vague way the whole body of Christian society, its power was incalculable. When this sentiment of the Holy Presence settled finally into a theory of Papal autocracy; when men could look at it as an institution and judge it as a law, its power began to wane. This is true on a wider scale. In every age and in every region of man's experience, how much vital vigour is lost in the transition from idea to institution, from sentiment to law.

Becket stands as the representative of the pure Church idea, which is not the same thing as the Romish system. With him it is not Pope against King, it is Church against King. Becket was a Latin churchman, and acknowledged the Pope as his earthly head. But the help of the Pope, though valuable, was not essential to his position. In the twelfth century, we repeat, the idea of the Church as a corporation of spiritual persons with their belongings, acting as the organ of the unseen and dreaded Lord, had not finally centred itself in Rome. It was gravitating that way, but there was much—papal schisms, papal avarice, papal corruption, and the like—to hinder it. To the great churchmen of those days the Church was a larger thing, a vaguer thing, a more spiritual thing, than it came to be when it was wholly embodied at Rome; and when the Mendicant Orders had placed an enormous number of clever talkers and fluent preachers, always roaming about Europe, at the absolute disposal of the Papal see. The struggle of Becket's life was not to make a foreign spiritual potentate supreme in England. The foreign potentate was a great element in the matter, but Becket's idea was a higher and nobler one: it was to make the Church and everything which in any way belonged to the Church, independent of all but spiritual judgment; accountable exclusively to the spiritual authorities on earth, as the organs of the ultimate spiritual authority on high. A churchman like Becket said in effect, 'That which is Christ's is Christ's alone, to be judged and ruled by His acknowledged organs; the interference of the secular power in a matter which has any spiritual aspect or interest, is like setting the Lord once more before Pilate, and putting Him to an open shame.' With Becket it was simply profanation of holy things and contempt of Christ's supremacy, to allow spiritual matters and interests to be called into question and judged in worldly courts. And surely there is *something* here which strikes one as right in assertion and claim. An Independent at any rate can sympathise with it—Christ's persons, Christ's things, amenable to the disposition of Christ alone. So far right. But when you substitute for Christ a company of ecclesiastics, it matters not whether they be Roman, Anglican, Presbyterian, or Independent (if there is such a thing as an Independent ecclesiastic), we pause. 'The rights of Christ' is a phrase which one always dreads to hear on the lips of a powerful body of ecclesiastics. It mostly means ecclesiastical tyranny of some sort, and of all tyrannies ecclesiastical tyranny is the most absolute, and the most withering to the happiness and progress of society. Christ Himself describes the only 'rights' for which He cared— 'everyone that is of the truth heareth my voice'—and such are found perhaps nearly as often outside as inside the visible churches.

The ground of the absoluteness of ecclesiastical tyranny is the tremendous sanction which is supposed to sustain its decisions, and the eternal issues which are believed to hang on its decrees. It is not selfish; some of the most conscientious men in the Church have been the fiercest persecutors, like Marcus Aurelius in imperial Rome. Its very unselfishness has not seldom made it the more stern and cruel. The struggle between Church and King was perhaps more purely and thoroughly fought out between Becket and Henry, than between Hildebrand and the Emperor, or Alexander III. and Frederic Barbarossa. It was, of course, quite a different contest from that with which we are brought into contact in Bernard's life. That was a struggle to make the truth, a spiritual thing, triumphant in the hearts and consciences of men. In these other cases it was a battle of systems and institutions. The battle was, as far as the visible actors are concerned, a worldly battle, and though spiritual names were used in it freely it is the names only that are spiritual. The name is Christ; the thing is the Church. We will look into this a little more closely; on a right appreciation of it depends very largely a true understanding of mediaeval history.

The 'spiritual persons' for which exemption was claimed, were not pious souls who only asked to worship in peace, and, as Carlyle says, 'to hear a sermon in their own manner'; they were prelates with sees as wide as provinces at the head of retainers as numerous as armies, together with every grade of ecclesiastics down to sextons and gravediggers and the menials of monasteries; and they comprehended, if con-

temporary history is to be credited, the scum of the rascality
of the land. The 'spiritual things' included castles, palaces,
and the fees of soldiers bound to the defence of the realm.
The simple truth of the matter is, and this was the strength
of Henry's case, that to exempt from secular jurisdiction
the men and the things which were covered by the term
'spiritual,' would have been to leave in irresponsible and
frequently lawless hands some of the strongest fortresses and
some of the largest estates in the realm; to release whole
provinces from the duty of taking their share in the defence
of the commonwealth; and to suffer some of the greatest
scoundrels in the country to cheat, and rob, and murder at
will. There were really two questions involved, that of the
relation of the Crown to the great ecclesiastical princes, and
that of legal jurisdiction over the persons and property of
churchmen generally and of their dependents. England, we
must remember, had but lately emerged from the bloody
confusion of Stephen's reign. The country had been reduced
to the lowest pitch of poverty and wretchedness. It had
been desolated by ceaseless petty wars; and the main movers
of it all, the turbulent men of the time, had been the bishops.
'The bishops at the close of the reign of Henry I.,' says
Milman, 'were barons rather than prelates, their palaces were
castles, their retainers vassals in arms; the wars of Stephen
and Matilda were episcopal quite as much as baronial wars.'[1]
The bishops were on the whole perhaps the most powerful
subjects in the realm. It had been to a great extent the
policy of the monarchs to endow the bishoprics largely, as
some kind of counterbalance to the overweening influence
of their nobles. The emperor and the kings of France and
England found their advantage in having powerful personal
feudatories whom they could play off against the hereditary
lords. In Germany, where the emperor was elected and

[1] *Latin Christianity*, Bk. VIII. Ch. 8.

rarely attained to the complete dominion which was possessed by our kings, the question was of the very first importance. There the battle about Investitures, which was really the question of the measure of authority which the monarch as representing the State, should exercise over these powerful ecclesiastical lords, had been settled, after the direst confusion and the most tremendous conflicts, on a basis of compromise by the Concordat of Worms in 1122, confirmed by the Council of the Lateran in 1123. According to this settlement, the ring and the crosier, the symbols of spiritual functions, were no longer to be given by the sovereign, while the sceptre, the symbol of temporal lordship, was to pass to the bishop from the monarch's hand. In England the controversy had been adjusted in 1107, under Anselm, on the basis that the prelate should take an oath of allegiance to the king. In Germany the Archbishop of Mainz was arch-chancellor of the Empire. The ecclesiastical princes were next in dignity to the dukes in its Diet. Three of the seven electors were churchmen; and the archbishoprics of Trier, Mainz, and Cologne, were among the largest and wealthiest provinces in the Empire. The relation of these influential subjects to the throne was a matter of vital importance, and successive monarchs contended as for their lives that these powerful and often turbulent churchmen should confess themselves their vassals for their temporal dominions, and give some security to the monarch as representing the common weal, that they would promote instead of trouble the peace of his realm.

The relation of the Crown to these greater ecclesiastical vassals had been settled, and on the whole with tolerable fairness, before Becket's career as a churchman began. The point at issue in his day was one of legal jurisdiction, and it was perhaps a still more vital one than the first, because it touched, not the great princes of the Church only, but the whole ecclesiastical estate. It concerned the liability of churchmen of all grades to be summoned before the King's courts, to answer for crimes which were destructive to the peace and the very existence of society. The King declared that he had sure information that some of the clergy were 'perfect devils in wickedness,' that the ecclesiastical punishments were entirely nugatory, and that the mischief was daily growing worse. The argument of the Church was that the Church courts were alone competent to deal with the matter, and that the Church penalties, degradation and confinement in a monastery, were sufficiently deterrent. But behind this there lay in the mind of a Church champion of those days, the idea of the Church as a complete spiritual kingdom, co-existent with, but independent of the State; an empire having its own laws, customs, and subjects; its own princes, tribunals, revenues, and rights. The answer of the secular authority was briefly, This is intolerable and impracticable; these spiritual persons are men; they are subjects; they share the welfare of the realm; they enjoy the benefit, and they must be amenable to the judgment of its laws.

However colourable, therefore, may seem the Church claim to judge Church persons, when we come to see to what kind of spiritual persons and things that claim extended, our sympathies pass over to the other side. It is quite possible that they may pass over too absolutely. The secular is the winning side from the first; the State is the fundamental institution. Society could exist without any form of bishop, but it could not exist without some form of king. In the twelfth century, however, the State needed profoundly the influences which the Church was able to bring to bear, and the independence of the Church of the secular power was the essential condition of their exercise. Secular society gravitated with a fearful proneness to brutality. Could we see

Henry IV. of the Empire or Henry II. of England as the men of their own day saw them, we should shudder at the idea of the supreme power being committed without restraint to their hands. They were able men, with a strong desire to rule for the good of their realms, but there was little in those days to bear up a monarch against this brutalising tendency, except the traditions and influences, one dare not say the Gospel, of the Church. William Rufus is a fair specimen of a ruler over whom the Church had little sway. He had sworn to Lanfranc that if he were made king he would preserve justice and equity and mercy throughout the realm; would defend against all men the peace, liberty and security of the Churches, and would in all things and through all things comply with his precepts and counsels. But after Lanfranc's death he kept the see of Canterbury vacant four years, seizing its revenues and wasting its property, and nothing but a serious illness frightened him into filling it. The revenues of the sees and abbeys which fell vacant were a mine of wealth to him, which he squandered on his pleasures. Monarchs left to themselves found the revenues of rich abbeys and sees convenient rewards for their minions, or marketable wares of price. The ravages of simony in the mediaeval Church were terrible. The most ignorant, the most debased incumbents were thrust into the richest benefices; and the idea that the Church and piety had anything to do with each other became in some reigns a tradition rather than a belief. Even Popes pursued the vile traffic. Boniface IX. (1389-1404) was constantly carrying it on, receiving the reports of his agents, and giving instructions, while he appeared to be saying mass.

The Church had to gather up her strength, by the help of her saints, to make head against this inward corruption, and against this proneness of secular life to the profane and brutal; and one cannot see how without her strong hierarchical organisation she could have done it with any measure of success. The miserable degradation of the Greek Church during the Middle Age, is a warning of the difficulty with which a spiritual office, unbacked by a powerful independent ecclesiastical system, maintains itself against all the secular influences around it, and especially the power of the Crown. It would have been a fearful thing for England if her prelates had sunk into the position of State officers of the sovereigns, like most of the Byzantine patriarchs or the Russian clergy at the present day. And in this very matter, the amenability of spiritual persons to secular courts, the Church had a witness to bear and a work to do. One ground of her claim to reserve these for her own judgment was her abhorrence of mutilation and torture, which her belief in the dignity of man through the Incarnation inspired. The secular claim triumphed; and the criminals of the Church were brought gradually under the stern hand of the law. Very rough was it, and fearfully savage were its punishments; but we must not forget in doing justice to both parties in a great controversy, that modern society has adopted fully the gentler and more disciplinary views of punishment, for which the churchmen, inspired by the traditions of their order, were contending in Becket's time.

Of course an easier solution of the difficulty occurs. Castles, domains, vassals, what had churchmen to do with them? Let them keep to spiritual things, and live as spiritual men, and the conflict with the temporal power would never arise. Strangely enough in 1111, seven years before Becket's birth, the same idea had occurred to a Pope. The young Emperor Henry V. was descending the Alps at the head of an army, and Pope Pascal II. met him with this remarkable proposal: Resume the donations on which your regalian rights and claims are founded, the towns, castles, duchies, and the like, out of which these conflicts spring. Leave us our tithes and private benefactions, and we will give ourselves to spiritual work. 'Let Heinrich renounce his right of Investiture, and the Church will immediately restore all that it has received from secular princes since the time of Charlemagne.' The proposal was received with a storm of indignation. German bishops and Roman cardinals loaded the poor Pope with execrations. It came to nothing; in those days it could but come to nothing. The two spheres drawing off from each other, and each living its own life, would have rent in pieces the very structure of society. And why? Because fundamentally, as we are learning now, the two spheres are one. Unity is the aim and the longing of society. The Church entered the secular sphere through its worldly organisation, and by that instrument wrought, not pure Christian ideas, but its own debased image of them, into the heart of worldly society. The end of it all is the consecration of the secular life, not by having always an institution which we call the Church working on it from without, but by the dwelling of the Christian mind and spirit within it.

We are far enough from this ideal, the one holy secular life; but we are working towards it. And we are able to disengage the spirit from the secular sphere and leave it free to devote itself to its own spiritual exercises and duties. If we recognise Christ as the sole Lord of the conscience, and leave a man's belief and conduct as a spiritual being untrammelled by any considerations arising out of his relations to civil society, it is because the two kingdoms have become so intimately one, not because we are content to recognise them as separate. It is because secular life has become so spiritual, so penetrated and leavened by Christian ideas, that we can unyoke the individual conscience and leave it free for nobler ministries than men dreamed of in Becket's days. The time will come—may God hasten it—when all the world will be a holy temple, duty a simple worship, and life a constant praise.

Becket, in contending so strenuously for the exemption of the subjects of the spiritual kingdom from any but spiritual jurisdiction, was the enemy of that unity towards which Christian society has been always working, and he would have made two realms of what should be only one. On the other hand, any unity based on the supremacy of the secular power, as it existed even in the highest examples of monarch and noble in those times, must have been partial, base, and tending to swift decay. It needed a long and stern assertion, on the part of successive Popes and Primates, of the claim for which Becket both stood and died, to work into the secular heart those ideas and sentiments of which the Church was the depository, and the possession of which is the essential condition of all noble and fruitful self-regulation in the State.

Becket was born in London, probably in 1118, at the house of his father, a man of repute and substance, connected in some way with trade, and called one of the 'barons of the city.' Becket was of Norman descent, but an Englishman to the backbone, which is a fact significant of the rapid welding of the conquering and the conquered race. He was brought up by the canons of Merton Abbey, and afterwards studied in London, Paris, Bologna, and Auxerre, the then most famous schools of canon and civil law. His education was a learned one, according to the standards of the time. He was a lad, as he became a man, of brilliant power: rapid, showy, energetic, with great capacity for business; but by no means a deep scholar or thinker. He was essentially a man of the world, and fitted by nature for the conduct of great affairs. Tall, handsome, accomplished in arts and arms, a gallant soldier, an able administrator, an astute diplomatist, a splendid courtier, a charming companion; fond of pleasure up to a certain point, but far from immoral, as Grim bears testimony, fonder still of pomp and power, he was one of those universal men who are sure to play a leading part in every scene through which the current of their lives may lead them, but who are wanting in that depth, self-concentration, inward simplicity and patience, which make the men of the very first mark in history. For a man like Becket, profoundly ambitious and with a position which justified ambition but not belonging to the noble class, there was but one great career, the Church; and to one of his endowments the churchman's career opened the first position in the world. In keeping such a career open to talent even in the humblest station, in putting the highest place in Christendom within reach of the poorest aspirant, the Church rendered, as we have already noticed, the grandest service to mediæval society.

A churchman in deacon's orders young Becket became. An ecclesiastic in minor orders was a clerk in name only. He could hold ecclesiastical preferment, and Becket was a great pluralist, like all influential churchmen in that day. The clerk could also, however, be a soldier, a statesman, a lawyer, or anything else of fair reputation that he pleased. Becket had gained some knowledge of knightly accomplishments in the house of a Norman noble, Richer of Laigle; and he afterwards acquitted himself more than creditably in the field. On his return from France we find him in the office of a relative, one Master Osbern Eightpenny, a citizen of London of the highest position and influence, not with the citizens only but with their superiors. He was perhaps a sheriff; at any rate we find Becket at this time in the office of the sheriffs or portreeves, where he no doubt got a good insight into public affairs. Here was a man who for a citizen's son had had a remarkably varied as well as complete education; and had been brought into fruitful contact with the various activities of his time. His

father Gilbert had some sort of friendship with Theobald
the Archbishop of Canterbury. Gilbert was from Rouen;
and Theobald was the third archbishop whom the celebrated
Norman monastery of Bec had given to the world. Their
acquaintance was probably formed there. Indeed 'Bec' =
'brook'—is probably at the root of Becket's name.

Becket was introduced to the service of the Archbishop,
with whom he became an immense favourite. Twice he
seems to have been sent by the Primate to Rome. The
question of the succession to Stephen was causing deep
anxiety. He wished to have his son Eustace crowned.
Becket seems to have hindered it by suggesting that it
could not take place without the consent of the Pope.
This is important to the understanding of his subsequent
position. He had already, before he passed into Henry's service, formed a high idea of the Papal prerogative; he was in
the service of the Church first and was naturally led to take
the Church view of affairs; and further it is evident that,
young as he was, he was trusted with important and difficult missions, and exercised a strong influence in favour of
Henry's right to the crown. The Archbishop made him an
archdeacon; but shortly afterwards on the coronation of
Henry II. he recommended him as chancellor to the young
King. Nothing can shew more strongly the opinion which
was formed of the capacity of Becket, than that he should
thus have been recommended by the Archbishop and
accepted by the sovereign. The truth is that he and the
King were congenial spirits; both of them consummately
able men, and both determined that order should reign in
the land. The chancellor is now the first lay subject, then
he was but fourth or fifth; but being always about the
King, and having the management of the whole royal
patronage, the chancellor was practically the most influential
person in the realm. Henry and Becket conceived the

warmest attachment to each other, and lived on terms of the most intimate familiarity. A man of Becket's capacity and determination was invaluable to the King; and his chancellorship marks a very distinct and important era in the development of the realm.

The reign of Henry II., it is now well understood, was the critical point in the evolution of our political institutions; it was then that the constitutional monarchy began to be. Henry when he came to the throne had almost to reconquer his realm. We can read ample evidence in the chronicles of the time, of the terrible condition to which the wars of Stephen's reign had reduced the country. Stephen had filled the land with Flemish mercenaries; and had allowed his barons to build some of the strongest castles in Europe, from which they tyrannised at will. The land was rapidly falling into the condition of France, in which the great vassals were stronger than the King. The misery of the country was so dire that John of Salisbury compares it to that of Jerusalem when besieged by Titus. Henry II., who had been knighted by David his great uncle the King of Scots, succeeded to this inheritance of anarchy, and set himself at work at once to bring his land into order. Within a brief space the Flemings had to depart, the castles were destroyed, and the realm was restored. Henry was but 21, but his ability and vigour carried everything before him, and within a year he had reduced every great baron to subjection, and made his people understand that he meant to reign. In all this he found an able coadjutor in Becket, with whom he crossed the channel in 1156 to make the same order in Normandy which he had made at home.

The attempt has been made to represent Becket's conduct in the chancellorship as tyrannous and brutal in the extreme. No doubt he struck hard, but always at the enemies of the State. His administration was evidently masterly, and all people blessed him for the order which he restored. The testimony is clear and explicit that he enjoyed the highest favour with all classes ; clergy, knights, commons, all agreed to look upon him with equal good will. His work, for we must give him the credit of a full share in the changes which signalised the earlier and best years of Henry's reign, was no less than the transformation of a State wherein the feudal order or disorder reigned supreme, into a compact and powerful monarchy, in which something more than the first rudiments of a Constitution began to appear. Henry developed the system of administration by skilled officials, who from his day manage more and more the affairs of State : while the great hereditary offices became confined to the household. He organised on a very complete basis the administration of justice, and did much to establish the system of trial, which is one of the glories of our State, and a sure safeguard of the liberties of the people. Having a distant war on hand at Toulouse in 1159, he set on foot a scheme of money payment—scutage—instead of personal military service, whereby he was able to carry on the war with hired soldiers, striking at the same time a severe blow at the independence of the vassals of the crown, and introducing a new and fruitful principle into the management of military affairs.

In all these great steps of progress we may be sure that we can trace the work of Becket's hand. About the last, and certainly not the least important, we know that it was mainly his work. In truth Becket was a masterly man of affairs, and during his brief administration he made the chancellorship the most important office in the realm. He was a born statesman, but he was only an ecclesiastical saint. His whole nature went spontaneously into the duties and toils of the one vocation ; he had to force his nature to make even a decent success in the other. Henry spoiled a very able coadjutor in his really noble life-work when he gave him the archbishopric; but as he had made him archbishop really as a stroke of statecraft—in the hope that he would thereby secure, in the Primacy, if not a pliant tool at any rate a man who would take a secular view of spiritual affairs—we have no need to spend much pity upon him, when he found that he had exalted to the Primate's throne, one who proved himself the most imperious of ecclesiastics.

A writer of the time draws an almost idyllic picture of the state of England after a very few years of Becket's rule as chancellor. It must not be taken too literally; but still there can be no doubt that he restored order and developed progress in the State, in a very effective manner. Had he remained at the head of affairs it is probable that he would have left one of the greatest names in our secular history; and he might so have consolidated the political order as to have spared some of the bloody struggles through which, in after generations, it had to fight its way. His great fault in his secular administration was a certain vulgar love of mere splendour and pomp of state. In intellectual gifts he towered, like Saul, a head and shoulders above his contemporaries; and being by nature vain and ostentatious, he was somewhat dazzled by his sudden rise from obscurity to power. He delighted in a sumptuous establishment, in troops of menials, in a great following of retainers. When he went as the king's envoy to Paris, he filled the Frenchmen with amazement at the magnificence of his appointments, and the lavish bounty of his gifts. There was policy here no doubt. Henry was the most powerful monarch in Europe, while for some of his domains he was vassal to the French king. Becket, from motives of State policy, may have been very desirous to impress the Frenchmen with the resources and splendour of his master's kingdom; but there can be no question that the parade was grateful to his vanity, and that he played the peacock with all his heart.

This was the weak side of Becket's character all through. He was too self-conscious; too much occupied with the effect that he was producing. He posed for the part which he had to play too dramatically; and that is never the weakness of the noblest and loftiest men. Becket was not in the first rank; he was not a man like St. Louis—a saint of as pure and lofty a type as St. Bernard yet moving through life by choice in the secular sphere, and mingling with keen interest in the congress of the great world's affairs. His place was however very high in the second rank, and it is impossible to think lightly of him; he was certainly no mere actor, no hypocrite; always there was a clear, consistent, resolute purpose behind his actions, though there were times when he shewed some tremor; his main aim was to do what seemed to him his clear duty in his office, as the best service which he could render to mankind. A man who went so calmly and firmly to his death at last must be credited with something higher than selfish scheming in the earlier stages of his career.

Now comes the great transformation. In the year 1161 Archbishop Theobald, Becket's early patron, died. In 1162 Becket was elected, virtually by the King's command, to the vacant see. The brilliant chancellor became the stern and scrupulous archbishop, and remained the most noted man in Europe, until his martyrdom made him one of the most noted men of the world. The present object is not to recapitulate the facts of a story which is very well known, and is easily accessible in the pages of any tolerable history. Our concern is with the right interpretation of the facts, and of the principles at stake on either side, in order that we may understand their true bearing both on the actors in this great tragedy, and on the welfare and progress of the State.

Perhaps the strongest charge against Becket, and that which weighs most against him in the popular mind, was that he treated the King, who had placed him generously by his own act in the highest ecclesiastical position in Europe next to the Papal throne, with signal ingratitude; the King placed him there as a friend, and a man of secular mind, to make things pleasant between State and Church, while he embittered their relations to the utmost of his power. It seems tolerably clear that as chancellor Becket had been strongly anti-clerical. He was called 'a despiser of the clergy'; and Foliot objected to him as a 'persecutor and destroyer of Holy Church.' Henry hoped that he would carry his secular spirit with him to Canterbury, and as Primate play into the hands of the King. Henry, like all secular princes in those days, and all secular premiers in ours, had a dread of the churchman's conscience. It is about the most troublesome thing upon earth this conscience towards God. Ahab once remarked on it to this effect to Elijah; but it has, nevertheless, been as the salt of the earth and the light of the world.

Henry was simply furious when he saw the pleasant, practical, worldly-minded Becket cast in a moment the slough of his worldly habits, and stand forth the very image of the conscientious churchman, impracticable to the backbone, with a vision of martyrdom as the appropriate end to his career. But the reason of this transformation it is not difficult to trace. Becket was one to carry out completely any part which he might find himself called on to enact. The King had misread his man. His devotion to the King as chancellor, was the way to make the chancellorship a power; to bring out all its possibilities, and to make it a position in which a man of large capacity might find full exercise for his highest faculties. To be the King's man and second all his designs for the unity and welfare of the realm, was the thing for an able and upright chancellor to do. When the archbishopric was forced upon him he saw at a glance that to be the King's man as Primate, would be to clothe himself with weakness, and cover himself with shame. He had been an ecclesiastic, we must remember, before he had been chancellor. He saw the position from the ecclesiastical point of view; he knew, as the King could not know, what it demanded, and in accepting it he accepted, not a splendid position, a large income, and unbounded adulation, but the part which it was becoming that the Primate of all England at that time should play. We may well believe that when this flashed on him, his generous heart was touched by the thought of all the sorrow that must grow out of his appointment to the King; and there is evidence that either in jest or earnest he warned him of it. None the less did his hand close firmly on the crosier, when Henry, taking no heed to his warning, forced it on his acceptance, and in a moment he became a new man; assumed, not a new nature, for he was the same Becket all through, but a new conception of duty, of the work which he had to do; and this conception he held with unflinching firmness till death.

There is no doubt that this power to throw himself entirely into two so opposite parts or schemes of life, detracts a good deal from his moral grandeur; saint and martyr though he was, there was a lack of that inner simplicity and highmindedness which in St. Bernard or St. Louis would have forbidden them to attempt anything but the one thing which they believed they had been set to do by a higher hand. These men who can play two such different parts with such consummate power are only in the second rank, never in the first; 'one thing

I do,' is the word of the loftiest spirits. This instant apprehension by Becket of the true *rôle* which it became him as Primate to assume, as a man under higher duty to God than to the King, was at any rate a far nobler thing than if he had been content to play the contemptible part of a secular churchman, letting the King have his way at will in Church as well as in State. Becket, made archbishop, was every inch an archbishop, and resolved at once that his supreme duty was to the Church and not to the King. Nothing but respect is due to that decision. In those days it would have been an unspeakable loss to civilisation had the Church as well as the State fallen helpless into the monarch's hands. Chancellors were generally rewarded with a bishopric, but then they resigned their chancellorships. The Primacy was quite another matter. The Primate was the counterweight to the Crown, and under the Conqueror and his son Rufus, he had done noble service by the strength of his restraining hand. It would have been a terrible thing for England had there been no Lanfranc or Anselm to plead the cause of righteousness and mercy, with these able but brutal monarchs on whom no other moral restraint could have been imposed. Had Becket consented to hold both offices as the King's man, he would simply have betrayed the best interests of the country as well as of the Church. Henry was a masterly ruler, but a stern one; and he had in him not only the brutality of his mother's house, but the devilish tincture of his father's. The kind of restraint under which a vigorous and high-minded prelate would place him would have been greatly for his good, and the good of his country. It is however characteristic of Becket that the work to which his sense of duty, and doubtless his ambition also, prompted him, he must do in the most arrogant, offensive, and imperious way. Through

the whole controversy his faults of temper were conspicuous.
He seems to have striven to make the King understand how
entirely he himself had broken with the past, and how little
Henry had to hope at his hands. He wielded his crook
just as he had used his seals, to make them the most
effective instruments of power; and by this he at once
satisfied his own large but not base ambition, and sought
what he honestly believed to be the public good.

Appointed to the Primacy he immediately commenced
to make such order in the Church's realm as he had
already made in the secular polity. There were the direst
irregularities in the estate of the Church, which needed
to be corrected, and usurpations demanding both the chas-
tisement of the offender and the exaction of restitution.
Becket set at once about the correction in the most imperious
and uncompromising spirit. His every act whether legally
right or wrong—to discuss that would be a long question—
was like a challenge; a defiance to the King as from a rival
throne. For reasons which have been explained we need
feel no great pity for Henry. The tone of Becket and the
animus of his proceedings from the first deserve however
to be severely condemned. He thought only of the
Church, and not at all of the realm, and acted so as to
make a fair compromise impossible. His commanding
powers and his personal influence with Henry, gave him a
great opportunity of settling these vexed questions on a
basis which would have been just alike to Church and
State. He showed, hovever, not the faintest disposition so
to settle them, but took the extreme Church ground from
the first.

It was the Church ground, notice, that he took. Becket
was not fighting for the Pope, and the Pope did little to
help him. Poor Alexander III. had an Antipope backed
by the emperor. He was in sore straits lest he should

offend Henry, and throw all the strength of England into the cause of his rival. So he trimmed and temporised, wishing in his heart probably as devoutly as Henry, that this terrible archbishop was out of the way. Indeed he seemed to Becket to fall so far short of common Christian courage and uprightness, that he wrote, 'At Rome it is always the same. Barabbas is let go, and Christ crucified. Come what may, I will never submit; but I will trouble the Church of Rome no more.' Thorough and hearty Englishman as he had been, the thought of what was good for England never seems to have crossed him; only what was good for Holy Church. It was no doubt better in the long run that he should have played the part of an arrogant churchman than of a worldly-minded truckling Primate; for what England most sorely needed, not for that moment only but for coming generations, was a power which should make monarchs feel that *they had a monarch*, and might not dare to play the tyrant at will. But there was a nobler part than either, which Becket did not play; perhaps which he was not great enough to play,—the part of the churchman who cared supremely for the best interests of the realm.

There can be no question, at any rate, that it was his firm and imperious demeanour before the King, which won the passionate admiration and devotion of the people. The secular power pinched them in those days fearfully hard; and this man who dared to beard the King in the name of a higher King, was a champion and a hero in their sight. At Northampton they thronged around him and attended him to his monastery with wild enthusiasm; and when he landed for the last time in England and entered it, as he may have known, to die, his progresses everywhere were triumphal processions; 'all the world went after him,' and his hold on the popular heart caused serious alarm to those who ruled the State. Henry and Becket had met again and again in hope of reconciliation; but always one thing stood in the way. Becket always made open or secret reservation of 'the rights of the Church,' or 'the honour of his God,' and Henry felt it; when he heard the dreaded phrase, 'Saving the honour of my God,' he broke forth into furious imprecations. He knew that there was a rock there against which both his passion and his force might spend themselves in vain. Alas! that the rights of the Church and the rights of the State in a world which Christ came to save, should be so constantly paraded as opposing powers! Alas! that man's pride, ambition and avarice have in all ages marred so miserably the benediction which the Saviour brought to mankind!

The history of the Constitutions of Clarendon is quite too large and intricate a matter to be treated in a brief lecture. We may simply note that in the Constitutions, the right of the King's court over criminal ecclesiastics was recognised, and Becket in some way was induced to accept them, though probably with a mental reservation, 'subject to the dispensation of the Church.' He bitterly repented his acquiescence, and the whole struggle of his life from that time was to recover for the Church the position which he felt that he had weakly betrayed. His long exile and his return in something like a popular whirlwind of triumph are familiar matters of history. He knew, probably, that he was returning to die. He was solemnly warned before he embarked that he would be certainly slain. 'It is of no consequence to me,' he answered, 'for if I am torn limb from limb I will go.'

He returned with a battery of suspensions and anathemas which he discharged at his enemies. It was to be war to the death; and we may conjecture that Becket saw his death might triumph where his life had failed. Warnings and omens were abundant. 'Archbishop, 'ware the knife, Archbishop, 'ware the knife,' shrieked a woman in the crowd that met him at Southwark. He foretold his fate to the abbot of St. Albans and returned to Canterbury to die. Then Henry, alarmed at the tales of the popular enthusiasm which reached him in Normandy, spoke those hasty passionate words which sent forth the murderers on their work of doom. Becket bore himself altogether nobly when he saw that the fatal hour had come. All the strength and dignity of the man came forth when he gathered up his courage and firmness to die. On the steps of an altar in his cathedral church they assailed him. Becket forbade his monks to exclude them, 'I came here not to resist,' he said, 'but to suffer.' They attacked him with great brutality, but they could not drag him from the church. Then, fearing rescue, they struck him down where he stood, and with the words, 'I am ready to die for the name of Jesus and the protection of His Church,' he fell.

He died, remember, the martyr of the Church, and not of Christ, or of mankind. But he died nobly, in what he believed to be a sacred cause; and the world justly keeps its high honour for the man who is ready to set to his life-struggle the seal of his death. Its highest honour it reserves for men like Bernard and Francis, and that pure and lofty spirit—the secular saint, St. Louis of France, whose pure simplicity and unworldliness make the glory of an arrogant and ambitious churchman like Becket look dim. Becket's death won for him the triumph for which he had struggled in life in vain. All know the tale of Henry's penance at the tomb of the martyr. The dark deed, the murder of the brave archbishop before an altar of his own cathedral, filled Europe with horror. Henry was, or professed to be, crushed by remorse. Henry grovelling a day and a night before the tomb in tears and prayers, and scourged by Becket's monks, is a spectacle

which means much not for Henry himself only, but for
English history. The happy thing for England is that
neither conquered, or both, in the long strife. Becket died
under the murderer's sword; Henry prostrated himself in
humiliation and shame before his grave; but 'benefit of
clergy' became a shield from the injustice and brutality of
the law, until the King's courts had learnt some precious
lessons; and then the whole administration of the law passed,
as it was bound to pass, under secular control.

Be sure that the lesson of Henry's humiliation was not lost
on monarchs. It drove home into their consciences the conviction that they were but the regents on earth of a higher
King. And so when the secular power had learnt lessons of
justice and mercy, and the spiritual power true reverence for
the secular life, the commonwealth of Great Britain, for Scotland has taken full share in both the conflict and the triumph,
came to master both the tyrannies which were struggling then
to play the despot over her life. It is the blending of the
two principles for which Becket and Henry stood, and not
the separate victory of either of them, which lends such
strength and dignity to our English freedom. And it is
because men like Becket and Henry have not been wanting
in any age of our history, because there have always been
men who have dared to stand even to death for each side of
that dual principle, which in its duality men call secular and
sacred but which in its unity constitutes the true grandeur
and glory of States, that the life of the English nation has
developed in such fair and stately proportions, and has become
the largest, the noblest, the strongest, and the freest in the
world.

VIII.

ST. FRANCIS OF ASSISI, AND THE RISE OF THE MENDICANT ORDERS.

VIII.

ST. FRANCIS OF ASSISI, AND THE RISE OF THE MENDICANT ORDERS.

1182—1226.

In passing from the career of St. Thomas of Canterbury to that of St. Francis of Assisi, we leave the sphere of ecclesiastial statesmanship, and enter once more the sphere of the religious life. St. Francis was saint pure and simple after his fashion; St. Bernard was saint pure and simple after another and a larger though not a higher fashion; St. Thomas of Canterbury was saint distinctly for a purpose, and was always at heart an able, ambitious, and resolute ruler of men. St. Bernard, as we have seen, entered the world, where he was the most powerful man of his time, with much sorrow and reluctance, while his heart remained always faithful to his beloved Clairvaulx; St. Francis, and the men of the order which he founded, entered the world much more freely than St. Bernard, and with a much more hearty feeling that it was there that their work lay; and this was a very remarkable change, may we not say progress, in the idea of the saintly life, the causes of which we must now proceed to examine.

There were, however, in those times, two ways of 'entering the world.' St. Thomas had lived in the world, but he lived in it as a man of the world, and the battle of his life to maintain the privileges of his order, was, as we have learned, a purely mundane battle.

It is in a far different sense that we can say of St. Francis that his life was passed in the world. His interests were of another kind altogether. The battles of systems and orders, the contests of rough kings and haughty churchmen, ruffle not the quiet serenity of his soul. We are back again in the calm region of saintly aspiration, a region of pure and earnest endeavour to live like Christ, to receive and radiate again the influences of His life, and to bring the powers of the spiritual sphere to bear on mankind. These powers of the spiritual sphere were not such powers as Innocent III. wielded, when, in what he believed to be a holy, a spiritual war, he went flaming with fire and sword through Languedoc, and stamped out heresy with the iron heel of the chivalry of Europe. The man whose life we have now before us aimed at the mastery of no such instruments. It is probable that he would have shuddered at them, for he was one of the humblest and gentlest of men. His only weapons were the purely spiritual weapons of example and persuasion. He sought by living and preaching to act on his fellows, and he cared for no other results than these would win. This is why we find ourselves now in another region than that into which the life of a great ecclesiastical statesman can usher us ; when we turn to St. Francis, and his mistress, holy Poverty, we are among the saints again, and close to the vital springs of the power of the Church.

Becket exercised a tremendous influence and Innocent III. wielded the same power yet more royally. He made himself absolute Lord of Christendom, and kings of great nations did homage to him for their crowns. But it was such men as St. Bernard and St. Francis who made the Beckets and the Innocents possible. It was the saints, the holy unworldly men, who furnished the standing ground for

Primates and Popes. The force which was directed by the hands of an Innocent, and which in his hands shook the strongest realms in Christendom to their very centre, was gathered by the lives of men like Bernard and Francis, whom the common people could, in their inmost hearts, reverence and adore. The word 'spiritual' covered all Becket's, Alexander's and Innocent's doings; though much of their work was begun, continued, and ended in selfish passion, in the effort after a dominion which was none the less worldly because it called itself by the most sacred name. But this word 'spiritual' had power with the people because there were living in Europe and before their eyes those who realised their purest imagination of what a spiritual man should be like, what life he should live, what work he should do. Worldly men might wield the power, but only unworldly men could create it. Unless in each generation such men as these had appeared, to renew that faith of men in the reality of purity, righteousness, humility, and truth, which the ecclesiastical policy and conduct of the Roman Church did its very best to destroy, the whole system must have perished of its own corruption. The Church died daily of its Priests and Popes, and was daily saved by its Saints. A life like that of St. Bernard and St. Francis gave it new centuries of existence, because it kept some reality that was Christlike, or was honestly taken to be Christlike, before the eyes of men. When saints became scarcer, Rome became feebler. When all were seeking their own, none the things of Jesus Christ, in the high places of the Church, the Reformation was born. Innocent III. saw in a vision the figure of this poor emaciated squalid monk St. Francis, supporting the great Basilica of the Lateran; and he was right. If no great priest of poverty, humility, and charity, had arisen in that age to revive the hearts and the hopes of men, the splendid

imperial policy of its great Pope, Innocent III., would have
been branded as heathen and cast out as hateful by every
true Christian heart. But men were little critical in those
days; Innocent adopted St. Francis; the virtues and graces
of the saint were credited to the system, and fed its
authority from a fresh spring.

St. Francis was born in 1182, and his youth was spent
in the early years of that thirteenth century, which is the
next great era in human progress to the apostolic age. It
ends the mediæval, and begins the modern epoch. Since the
establishment of the Roman Empire, and the advent of the
Lord into the bosom of the Universal Society which Rome
had founded and whose unity she guarded with her shield,
there had been no movement for the progress of humanity
comparable in its importance with the rise of a national life,
a national monarchy, a national language and a national
literature in all the great countries of the West. The age
of this momentous development of the national spirit in
the West of Europe is the thirteenth century, and it is the
great landmark of history between the establishment of the
Roman Empire in the first century, and the French
Revolution in the eighteenth. One of the most remarkable
features in the movement of this thirteenth century is the
development of a vernacular literature. Scholars then
began to use the language which was understood by the
people, instead of the Latin which was understood only, in
the main, by the priests. The result of this was an
immense enlargement, not of the knowledge only, but of
the interests, the concernments, of the mass of the people.
They began feebly and dimly, but very really, to take an
interest in matters which till then had been held to be
quite above their sphere. Educated men found the common
language sufficiently perfected to become the vehicle of
their ideas. The poor and ignorant folk began to have

thoughts of their own about politics, about the conduct of life, and even about theology; they began to be critics in their own dull way; it is true they knew but a little, yet they exercised this knowledge as an instrument for the acquisition of more. A free circulation of thought began, and though it was very feeble and very slow, it was the origin of the movement which culminated in one direction in the Teutonic Reformation, and in the other in the French Revolution. Both of these really have their springs in the thirteenth century, when thought freed itself from the two main grooves, the classical and ecclesiastical, in which for centuries it had travelled, and went forth in vernacular freedom to find what entertainment it might in humble human homes and hearts.

The consequent rise of secular life in dignity and import-ance is the broadest fact of the thirteenth century. The great saint of the middle of the century, St. Louis, is a layman, a thorough layman, and that means much. The Crusades had greatly stimulated the growth of the popular mind, and the development of the popular estate; commerce, knowledge, and great purposes which the poorest and the richest equally shared, had elevated the population of the chief European kingdoms; and from that time men of the people began to take, not an accidental, but a constant and recognised part in the conduct of public affairs. As secular life grew larger and took in a wider field, it would inevitably assert its right to something of that sanctity which till that time had been supposed to attach to the religious life alone. Two centuries earlier a man so holy as St. Louis would have been almost driven into a cloister; in the thirteenth century he could feel that holiness had a wide field of influence even in the most eminent places of the world. Questions of morals, of religion, had their interest for secular men, and were dealt with apart from the mere

authority of their spiritual guides. Men would be thinking about the deepest problems of life under the monarch's
crown, the soldier's helmet, the scholar's cap, as well as
under the monk's cowl; nor would the peasant be quite
shut out from interest in what king, soldier, and scholar
felt had come within their sphere. On many subjects
which till then had been the exclusive concern of churchmen, the appeal would be thenceforth to the secular
judgment, and unless the Church could win the homage of
the secular intellect to her presentation of truth, there was
some likelihood that she would sink down into a mere
directress of devotion. Truth must come out of the schools
and frequent the forum; the Church must throw herself
into the thick of the intellectual and moral controversies
which this breaking forth of the secular life into freedom
and honour would inevitably generate, and must either hold
her own by superior intellectual power, or else retire from
the headship of the movement, and leave the secular spirit
in the world of political, intellectual, and martial strife,
to run into extravagance at will. If all that was most
spiritual in the Church should continue to withdraw itself
and hide itself in the cloister from all contact with the
world, very plainly the world and the Church would cease
to comprehend and to act upon each other, and civilisation
would miss that inestimable advantage which their close
relation and interpenetration alone would secure. A new
idea of saintliness, or rather a new form of it, and a
new view of its relation to the world, were imperatively
demanded. We shall see how these were supplied.

M. Michelet says, in his rapid brilliant way of disposing
of the characteristics of an era, that Innocent III. used
the Mendicant Orders to prop up the tottering Church.
That seems to imply in Innocent an altogether clearer
discernment of the special character of a time, than any

man living in it would be likely to possess. We must not credit even the ablest men living in an age, with that insight into its character and tendencies which our own more remote perspective affords to us. The Mendicant Orders forced themselves on the Papacy. It was very unwillingly, very doubtfully, that the Roman Church accepted their aid. The truer account of the matter seems to be, that they grew out of the necessities of the times, of which neither they, nor the Roman Church, were very fully conscious. The times and they grew together out of one root. It is only on looking back over the gulf of ages that we can see how wonderfully they fitted each other, and how the new Orders served to prolong (on the whole greatly to the advantage of Europe) the influence of the Church on the formative movement which was then beginning to gather force in all the great European kingdoms of the West.

At the time when this grand stir began through all the spheres of secular society—a movement of humanity at large up to a higher line of thought and life, a movement of which a great layman, St. Louis, was to be the consecrating priest, and a greater layman, Dante, was to be the poet and seer—two men appear upon the scene, who show at once, though differing very widely from each other, a most remarkable adaptation to those special features and needs of the times, which we can see clearly enough, but which could have been only very dimly discerned by the men who were active in those times, and who partly were made by them, and partly made them.

St. Dominic and St. Francis now take their place upon the stage. St. Dominic was born in 1170, St. Francis in 1182. They both play their part in the world during the first half of the thirteenth century. Dominic died in 1221,

Francis in 1226. The first quarter of the century we may say witnessed the commencement and the close of their labours, but they left behind them, when they died, two numerous and powerful Orders, which soon gathered into their fellowship some of the ablest scholars and administrators in Europe, and for two centuries wielded the chief spiritual and intellectual power in the Western World. Thomas Aquinas and Albertus Magnus on the one side, and Duns Scotus and Roger Bacon on the other, were four of the very ablest men in the annals of the Scholastic Philosophy, and they are but the foremost of a long line of illustrious men whom the Mendicant Orders trained for the highest service of mankind.

The two Orders had different spheres, but they had this in common; they went into the world. Their votaries had vowed to go about and mingle with their fellows; as preachers, as scholars, as administrators, they sought out the most frequented highways of the world, and there they brought their influence and the influence of the Church to bear on men. They became as Dr. Milman justly observes, 'a kind of Papal militia, always mobilized, ready to be moved hither and thither at the Papal will.' Again, however, we must guard ourselves from supposing that this tendency to mix with men and take their saintliness down into the world, was the fruit of any deep laid scheme of influence. St. Francis had sore struggles of spirit before he could discern which was the path of saintly duty, the life of the recluse · or the life of the missionary; and when he finally elected the latter, he was but obeying unconsciously a certain spirit of the age which was in him, and with little prevision of the momentous importance of his decision to the highest interests of the Church.

St. Francis was born at Assisi, a picturesque little town among the Umbrian hills, the son of Pietro Bernardone, a thriving merchant not without pretension to noble blood, and he seems to have been a youth of brilliant promise. John was his baptismal name, but his father had much traffic with Frenchmen, and made his son a thorough French scholar, and it is said that from this circumstance he derived the appellation which he has made illustrious in the annals of the world. He was a general favourite, gay, brilliant, lavish, though clever and assiduous in business, and high expectations of his future were entertained by his father. And not unjustly, for he was born for greatness, though of a kind of which his father little dreamed; and some evidence of his remarkable power must have been apparent to all who had an eye to discern spirits, even in his prodigal days. From the first, however, we are told, even when he was wildest and most wanton, he had a quick eye and a tender heart for the necessities of the poor. We have a picture of the man sketched by a comrade :—

'He was,' says his biographer, 'of a cheerful countenance and kindly mien, free from both indolence and pride. His stature was of the middle size inclining to smallness. He had a small and rounded head, an oval face with forehead smooth and not large, black eyes with no malevolence in them, straight eye-brows, straight and thin nose, small pricked-up ears, sharp and ardent tongue, earnest and sweet voice with clear and musical tones, white, equal, and compact teeth, thin lips, little beard, slender neck, straight shoulders, short arms, long fingers and nails, a poor leg, a small foot, tender skin, and little or no flesh on his bones.'[1]

Long before the time which may be fixed on as the date of his conversion, he reveals the tender and compassionate nature to which he resigned at length the government of his life. His ministry to the wretched began early. He was ever ready to give an alms to the poor, but one day, being much occupied, he sent one away without giving him anything. Reproaching himself immediately for his want of

[1] Thomas of Celano, *Vita S. Fran.*, I. 10. in *Acta Sanctorum*, Oct. II. p. 706.

charity, he ran after the unfortunate man whom he had refused and repaired his fault. He bound himself from that time with a vow, to give an alms to all those who asked it for the love of God; and he kept it faithfully till his death.

Francis must have been endowed with an intensely sensitive and sympathetic nature, open to impressions and influences to an extent which to most of us would reach the point of agony. Indeed it would not be too much to say that his heart agonised over the sins and the sufferings of mankind. From the time of his youth any spectacle of distress not only tormented him, but so moved him that it became a positive necessity to him to put forth his hand to help and to save, no matter at what cost. A severe illness, as with many of the great saints, was probably the turning point in his life. On recovering from it he mounted his horse and rode out to enjoy himself. Meeting a poor gentleman, who had fallen into utter poverty and was clothed in miserable rags, he was so touched by the sight that he dismounted, stripped himself of everything, clothed himself with the rags of the poor soldier, to whom he left his own garments, and went light-hearted on his way. That was the spirit of the man. He was of an impassioned, imaginative, and highly mystical nature, with a wonderful power of projecting his imaginings in forms which reacted mightily on his own life. He was a man of visions; he lived in an atmosphere of marvels. Few poets have seen such depths of beauty in the creation, and have felt so vividly the kinship of all animate and inanimate things: while as the mystical devotee of the Crucified, the young Bernardone gave himself up with all the passion of a lover to the contemplation of the Saviour, and moulded his life even to the minutest detail on the outward likeness of the life of his adored Master.

The night after this adventure with the soldier Francis saw a vision, and henceforth visions are the most important part of the outward apparatus of his life. He beheld a splendid palace filled with weapons, each having on it the sign of the cross. On asking for whom they were provided he was answered that they were 'for him and for his soldiers.' It is a sign of his perfect simplicity of heart that he took this as a literal command to go forth to the wars. Walter of Brienne was then fighting for the Italian cause against the Emperor. He thought that that must be the cause of Heaven; so he armed himself, caring for nothing but the heavenly commandment, and started off for the Neapolitan States to offer his sword for the good fight. On his way another vision arrested him. Bonaventura gives the curious colloquy which ensued. 'Francis, who can do the best for thee, a master or a servant? a rich man or a poor?' Francis answered that a lord and a rich man could do the best for him: another voice replied, 'Why then leavest thou the Lord for a servant, and for a poor man the rich God?' Francis submissively replied, 'Lord, what wilt thou have me to do?' The Lord answered, 'Return unto thy land, for the vision which thou hast seen prefigures spiritual and not human work, and should have its fulfilment within.' At once with haste he returns to Assisi, and waits there the word of the Lord.[1]

Not a spiritual person is he at present, or in any wise separated from secular work, but a man who had all his eyes and ears open to every sign which might come to him from the world of spirit; and who in such an age could in the end devote himself to no other than spiritual work. He was a young man of twenty-four when this critical vision appeared. From that time he commenced to devote himself, with the intensity which always characterised him, to

[1] S. Bonaventura, *Vita S. Fran.*, c. 1. In *Acta S.S.*, l.c.

religious exercises ; and he began to be conscious of earnest longings after a more perfect and heavenly life, though how to satisfy them remained hidden from his mental sight. 'The will was present with him, but how to do he found not.' It is to this period that the birth of his passion for his bride, Poverty, is to be referred. It is said that he returned to his worldly courses at Assisi, and that in the midst of a revel, a shadow gathered over his face. 'Why so sad, Francis,' cried one of his boon companions, 'Art thou going to be married ?' 'I am,' was the answer, 'and to a lady of such wealth, and rank, and beauty, that the world cannot produce her like.' He burst from the throng to search for her, and ere long he held her in his embrace.[1] The lady was Poverty—Holy Poverty—of whom he always spoke as his bride, to whom he remained loyal through life with a rare fidelity, and whom he held to be the mother of the whole Order of Franciscan friars. This was his manner, not of talking of it, but of realising it ; thoughts with him easily became things. Still he was searching for the way. His was a simple, childlike heart, very unversed in the methods of the religionists ; all uncertain as to what might be the acceptable way of fulfilling the divine command, he was content if he could see only a day's length of the journey before him, and was mostly in sore perplexity and distress because he could not see even that.

The stories of his literal interpretations of divine admonitions would be almost laughable, but for the noble, touching simplicity of spirit which they reveal. Here is a notable instance. Wandering one day in the country, he went in to pray in an old ruined church that was dedicated to St. Damian. In his rapture he heard a voice from heaven, 'Francis, arise and repair my house, which, as thou seest,

---

[1] *Vita S. Fran.*, Auctoribus Tribus Sociis, c. 1, in *Acta S.S.*, l.c.

is wholly falling to destruction.' In his simplicity he thought it was the poor old church of St. Damian which he was to build up again, so he straightway goes home, loads a horse with silks and stuffs, starts off for Foligno, sells both horse and goods, returns to St. Damian and offers the money as a free gift to the poor priest. The priest was a wise man in his generation. Knowing Francis, and something probably too of the temper of the old Bernardone, the father of the future saint, he refused the money, but he gave the youth permission to remain with him. Francis in scorn threw the money into a window, and when search was soon after made for him by his father, he betook himself to a hiding place in a certain cellar where he lay quiet seven days and prayed. Ashamed of his fears he soon after resolved to return to the city. Squalid, dirty, in rags, pale and emaciated by fasts, the citizens took him for a madman, and pelted him with mud, filth, and stones. Francis walked calmly on. But old Bernardone, a dour old man it appears, heard the clamour, got news of the return of the fugitive, and rushed forth to seize him, and knock the nonsense out of him if he could. Abusing him and thrashing him soundly, he dragged him home, bound him with a chain, and left him to chew the cud of his meditations, and come to his right mind once more.[1]

Right or wrong, however, Francis had but one mind. It never wavered till death. His mother, touched by his sufferings, and with a woman's sympathy for high and unworldly ideas, after loving remonstrance and entreaty, loosed him and let him go. He went straight back to his hiding place at St. Damian. His father, furious, swiftly followed him. Francis calmly protested that neither words nor blows could alter his resolution, and his father, resolved to save what he could from the wreck, had him before the magis-

[1] S. Bonaventura, c. 2.

trate that he might compel a legal renunciation of his goods. Francis would hear nothing of the civil magistrate in such a transaction, so he was had before the Bishop. The good priest of St. Damian gave up the money, Francis signed a renunciation of his patrimony, and to make the matter complete stripped himself of every rag of clothing which he owed to his father's bounty, and stood there before the amazed and delighted Bishop a free man in a plain hair shirt. Francis never did anything by halves. There are grave doubts whether the shirt did not follow the rest of the attire. The people burst into tears. The Bishop took him to his embrace, and in pity on his nakedness, procured for him the dress of a poor peasant, a serf of the Episcopal house, and Francis donned the beggar's gown, which he wore on through life till he stripped himself of it to die.

Filled with a transporting joy as he realised his freedom, he wandered forth, making the air vocal with songs of praise. Some robbers caught him in a wood, and asked him of his business. 'I am the herald of a great king,' he answered, and sang on. They thought him mad, beat him soundly, and tossed him into a dyke which was deep in snow. When they had turned their backs, Francis jumped up and sang the louder, glorying in the shame and pain. Meeting some lepers, he tended, washed, and even kissed their ulcers, and devoted himself very solemnly to what was held then, and was in truth, a very terrible ministry to these wretched pariahs of the human race. But the tenderness of Francis knew no fears and no bounds. Miracles of course attended on his ministry—and results which it would be hard to distinguish from miracles no doubt appeared. We have no need to brand as fictions or delusions all the tales of apparently miraculous cures which we meet with, supported by overwhelming testimony, throughout the whole Middle Age.

The next thing to be done seemed to him the rebuilding of this ruined church. Poverty was the only helpmeet he invoked. Begging wood and stones, and paying for them faithfully with prayers, he bore them in his wasted arms to the builders, and in the end the work was nobly done. Near Assisi was another poor dilapidated church, La Portiuncula, sacred to Santa Maria de Angelis. He gave himself no rest until he had restored it after the same fashion. It became the holy place of his Order, and a magnificent church stands there to this day, plainly visible from the hill on which Assisi stands, defying every precept of his life by its splendour while it professes to honour his name.

The wonderful success which crowned the efforts of Francis began to open the eyes of men to his remarkable power. Those who had laughed at and pelted him, began to reverence and love. Money and offerings of all sorts poured in upon him; he was fairly embarked on a great career. The decisive step was at hand. Worshipping in the Church of Sta. Maria he heard the Gospel read, '*Provide neither gold, nor silver, nor brass in your purses, neither scrip for your journey, neither two coats, neither shoes, nor yet staves.*' After mass he asked the good priest to explain it. The words struck home. 'This,' he cried, 'is what I have been seeking for. Now I see my path.' Straightway he loosed his sandals, laid down his staff, cast aside his girdle, and flung his purse on the ground; he dressed himself in one coarse cloak of serge, girded himself with a rope, and went forth to preach the gospel as poor, as homeless, as penniless as his Lord.

The man who could *do* such things in the Middle Age could sweep a vast throng of followers in his train. The common life of the world was so unlike all that is pictured in the life of Christ as good, beautiful, and blessed, that there was a deep) chronic sadness and unrest in the heart of all the nobler and purer souls ; so that any plan of living which promised to make life more Christlike had an intense attraction ; and there was something very deeply in tune with the best thought and aspiration of the age, in the poverty and self-renunciation · which the rule of St. Francis enjoined, and the life of St. Francis expressed.   But as yet it was simply a life. It had not yet become a rule.   The history of his first converts of importance may here be given from the Life by the Three Companions.   The first was one Bernardus (of Quintavalle). He had watched the way of life of the saint and coming to him asked him to spend the night with him.   In the course of their conversation Bernard asked Francis what a man should do who had received possessions from his Lord which he wished no longer to keep ?   He should give them back, answered the saint, to the Lord from whom he received them. The narrative then continues.   'And Bernardus said, "I wish, my brother, to give up all my goods for the love of my Lord who gave them to me, and will perform it as seems best to thee."   To whom the saint, "At morning-tide we will go to the church and will learn through the Holy Gospel-book, as Christ taught His disciples."   Rising therefore in the morning with one other, Peter by name, who also desired to become a brother, they came to the Church of St. Nicholas by an open place in Assisi.   Entering this to pray, because they were ignorant and knew not how to find the word of the Gospel touching the renunciation of the world, they humbly asked the Lord that He would vouchsafe to show them His will, by the first opening of the book.   After they had prayed, the holy Francis took the closed book, and kneeling before the altar unclasped it, and where he first opened the leaves there met his eye this counsel of the Lord, "*If thou wilt be perfect, go, sell all thou hast and give to the poor, and thou shalt have treasure in heaven.*"'   The *sortes* were tried a second and third time with the like result, and Francis, turning to his companions, exclaimed, 'Brethren, this is our life and our rule, and that of all who shall wish to join our society. Go ye, therefore, and as ye have heard, so do!' Thereupon Bernard (who was very rich) and Peter sold all they had and gave the money to the poor, and adopting the same dress as Francis 'from that hour lived together with him according to the fashion of the Holy Gospel revealed to us by the Lord.'[1]

This was truly the birth of the Order, and the most notable thing which in that generation happened in this world. The next step was to obtain the confirmation of the Pope. Seven poor men were gathered round Francis, and one morning, after long prayer, he called these brethren around him and gave them this solemn charge:—

'Take courage, beloved ones, and rejoice in the Lord. Be not depressed to think how few we are. Be not alarmed either at your own weakness or at mine. God has revealed to me that He will diffuse through the earth this our little family of which He is Himself the Father. I would have concealed what I have seen, but love constrains me to impart it to you. I have seen a great multitude coming to us, to wear our dress, to live as we do. I have seen all the roads crowded with men travelling in eager haste towards us. The French are coming. The Spaniards are hastening. The Germans and English are running. All nations and tongues are assembling together in haste.'

'We may seem contemptible and insane. But fear not; go rather and preach repentance for the remission of sins. Faithful men, gentle and full of charity, will receive you and your words with joy. Proud and impious men will condemn and oppose you. Settle it in your hearts to endure all things with meekness and patience. The wise and noble

<hr>

[1] *Vita*, auct. Trib. Soc., c. 3.

will soon join themselves to you, and with you will preach to kings, to princes, and to nations.'[1]

Soon after the humble tattered squalid company bent their steps towards Rome. Few things in history are more striking than the meeting of Francis of Assisi and Innocent III. We must pause here to look at the character and position of the man to whom the poor beggars of Christ draw near.

Innocent III. was, probably, on the whole the ablest man, the greatest ruler, who has ever occupied the papal throne. If Hildebrand, Gregory VII., was the Julius, Innocent was the Augustus of the Church. Hildebrand had spent his life in fierce and constant struggle. He had fought a tremendous battle for the supremacy of the Church. He won the battle but at the cost of life. 'I have loved righteousness and hated iniquity, and therefore I die in exile' were the bitter words which faltered from his dying lips. After one hundred years Innocent entered into the full enjoyment of the legacy which Gregory bequeathed. He was the author of that memorable simile which carries to the highest pitch the papal claims, 'As God has placed two great luminaries in the firmament, the one to rule the day, and the other to give light by night, so He has established two great powers, the pontifical and the royal, and as the moon receives the light from the sun, so does Royalty borrow its splendour from the Papal authority.' Innocent made this a reality and was the supreme man in Christendom. Bernard and Becket, as well as Hildebrand, had prepared his way. The proudest monarchs submitted themselves to his authority. No power in Europe was strong enough to stand up against his will. Philip Augustus of France, John of England, Otho of Germany, Pedro of Arragon, had all been humbled to the very dust before his footstool. Frederic, the young, the brilliant emperor, the last of the great Hohenstauffen line, was his ward;

---

[1] Thomas of Celano, c. 4, and the Three Companions, c. 3.

while the conquest of Constantinople by the Crusaders brought the whole East under the control of his hand. Never did man in this world stand on such a pinnacle of power; and never did Innocent realise more fully the meaning of those tremendous words with which he entered on his papal reign, 'The Pope stands in the midst; between God and man, below God, above man; less than God, more than man,' than in the hour when the company of beggars drew near.

It was evening. The rays of the setting sun were slanting on the Campagna, and flooding the lofty terrace of the Lateran Palace, where a group of splendidly attired churchmen were walking, drinking in the balmy breath of the evening air. One walked apart, simply clad, but with the mien of a monarch, and the lordly brow on which sat gravely the care of the great world's affairs. He was plunged in the deepest thought, meditating doubtless the tremendous problems of a dominion wider and grander than any of which Nebuchadnezzar or the Cæsars dreamed, when the squalid travel-stained mendicant approached. Innocent, immersed in care, had few words to waste on such an object, and repulsed him with some scorn. Francis, humbly accepting the rebuke, withdrew, and left the matter in the hand of Heaven. Nor in vain. That night the Pontiff, like another great ruler of old, was haunted by visions, and they shaped themselves into a form which tradition has handed down to us. He seemed, we are told, to see a palm tree slowly growing between his feet, and rising into a beautiful tree. Greatly wondering and questioning what this vision might reveal, the divine light fixed in the mind of the vicar of Christ the thought, that the palm represented that poor man whom the day before he had repulsed.

Innocent in his turn accepted humbly the higher rebuke, and caused proclamation to be made in Rome for the mendicant whom he had so scornfully dismissed. Francis was speedily discovered, and brought once more into the presence of the Pope. We can lift the curtain, and hear the debate, and we shall find it interesting from the highest point of view. The scene is sketched in Bonaventura's life. Innocent heard the simple tale of the mendicant, who asked only to be allowed to found an Order, which would compel its members to be paupers and to preach the Gospel. The only thing he asked in fact, in addition to the Benedictine rule, was the allowance of this absolute, utter poverty. The Pope, though greatly struck by the earnestness and simplicity of the man, hesitated. Some of the cardinals thought it 'a new and questionable matter, and arduous beyond human strength.' It had slipped from their thoughts on their spiritual thrones, that on their theory Christianity could never have planted itself in the world. Then arose a venerable cardinal, John of St. Paul, Cardinal Bishop of Sta. Sabina, 'a man of all holiness, and a helper of the poor of Christ,' who, fired by the Divine Spirit, spoke to the supreme Pontiff and to his brethren thus :—' If we reject the petition of this poor man as a thing new and too arduous, when he seeks confirmation of the form of the evangelical life, let us beware lest we be found to offend the Gospel of Christ. For if any man says that within the observance of evangelic perfection is contained anything new, irrational, or impossible to keep, he is convicted of blasphemy against Christ, the author of the Gospel.'

These words of the second and nobler Gamaliel prevailed. The Pope turned to Francis, and besought him to pray that God would make known to them His will. A second vision ended Innocent's hesitation. He dreamed again. He saw the Lateran Basilica falling into ruins, and a certain poor man, of humble and despised aspect, stooping beneath the crushing burden, and sustaining it. 'Truly,' he cried, 'this is he who by labour and doctrine shall sustain the Church of Christ.' Innocent granted the request. A verbal, not a

written, confirmation of the rule was given; Francis was
sent forth with the Papal benediction to beg and to preach
the Gospel; and Innocent by that day's work added two
centuries to the dominion of the Roman Church.

Poverty, humility, labour, again saved the Church. And
it was time. Rome in all ages has done her best by her
morals and her influence to destroy the power, which the
holiness and self-devotion of her saintly men have enabled
her to wield. The dominion of Innocent to the eye was
absolute and splendid. To those who looked at it closely
it was rotten to the heart's core. He triumphed *in form*
in every conflict which he undertook, but he met everywhere
a spirit which no authority and no victory of force could
put down—the new born spirit of free thought and national
life. He had made King John his vassal. But he had
cursed the Magna Charta and all who supported it, and the
barons and people of England only laughed at him. He
had compelled Philip Augustus to put away his Agnes de
Meran, but Philip had won the battle of Bouvines, and utterly
broken up the Pope's German combinations. He had hounded
on the terrible Simon de Montfort through Languedoc on
his mission of extermination; the most brutal cruelty, the
most savage bloodthirstiness which find any record in history
had raged through the fairest land in Europe. Cities and
provinces had been given up to pillage and slaughter; 400
men and women had been burnt in one great funeral pile,
which we are told ' made a wonderful blaze, and caused great
rejoicing in the camp.' The literature, the national life, of
the Provençal population had literally been quenched in
blood; but one thing escaped Innocent—the spirit at which
he aimed the tremendous blow, the anti-sacerdotal, anti-
sacramental, anti-Roman spirit, the spirit of free, pure,
scriptural Christianity, that lived on, nursed by the awful
persecution through which God had sustained it—and a far-

sighted man like Innocent might well be musing there moodily on the Lateran terrace, as he saw this free spirit breaking out in every land. The truth is that the century of Imperial power and splendour had simply pampered the Church. It was an unwholesome and unlovely greatness—grossness, rather —which she had reached, and which the world wondered at and began to criticise with bitterness. Rome, grand as was her form in the eye of the nations, was becoming every-where a scandal and an offence; and the cry of the heretical sects, Waldenses, Albigenses, Poor Men of Lyons—no matter what their names—was for more simplicity, more purity, more power, more of Christ, more of the Holy Ghost, in the system and the life of the Church.

The extent to which this demand was spreading in Innocent's days, would be little apprehended by those who looked only on the gorgeous form of the dominion over which he swayed the sceptre, and the peace which it enjoyed. Here is the picture of the situation as sketched by Dr. Milman :—

'From almost every part of Latin Christendom a cry of indignation and distress is raised by the clergy against the teachers or the sects, which are withdrawing the people from their control. It is almost simultaneously heard in England, in Northern France, in Belgium, in Bretagne, in the whole diocese of Rheims, in Orleans, in Paris, in Germany, at Goslar, Cologne, Trèves, Metz, Strasburg. Throughout the whole South of France, and it should seem in Hungary, this sectarianism is the dominant religion. Even in Italy these opinions had made alarming progress. Innocent himself calls on the cities of Verona, Bologna, Florence, Milan, Placentia, Treviso, Bergamo, Mantua, Ferrara, Faenza, to cast out these multiplying sectaries. Even within or on the very borders of the papal territory Viterbo is the principal seat of the revolt.'[1]

The most daring satires began to be written against the Papal luxury and tyranny, they were chanted by monks, it is said, to holy tunes, and passed on from convent to convent, while princes and people added their hearty Amen.

[1] *Latin Christianity*, Bk. IX. ch. 8.

Here is a specimen of what is reported to have been actually chanted at service time:—

> *' Quidquid male, Roma, vales,*
> *Per immundos cardinales,*
> *Perque nugas Decretales;*
> *Quidquid cancellarii*
> *Peccant vel notarii,*
> *Totum camerarii*
> *Superant Papales.*[1]

It would be easy to quote passages, not from enemies but from bold champions of the Papal See, unquestionable witnesses, to shew how the very name of Rome was growing hateful to all that was righteous and merciful in the Christian world. And there were, moreover, preachers about Europe whom the omnipresent power of the head of the Church was impotent to silence, who with more or less purity and earnestness were urging upon the people the pure Christian ideas which the Waldenses, the Poor Men of Lyons, and other anti-sacerdotal sectaries had sealed with their blood. The position was critical when such doctrines as the following were abroad. These latter preachers, writes the author of *Latin Christianity*,—

'Threw aside the whole hierarchical and ritual system, at least as far as the conviction of its virtue and efficacy, along with the priesthood. The sanctity of the priest was not in his priesthood but in his life. The virtuous layman was a priest (they had aspired to reach that lofty doctrine of the Gospel,) and could therefore administer with equal validity all the rites; even women, it is said, according to their view, might officiate. The prayers and offerings of a wicked priest were altogether of no avail. Their doctrine was a full, minute, rigid protest against the wealth of the Church, the power of the Church. The Church of Rome they denied to be the true Church; they inexorably condemned homicidal engagements of popes and prelates in war. They rejected the seven Sacraments, except Baptism and the Eucharist. In baptism they denied all effect of the ablution by the sanctity of the water. A priest in mortal sin cannot consecrate the Eucharist. The transubstantiation takes place, not in the hand

---

[1] Quoted by Milman, *l.c.*

of the priest, but in the soul of the believer. They rejected prayers for the dead, festivals, lights, purgatory, and indulgences.'[1]

In the midst of all this luxury, splendour, lavish expenditure, and shameless venality of churchmen, and amidst the gathering discontent which the preachers of the heretical sects throughout Europe were fanning into a blaze, the Franciscans and Dominicans uprose. Pure Poverty was their fundamental rule, pure preaching, pure persuasion their fundamental work. They multiplied immensely. They threw themselves with intense and fearless zeal into their ministry. Europe, Africa, Asia, were fairly overrun by a crowd of courageous, self-sacrificing, and believing preachers; men whose lives, and whose readiness to die, lent immense weight to their pleadings: they outpreached in their intense and passionate fervour the preachers of a purer Gospel; their holy, self-denying lives, their impressive demeanour, and their picturesque figures in gown and cord, swept the sympathies and the hopes of the multitude in their train. They invaded the seats of learning, they furnished the ablest scholars and thinkers to the schools and universities, the ablest administrators to the Episcopal and even the Papal Chairs; in a word, they stormed the conscience and the heart of Europe, and for the time the Papacy was saved.

Francis having won the confirmation of his rule, went back in a kind of triumphal procession, joyously to his task. The Benedictines gave them the church of Sta. Maria de Portiuncula for their own, to be the headquarters of the Order. Francis refused even that as a possession, but gratefully accepted the use; sending to his benefactors, as a kind of acknowledgment, a pannier of fish year by year. Then he devoted himself with passion to the pursuit of Poverty, and strove to kindle in the hearts of his disciples the same absorbing enthusiasm by which he was himself consumed.

[1] *Latin Christianity, l.c.*

'Poverty,' he cried, 'is the way of safety, the nurse of humility, and the root of perfection; its fruits are hidden but they multiply themselves by an infinity of means.' His personal habits were of the severest rigour, and his ingenuity in mortifying his body is celebrated by his panegyrists. The bare ground was usually his bed and he slept sitting, his head leaning against a billet of wood or a stone. He rarely ate cooked food. But when his health compelled an exception, he took care to mingle cinders with it, lest his palate should relish it unduly. He kept eight great fasts a year, and in his holy meditations and contemplations he was constantly bathed in tears. But he was not a self-deceiver as to the virtue of these austerities. 'One must not praise a man,' he said, 'who is not sure of his lot, and who knows not what he may become. A man should not glorify himself because he fasts, because he weeps, because he chastises his body, all which things a sinner can do. There is but one thing which a sinner never does, and that is serving God faithfully, and rendering him the praise of what he bestows.' And yet his simplicity allowed him to indulge in strange excesses. Once, poor man, when he was nearly famished, he had eaten a bit of fowl. Thomas of Celano tells us that he had himself drawn, naked, through the streets, and well scourged, while proclamation was made 'See the glutton who gorged himself with fowl unknown to you.' Once at Christmas he had a stable arranged to preach in. There were the ox, the ass, the hay, and, that nothing might be wanting, he bleated like a sheep while uttering the word Bethlehem; and when naming the sweet Jesus, he licked his lips with his tongue as though tasting honey.

We must not however take up the idea that the man was a witless enthusiast or an ecclesiastical buffoon. There was stern work in him, daring courage, strong sense, and far-reaching wisdom. He was of the stuff of which the rulers of ages are made. His name echoes, and the influence of his life thrills, through Europe to this day. He had a direct and practical way of enforcing his commands. A rebellious brother, who shewed some lingering remnant of the old Adam of self-will, he had buried up to the neck in the earth, and was proceeding to bury him entirely, when the man capitulated. 'Art thou dead, my brother,' cried the saint. 'Yes,' the culprit stammered. 'Then come forth, and remember in future that I want dead followers, not living ones.'

The Order grew, as we may believe, mightily. There was something in the idea of St. Francis which high-minded women would not be the last to honour and love. Clara, of the noble house of Ortolana, under the counsel of the saint, forsook her home, and founded, in defiance of parental authority, a convent of nuns who have made famous the name and the rule of St. Clare. Sta. Clara was one of the chief instruments in directing St. Francis to the life of a missionary rather than the life of a recluse.

A great chapter of his Order was held at the Portiuncula, in May 1219. Five thousand mendicants assembled. Huts of straw and mud received them, the inhabitants of the province delighted to supply their simple needs. They were broken into groups of sixty or a hundred, each forming a little congregation, joining in prayers or listening to discourses, the theme of which was the conquest of the world. Thither Cardinal Ugolino came, afterwards the vigorous Gregory IX., and casting off his purple mantle, his hat and shoes, he was conducted in the dress of a minor brother to the place of the great assembly. 'Behold,' he cried, as he looked upon it, 'behold the camp of God. How goodly are thy tents, O Jacob, and thy tabernacles, O Israel!' Francis had reason enough to wish that his disciples should have as little as might be to do with Popes and dignitaries of the Church. He dreaded the temptations of mitres and cardinals' hats; and in the chapter he lifted up his voice against the seduction, and besought his followers touchingly to be faithful to the simplicity and foolishness of the Cross.

He then formulated a scheme for the spiritual conquest of the globe. Dividing the realms of the world among his followers, for himself he reserved the post of danger, and resolved to devote himself to a mission to the Saracens, then struggling with the Crusaders under the walls of Damietta. In 1219, with eleven companions, he set sail for the East. His clear strong sense penetrated the weakness of the Crusaders' operations. He had not much hope of the martial success of the soldiers of the Cross. But his business was with their enemies. And here is in brief the history of his enterprise.

While the two armies were in the field, Francis, carried away by the warmth of his zeal, went into the camp of the Saracens without fearing the dangers to which he exposed himself. On being stopped by the scouts of the Infidels, he cried, ' I am a Christian, take me to your master.' He was accordingly led before the Sultan, who asked him what had induced him to come into his camp? ' I am sent,' answered Francis with intrepidity, ' not by men, but by the Most High God, to shew to you and to your people the way of salvation, and to announce to you the truths of the Gospel.' This firmness impressed the Sultan, and he invited Francis to remain with him. But the man of God answered him thus: ' If you and your people will listen to the word of God I consent willingly to remain with you. But if you are wavering between Jesus Christ and Mahomet, cause a large fire to be lighted, into which I will enter with your priests in order that you may see which is the true religion.' The Sultan replied that he did not think there was any priest of their law who would accept that challenge, nor expose himself to torments for the sake of his religion; he feared besides that some sedition would spring up. He offered the saint several presents, all of which he refused. Some days after he sent him back with a good escort to the Christian camp.

His wider knowledge of men now suggested to Francis the establishment of an Order, content to aim at a minor perfection, which should lay men and women under *some* spiritual constraints, but should yet allow them to remain in, and to transact the business of, the world. The idea wrought, as far as numbers were concerned, with singular success. The members were bound by an agreement rather than a vow, and their habits of life were not so unlike those which George Fox laid down for the Society of Friends. He called it the Order of Penitence, and the association spread so rapidly that during the life of St. Francis and his immediate successors 'the Franciscan cord was to be seen on countless multitudes, in the market place, in the universities, in the tribunals, in the camps, and even on the throne.' After the death of Francis the Order continued to increase with even greater rapidity. In 1280 there were reckoned 1500 houses of Franciscans and 90,000 friars. But long before 1280 corruption had commenced its work. The Order rapidly rose to power and wealth and as rapidly grew rotten. The wandering friars begging through Europe, losing their first inspiration, would be in the way of all knavery, folly, and lust. There was little conservative force in the system of the Order; when the spirit of St. Francis died out of it we can well believe that morally it very rapidly decayed.

The expedition to the East is the main external event in the latter years of the life of St. Francis. Never of a strong constitution, and worn out by fastings and tears, he was a broken man before he had reached his prime. He had lived much in vision: and there was wrought into his heart and into the heart of his disciples an intense conviction that there was a special closeness of likeness between the outward fashion of his life and that of his Lord. His biographers tell us that they had often seen him lifted up from the earth so that they could only touch his feet, and even to a greater height. In truth nothing was miraculous with him, because all was miraculous. His life was so purely spiritual that it seemed to his disciples to have a wondrous power over the material elements and limits which shape the conditions of the lives of more earthly men. They seemed plastic in his hand. And there is a region here of wonder and mystery the secret of which has not been fathomed yet. It is not easy to make up one's mind amid all the difficulties of the wondrous tale of the stigmata, and we may pass over the subject with the words of Dr. Neander, who does not see his way wholly to dispose of it, but calls it 'a story with regard to which it still needs and deserves enquiry, to what extent in certain eccentric states of the system, a morbidly over-excited fancy might react on the bodily organism.'

The work of the saint was well nigh done. Twelve months of prostration followed the ecstasy in which the marks of the stigmata are said to have made their appearance. The autumn brought some intermission, and his voice was heard in simple, brief, pathetic words preaching the Gospel of the love of God, and when unable to preach in words, he presented himself to the crowds on whom he gazed earnestly as they thronged to touch his garments and receive his benediction. As death drew near he wrote a strange letter, which is preserved, to a Roman lady, in which he requested her immediate presence, with a winding sheet and tapers for his funeral, and with cakes which she had been used to give him during his illness in Rome. She came; some say she was already on her way. The cakes were eaten, but there was no abatement of his malady. His disciples Elia and Bernard de Quintavalle were kneeling by his bed. To each he gave a piece of the cake, and crossing his arms to reach Bernard with his right hand, he laid a hand on both and blessed them, bequeathing to Bernard the government of the whole Franciscan Society. He then dictated his last will, and solemnly commended his followers to the Most High. His last work done, he was laid on the bare ground. The evening—it was Oct. 4, 1226—was soft and calm. The western sun was glowing in the balmy autumnal air. The requiem for the dying ceased, and the faltering voice of the saint was heard. '*With my voice have I cried unto the Lord, bring my soul out of prison, that I may give thanks unto thy name.*' A moment, and Francis was free.

Whatever judgment we may form of the life of St. Francis as the founder of a powerful Order, none who have read the tales which loving biographers have delighted to treasure up and hand down to us, can question that Francis was one of the gentlest and tenderest of men. His love for dumb creatures was a beautiful and winning trait in a rude and blood-stained age like that. They evidently felt some magnetic power in the earnest and holy preacher; the tales of the trust and ministry of these dumb creatures to their friend cannot all be false, nor need we question the truth of them merely because they seem so marvellous to our own prosaic minds. The bees are said to have settled harmlessly on his lips. The birds flew round him in flocks, and when the twittering of the swallows disturbed him as he was preaching, 'Hush, my sisters,' won instant silence, that he might declare his Lord's will. One of the earliest Italian poems is a simple outpouring of his heart to his brother the sun, his sisters the moon and the stars, his brother the wind, his sister the water, his brother the fire, his mother the earth; he calls them all in words of touching pathetic simplicity to awake and join him in praise. And it is in beautiful harmony with this strange sense of kindred with nature, which made the bees, the birds, the beasts his tender and vigilant ministers, that when he felt the death shadow falling around his spirit he could breathe out the words, ' Welcome—my sister, Death.'

IX.

ST. LOUIS OF FRANCE: THE SAINT IN SECULAR LIFE.

IX.

ST. LOUIS OF FRANCE: THE SAINT IN SECULAR LIFE.

1215–1270.

ST. LOUIS of France characterises more perfectly than any of his great contemporaries the most important era in the history of Christendom—the era when men began to have some clear glimpse of the truth, after which they had been blindly feeling through all the ages of Christian history, that secular things and spiritual things are substantially the same things, though looked at in a different way. Secular things become spiritual things when spiritual insight and energy are brought to bear upon them; and this truth began to shine out in Christendom in St. Louis' life.

Louis IX. of France, grandson of a great French king, Philip Augustus, and grandfather of a great French king, Philip le Bel, was as true and pure a saint as St. Bernard in his monastery, while he was king, statesman, judge, warrior, husband and father, and spent his life in the management of great secular affairs. How much that meant in those days we are not able fully to measure in ours. It meant that an entirely new order of things was dawning; that the monastic age of Christendom was ending; that the day of the priest was drawing to a close: that the noble and sacred development of secular society in national life, with all its various organs and activities, was about to begin. St. Louis, king and warrior, was a man whose saintly ideal was as high and pure as that of either of the two great monastic saints, and of a far more elevated type than that of St. Thomas of Canterbury, whose saintship was mainly an organ of ecclesiastical power. With St. Louis the desire to live soberly, righteously and purely in the world, and to make his life, as far as a man's life might be, holy and beautiful as his Lord's, reached down to the springs of his thought and will and penetrated his every act and utterance. But the object of his saintly thought and interest was not the cell, nor the cloister; not the exercises of devotion, nor the services of the Church, but his duty in his secular work of ruling, fighting, and judging righteously, as the regent of Christ his King. He was one of the most pious of men, and the exercises of devotion occupied a large part of his time and thought; but they never became the end, as they tended to become among the Ascetics—as if life were made for devotion and not devotion for life. With St. Louis they were always means to the end which he had ever in sight, to follow wisely and nobly his secular calling. St. Louis had looked more deeply than most men into the meaning of that sentence of St. Paul, which is the true consecration of the secular life of men, ' Brethren, let every man, wherein he is called, therein abide with God.'

St. Louis was born in the year 1215. He died in 1270. So that his life falls wholly within that wonderful thirteenth century, which really marks the end of the childhood of Christendom; the century in which it began to feel that it had done with tutors and governors, and would manage its life henceforth for itself, with the help of its King, in whom it firmly believed, on high. It is the century of Edward I. and of Frederic II., who was one of the ablest men that ever occupied a throne. As head of the Holy Roman Empire, Frederick filled a larger place in the eye of Christendom, but from this distance St. Louis stands out as quite the noblest personality in that the dawning age of modern history. Five years before the death of St. Louis was born Dante, with whom the modern era fairly opens. The great Italian poet belongs to the world in which we now are living. There is always in each great era of transition some one writer of transcendent genius, who, connecting the old with the new, receives and hands on the sacred fire, and thus Dante closes the feudal era and opens the national era of Christian history.

Of this national era, as it expressed itself in the new-born polity of France, the saintly kingship of St. Louis was the consecration. A kind of sacredness attached to the kingly power through that man's life, which lent to it a very precious support in a world teeming with lawless men, who, full of daring before all human forces, had a humble, reverent fear of aught which seemed to bear the seal of a higher sphere than this.

In connection with St. Bernard, reference has already been made to the strong support which the sanctity of saintly men lent to ecclesiastical institutions, which but for that sanctity might have gone rapidly to wreck. The hierarchy, by their avarice, ambition, and lust, were always destroying that influence of the Church on the conscience of men, which the purity and self-sacrifice of the saints restored. An age that talks drearily of fate, or chance, or law, as accounting for all things in heaven and earth, is an age we may be sure in which the cant of the Church has drowned the music of the Gospel. For men in the main do long to believe— if the theologians would let them, and not sadden their hearts by claiming monopoly of the Divine Counsels, and branding as heretical every movement which promises enlargement of thought, life, and hope to mankind.

The thirteenth century is the age in which the things with which we are all familiar took, so to speak, their modern forms.   Kings, nobles, peoples, towns, navigation, trade, banks, manufactures, art, literature, constitutions, reformations, in the modern sense began to appear.   The central feature of all is the growth of the national life, round this as the sun all the others range themselves as satellites, and from this they derive their main motive power.   France in that century grew into a nation, and St. Louis marks the age of the transition.   His grandfather Philip Augustus had commenced the work, his grandson Philip le Bel completed it, and the result seemed a more holy and beautiful thing to the eyes and the hearts of men through St. Louis' life.   In this century the awful and oppressive shadow of the Holy Roman Empire really vanishes. After the death of the last great Hohenstauffen Emperor, it falls rapidly from a Catholic to a German State. France becomes a kingdom with an individuality as strongly marked, and with a right to recognition as clear, as the Empire itself; and we discern the beginning of the balance of power—that is the action and reaction of independent and tolerably well matched European nationalities.   The battle of Bouvines, won by Philip Augustus in 1214 over the Empire, established a new relation; thenceforth France and Germany become finally separate and opposed in their ideas and interests, with Italy and Flanders for their battle-fields, and England the spectator, the moderator, and not seldom the arbiter of the strife.

In the break up of the Carolingian Empire at the end of the ninth century the inheritance of the Imperial idea fell to the German branch of the House.   The symbol of the Empire was the possession of Rome.   The Holy Roman Empire was conceived of through the earlier Middle Age as the ancient Imperial realm of Christendom—the one fair realm of Christ co-extensive with the profession of His Gospel— over which the Emperor ruled by His commission and in

His name. It is impossible for us to imagine how the shadow of that great Roman Colossus, after the complete extinction of the Empire of the West by the Teutonic tribes, continued to awe and rule mankind. The barbarians who shattered it continued to regard with something like religious veneration the civilisation which they had destroyed. They despised heartily Roman rulers and Roman morals; but Roman ideas mastered them, and no sooner were they fairly settled in the noblest provinces of the Empire, than they set themselves to restore in government, literature, and art, as much as they could imitate of Rome. Especially the image of the Empire haunted them; one Imperial head of Christendom; one rule, one law, one belief, through the whole Christian world. They looked upon this grand institution with its sublime idea of unity, as having in it something Divine. It was the form of Christendom, and holy with an inherent sanctity. There was a sacredness in the person of a Roman Emperor which only very slowly passed over to the Roman Bishop. The earlier Popes regarded and addressed the Roman Emperors with profound reverence. The first man in the world was the Roman Emperor, and not the head of the Roman Church. Charlemagne restored the image. On Christmas day, 800, he was crowned Emperor of the West at Rome. He considered, and men considered in his day, that in his person the Holy Imperial rule was restored. Dying, he bequeathed the idea as a legacy, and his German successors endeavoured to grasp it, though it was constantly slipping from their hands.

Those will quite misunderstand the history of the Middle Age who lose sight of this vague, mysterious, but impressive image—the Holy Roman Empire—which from the ninth century to the thirteenth, haunted the imagination of the West. Nay, readers of Dante's *De Monarchiâ* will know how powerfully the idea acted on great minds up to the close of the Mediæval epoch. The German Emperors aimed at rule in Italy and Rome, on quite other grounds than those on which Philip Augustus aimed at rule in Normandy, or St. Louis in Provence. Masters of Rome, they ruled by sacred right and were the suns of Empire: while kings of kingdoms like France and Spain were but attendant satellites. England occupied a special position, and held that she had an imperium of her own, beyond the bounds of the Roman world. But a French king would find it hard to shake off the idea that an Emperor reigned by a right of which his own was but a reflection, and would at first find it difficult to comprehend, or at any rate to find a place in his political system for, his own right to reign in independent sovereignty at all. The idea was ever before the minds of such that the normal condition of Christendom was that of one vast State under one Imperial head; and the rapid growth of independent monarchies having no visible relation to the Empire, would be a perplexing thing to the minds of the very men who were most busy in building them up. For men obey the behests of present and near necessities: and are often startled by the shape which their work assumes, and puzzled to reconcile it with pre-existing ideas. The French kings were driven by sharp necessity to create a French kingdom; but it was not until the age of St. Louis that it disentangled itself from the meshes of the Imperial conception of Christendom, and claimed on its own behalf a sacred right to be.

During these five centuries the Imperial idea is really the dominant thing in Christendom, but happily for Christendom it had a twofold embodiment, in the Empire and in the Church. In the Eastern Empire the secular power was master, the Empire was forced into unity, and progress was killed. In the West the government and the Church grew separately. The headquarters of the former were usually in Germany, while Rome was mainly under the rule of the Popes. How essential this separateness was for the full development of the Church, is revealed by the miserable decrepitude of the Papacy when the French kings had it under their own hand, during the 70 years' captivity at Avignon. The same idea of the essential unity of Christendom was in the minds of both, and while the Emperors sought it in a secular form, the Papacy sought it in a spiritual, or what in those days passed for spiritual. It is important that we should realise clearly that this duality was the condition of a high development, and of advance towards a real and surely-grounded union. Because there were in the West two co-ordinate powers struggling together for the supremacy, and each doing its utmost to help forward the progress on its own lines, Christian society was developed more nobly in Western Europe than in Eastern Europe, where one power had it all its own way. It is by the harmony of strongly developed and opposing forces that the highest progress is realised. Christendom is the product of two forces, and is vigorous and progressive. Islam is the product of one force only, and when its first impulse was spent, it fell rapidly into decay. There were two things which prevented the Imperial system of Charlemagne from becoming absolutely dominant in Europe, and overshadowing the development of the various nationalities included under his rule. The one was the growing influence of the Papacy, which had its independent centre at Rome, and was largely a rival power; and the second was the elective principle of the Empire. The electors were powerful Princes and Prelates, who were able to limit the monarch's ambition, and among whom the Pope could always stir up formidable discords and so prevent the ablest Emperors from carrying everything before them in the realm. In the hands, however, of the great Saxon, Franconian, and Swabian rulers, the power was very formidable, though crippled much in practice by the influences just referred to.

The French kings before the thirteenth century were very petty princes as regards the extent of their dominions, compared with the head of the Empire, or even the great lords of their own realms. Five departments, out of the eighty-nine into which France is now divided, were all that the king could call his own, and within that little circle he had to carry on a constant struggle with the Counts of Chaumont, Clermont, and half-a-dozen others, who were the torment of his life.

Louis le Gros was the first king of the Capetian house (a house we must remember quite unconnected with the Empire, and inheriting nothing but the vague title and authority of king from the Carolingians), who made the name King something of a substantial reality in France. That is, he asserted and exercised a practical overlordship, as the dispenser of justice and the protector of the poor, over the feudal nobles ; an authority quite outside the feudal régime. From that time in France the king begins to act with vigour in a very visible and practical way. But Philip Augustus in the first years of the thirteenth century really created the realm. His predecessor, Louis VII., had married Eleanor of Aquitaine, who brought the South of France as her dower. Divorced subsequently, she married the able and resolute man who afterwards became Henry II. of England, and has won a by no means enviable place in our history. With her she took her whole domains, and Henry became lord of the extent of France between the Loire and the Pyrenees, besides Normandy and Anjou which were already in his hands. When Philip Augustus ascended the throne in 1180, perhaps three-fourths of what is now France obeyed a foreign lord. Poor Philip is said to have exclaimed, when he began to feel the burden and to realise the helplessness of the Crown against the turbulent vassals, 'Whatever they may do now, they are so strong I must bear their outrage and villanies, but please God they shall become weak, and I shall grow strong and powerful, and then, in my turn, I shall take vengeance upon them.' His whole life was devoted to making that promise good. While Henry II. lived he could not accomplish much. John gave him the longed-for opportunity. He was his vassal for the French provinces. On the murder of Arthur he summoned him before his Court as his lord, condemned him, and took possession of his lands; recovering in the end by legal process, which was not strictly legal but had a show of justice about it, almost the whole of the lands which the divorce and the re-marriage of Eleanor had transferred to the English Crown.

One other grand acquisition was made before St. Louis began to reign. Into the moral aspect of the Crusade against the heretics in the south of France we must not enter. From our point of view it was simply horrible. But it is important to understand why it did not seem horrible from theirs. Politically, the Crusade was a complete success. Free thought and spiritual life were for the time quenched in blood. A vigorous young literature, the first-born of modern Europe, was destroyed. But a great province which had been almost as independent as a separate kingdom, was brought into vital relation with the French monarchy, and this gave Louis IX. the mastery of the whole realm from the English Channel to the Mediterranean Sea. It was a fearfully blood-stained legacy. St. Louis was one of the most merciful of men; but he had no shadow of scruple about the sharp punishment of heretics. He was emphatically a man of his time; and in the judgment of his time heresy was not an intellectual aberration, far less, as *we* see that it often is, a nascent truth; it was a moral rebellion against a lawful authority, a breach in the sacred order of the home, the one household of Christendom, and was to be put down as the rebellion of a presumptuous child is put down, swiftly and with the strong hand of power. Louis, accordingly, not only accepted the legacy of the conquered, the murdered, province, but shewed great skill and energy in making his conquest complete; and thus the kingdom grew under his hand. The King of France now became the great power in Europe, in the period when the Empire and the Papacy had begun to decline, and before the rise of England. To this monarchy, which was really a new thing in Europe, the personal saintliness of Louis IX. gave, as we have said, a kind of consecration, which in that age was of inestimable worth. Louis VII. and VIII. had kindled a strong enthusiasm; under St. Louis something touching on worship was added, something which made a national King holy as Emperor or Pope.

There is generally to be observed a striking correspondence between the great characteristic of the leading man of an era, and the general tendencies of his times. St. Louis, the leading man of his age, was a secular saint. The broad feature of the thirteenth century is the growing dignity of secular life.

In that century the life of a man in the world emerged from its former feudal narrowness and monotony. It had to do with wider and more important interests; it was sanctified by higher aims; and it is quite natural, nay, in a sense inevitable, that the transition should be marked by the life of a great secular saint. The feudal age was, like the era of the Judges in Israel, an age of the disintegration of political society—its disintegration with a view to a reconstruction on a higher and larger plan. Each castle for the time became the centre of a petty state, and in the feebleness of the royal power, everyone, as of old, 'did what was right in his own eyes.' If it had not been for the existence of this royal power, feeble as it often was, all national and imperial interests would have vanished from the eyes of men. We must remember that the feudal ages, savage and contracted as was their life, had an order of their own not without its nobleness; their great and important work being to attach the idea of duty to power. They established a system of relations in which, within its limits, every man had a definite position with regard to every other man, and definite claims upon him. The bonds of men and classes were accordingly tightly riveted under the feudal law, but society was under the yoke and life was contracted and depressed. Feudalism left to itself would have lived an ignoble life in a dull soulless world; the thirteenth century, like the age of the Kingdom after the Judges, began that enlargement and elevation of the secular life which has continued to the present hour. Men were brought out of their narrow feudal relations and realised that they belonged to a wider world. National interests, national enterprises, national sorrows and joys, began to affect them, and the life of the world was seen to offer to them as fair a field for the exercise of high qualities as the cloister of the monk or the episcopal throne.

Among the causes which tended to this elevation of the secular life, four seem to stand out with peculiar prominence, at which a passing glance may be thrown :—

    I.   The rise of the vernacular literatures.

    II.   The growth of the towns and commerce.

    III.   The influence of the Crusades.

    IV.   The development of the kingly power.

I. It has been noticed on a previous page that so long as thoughtful men only expressed their ideas in a learned language, there was a certain stigma of contempt upon ordinary existence. Thought is the salt of life, but thought in the feudal ages was hidden from the multitude, and the common life was left poor and unsavoury. In the thirteenth century, however, the language of the people began to be used freely by the cultivated to express their thoughts. The life of St. Louis was written by a layman in the vernacular speech, and in the next generation Dante gave to the world one of its grandest works of literature in a language which could be understood by the people at large. Imagine the elevation of secular life which would arise from this source alone; the richest and the poorest having a common organ of communication; the best thoughts of the best minds enshrining themselves in, and thereby purifying and elevating, the language of the poor.

II. The growth of the towns and of commerce. The reign of Philip Augustus was marked by the rapid growth of the towns. He re-founded Paris; he gave it its cathedral, market, pavement, hospitals, aqueducts, boundaries, arms, and above all, a university, which dates from the year 1200. Population increased and tended to centres. The people were beginning as a class to feel their power, and they naturally drew together. Towns waxed strong, obtained charters, and attracted citizens by the security they afforded. The intercourse of town life develops intelligence and diffuses interest in political affairs. And thus in a score of ways these centres of population grew, and in growing enlarged and elevated the secular life of men.

III. The influence of the Crusades in the same direction was immense. They extended commerce, enriched new classes, created an order of men of business to attend to the carrying on of distant enterprises, and spread a taste for a more refined mode of living, though they did also much to corrupt the simplicity of feudal society. The age of St. Louis saw the close of the Crusades. Why? Because men saw their folly? Not in the least. Columbus, one of the greatest of modern men, was at heart a Crusader. The Crusade was very largely an outlet for the imagination and for the energy of men, shut up to a narrow and miserable life. It was the romance as well as the devotion of it which attracted them. Christianity had done thus much for men at large. It had made them conscious of other than local interests, and given them a community of thought and life with distant people, which made the stormy and often brutal existence of a feudal province seem very narrow and poor. They craved some higher excitement, some enterprise which would take them out into a larger and nobler world, would associate them with fellow-believers and band Christendom in a visible unity of aim, interest and hope. This in a great measure the Crusade supplied. Here was a holy enterprise in which the layman—king, duke, baron, nay peasant—was more important than the priest. The secular man with the cross upon his breast had a sanctity which the priest could neither give nor take away. He too could be a soldier of Christ in his own rude way. And so the Crusade had an immense direct influence on the elevation of the secular life of men; while the wider observation, the larger knowledge, the higher culture which it secured indirectly to all who had any concern with it, tended to establish and perpetuate the elevation which it won.

IV. Co-ordinate with this, and in some measure rising out of it, was the growth of the royal power. The king in that age represented the unity and the majesty of the nation, as against the provincial despot. Through the king, the distant members of the body politic realised their connexion with each other. The king really related the citizen to a larger world; and gave him some faint interest in the condition of Christendom and the conduct of great political affairs. And so this desire for an ampler existence, and for contact and concert with the great world of Christendom, which had been one main element in the fascination of the Crusade, found growing satisfaction, as the national life developed itself through the extension of the royal power, in the ever enlarging interests of the circle of their daily lives. Men ceased to feel the glamour of the Crusade, because they were beginning to find so much noble work to do at home. They began to understand that their Jerusalem was at home, or nowhere. 'Preach the Gospel to every creature,' said Christ to His disciples, 'beginning at Jerusalem.' Every great mission must begin at Jerusalem, that is in the circle close round us, if it is ever to accomplish much in a wider world. It is idle to be regenerating Africa, China, India and the islands of the Pacific, while we leave the poor at our own doors to herd like brutes, and to wallow in worse than heathen ignorance and brutality. Begin at Jerusalem, your native city, the home and centre of your daily lives; instruct its ignorance, clothe its nakedness, cleanse its foulness, give it homes to dwell in where a Christian household may live with some decency and dignity, overcome its idleness, drunkenness, and lust, and then you will not only have earned the right but won the power to bear your civilising Gospel all round the world!

Into the midst of this stirring growing life of secular society St. Louis was born, and he was born to be its consecrating priest. When he died he left a benediction upon it which men felt to be the benediction of Heaven. That the most spiritually-minded man of the thirteenth century felt no temptation to turn monk, but found room for all his saintly impulses and aspirations in ruling a kingdom, judging a people, and leading his armies in righteous wars, is a fact of the first importance in modern history.

It was the emancipation of the religious life. Then it burst the shell of the cloister, and took its place by the great world's hearth-fire. It meant much when a saintly monk or a saintly mendicant wielded an influence in virtue of his goodness which cast the power of the hierarchy into the shade; it meant very much more when that supremely Christlike man was seen to be a secular king. It is the starting point of that modern progress, which will end at last—we have not reached it yet—in the emancipation of the sphere of man's higher life from the despotism alike of the creeds and the churches, while it accepts joyfully all the help and guidance which they can give it, as it does its work and fulfils its destiny, under the headship of Christ alone.

Having now glanced at the spirit of the times in which the lot of St. Louis was cast, and on the political and spiritual significance of his life and reign, we will pass on to study the man himself, of whom we fortunately know much from reliable records of his words as well as his works. Quite the most valuable of these is the life of St. Louis, by one of his most trusted friends and followers, the Sieur de Joinville of a noble family in Champagne. It is fortunately a rambling familiar gossiping narrative, full of graphic records and descriptions, and makes no pretence to be a fine artistic production by a man who had a classical model before his eyes, as is the *Philippide* of Guillaume le Breton, in which the *Æneid* is followed so closely that we are in doubt sometimes whether Philip Augustus or Æneas is the real hero. Joinville's is a homely unmethodical account, but its value lies in the fact that it was written by a man who almost lived with Saint Louis, and who had an eye to discern and a heart to reverence the moral beauty and grandeur of his life. He was constantly at court, he accompanied the King on his

Crusade, he loved him with a passionate devotion, and though no saint, was a man after his own heart. Joinville set himself honestly to record what he saw and heard, with all manner of minute loving touches which only his tender reverence could have inspired. Moreover he wrote in the vernacular French of the day, inditing no learned book for an educated class, but a simple tale to be read by laymen, and, it might be, to make his great master known in some measure to the poor. Like Asser's life of Alfred, the work is an invaluable portrait of one of the few greatest men of the world by a friend and follower, written not to draw attention to the skill and talent of the author, but honestly to make the subject of it known to mankind. Alfred the Great was a man worthy to be set in the same rank as St. Louis, and it would be hard to find the third who can be placed by their side. Our own great Alfred was probably on the whole the nobler man and the greater king. There was the same moral dignity and purity in Alfred as in Louis, the same justice, the same absolute devotion to the good of his people, but in the former there seems to have been greater moral and mental robustness, a stronger mind, a firmer will, and a larger capacity for ruling men. Alfred was free from that touch of fanaticism which appears in St. Louis; not even in the thirteenth century, we may think, could Alfred have been induced to invoke the Inquisition or to lead a Crusade. But there is a special delicacy and beauty in the character of St. Louis which perhaps even Alfred cannot rival, but these were connected with certain saintly qualities in his nature which were an element of weakness to him in the management of practical affairs. From these Alfred was absolutely free.

St. Louis was probably the most purely just-minded man whom we meet with in history. Just all round, to friends, kindred, vassals, enemies, and infidels, he had the simplest belief that what is just is not only the rightest but the wisest thing to do. He seems never to have hesitated a moment, nor to have allowed any interest however large to obscure in the faintest degree his vision of the right. He was not a constructive legislator like Alfred, nor yet a political reformer. Though the feudal system was wearing out in his days, he did not try to destroy it or even to hasten its overthrow, nor did he make any attempt to strengthen the monarchy that it might occupy its room. And yet, as a fact, he greatly hastened the overthrow of feudalism and the growth of the monarchical power in France, and this partly by dealing justly with his vassals and imposing on them the same duty in their turn, and partly by the strong personal influence which his upright, pure, and unselfish nature established over men. He extended widely the limits of his kingdom, though never by aggressive wars, and under his hand it became consolidated and grew rich and prosperous, so that the reign of St. Louis is certainly a conspicuous proof that a righteous political course, fearlessly pursued, enlarges, enriches, and edifies States.

St. Louis was born at Poissy. His mother was Blanche of Castile, a remarkably able woman, who ruled France as regent during his minority with singular firmness, and who established over her son a very powerful influence, which remained unbroken till her death. She was a woman of this sort—one likes to know something of the mothers of such men as St. Louis—when he was born they stopped the bells of the church close by lest they should disturb her, and upon her discovering the reason, she ordered that if needful she should be removed, but that nothing should hinder the summoning of the faithful to prayer. And her son often in after life repeated, that Madame used to say, 'that if I were sick unto death, and could only be cured by committing a mortal sin, she would rather let me die than utterly offend my Creator.' It is notable that Queen Blanche called the people to the coronation of her son, as well as the barons and clergy, and once when there was a plot of the barons to seize him, Blanche summoned the burgesses of Paris and the people of the country round, who responded in such overwhelming numbers that the great vassals were foiled and withdrew. While young, his mother married him to Margaret, daughter of the Count of Provence. But like many another strong-minded mother-in-law, she could not bear the young people to be much together, and made Margaret's life very miserable. Margaret made him a devoted wife, and St. Louis loved her tenderly, but it is characteristic of his strong good sense and clear sight, that he marked in her an ambitious temper and a want of political wisdom, and would never during his absences leave the realm in her charge; whereas his mother while she lived was regent as matter of course. But poor Louis and Margaret had to meet almost by stealth. Joinville says that when they stayed at Pontoise, Margaret's apartments were on the floor below his own, and there was a winding stair between them on which the pair used to sit and converse, while her attendants and his watched at the doors lest this terrible mother-in-law should draw near, in which case they would fly to their own rooms.

Louis' sense of justice with regard to all matters but heresy seems to have been perfect. A charter was brought to him by the heir of the late Countess of Boulogne promising him the County of Dammartin. The seal was almost effaced. His whole council assured him that he could not be bound by it. There was just a little portion of the seal visible. He sent for a document sealed with the seal which he used when he gave the charter. He compared them minutely, determined that the seals were the same, and said, I cannot with a clear conscience keep back the County. Being very ill once he summoned his eldest son and said, 'Fair son, I beseech thee to make thyself beloved by the people of thy kingdom, for in truth I should like better that a Scotsman, fresh from Scotland, should govern my subjects well and loyally, than that thou shouldst rule them wickedly and reproachfully.' His last instructions to his heir form one of the noblest documents in history.

Louis was emphatically the peacemaker among his Christian neighbours. War between Christians, except for the sake of justice, was hateful to his heart, and when his council reproached him with the foolishness of this policy, because if his neighbours were suffered to fight it would weaken them and leave his realm relatively stronger, he wisely as well as piously answered, 'If the neighbouring princes see that I leave them to fight they may well take counsel together and say, The King has some evil design in allowing us to attack each other, and then out of the hatred they would bear me, they would all run-a-muck against me, and I might lose everything, without taking into account that I should earn the enmity of God, who has said, Blessed are the peacemakers.'

Perhaps the sorest trial of his love of justice occurred in the Holy Land. The Crusade to Egypt had been a miserable failure and the King had been made captive. He had paid an enormous ransom, though it is worth noting that such was the dignity of his demeanour, and so indomitable was his resolution to submit to no terms which would bring moral shame on the Christian cause, that the Sultan said to him, 'You say that you are our prisoner, and in truth we thought so; but you treat us as if we were held captives by you.' There was strife at the time between the Sultan of Damascus and the Emirs of Egypt, and the Sultan offered to restore the kingdom of Jerusalem to St.

Louis, if he would help him against his Egyptian foes. It was the dream of Louis' life, his one absorbing passion, to see that kingdom restored. But no. He had made a ten years' truce with the Emirs and they had faithfully released their Christian captives. He would not break his word, even under that tremendous temptation, and he sorrowfully saw the restoration of Jerusalem vanish out of his sight.

On the other hand he was no easy, soft-hearted ruler, disposed to make everyone happy by letting vassals, subjects, and servants riot at will. He had no idea that he could make anyone happy except by making him just and good, and he was remarkably firm in securing that everyone did his duty, while his stroke was swift and stern against high-handed wrong. A certain Count de la Marche refused homage where it was due. Louis called his vassals together and asked them, 'What ought to be done to a vassal who wishes to hold his lands independent of any liege lord, and who refuses the faithful homage which has been paid time out of mind by him and his forefathers?' They answered that the lord of the soil ought to resume the fief as his own property. 'By my royal name,' said the King, 'this Count de la Marche pretends to hold lands after this fashion—lands which have been the fief of France ever since the time of the brave king Clovis!' The vassals having been first consulted (this was Louis' wisdom), promised hearty support. He gathered a powerful army well supplied with munitions of war and fell upon the foe, with whom Henry III. of England was in some way associated. He shewed brilliant military conduct; won two great battles and drove Henry a fugitive into Bordeaux. He resumed the fief, and only on his abject submission accepted the Count as his vassal. Thus his kingdom grew. It is a beautiful trait of his generosity that he allowed Henry to travel home to England through France, and that once, when his courtiers were making a jest of the English king, he said, 'Cease, I forbid you either to ridicule him or to cause him to hate me for your folly. His charity and piety will save him from all danger and all disgrace.'

One anecdote may be quoted to illustrate his admirably wise and firm administration of his realm. In former times the Provostship of Paris was sold to the highest bidder, and robberies and other crimes abounded. The common people were afraid of dwelling in the open country, which became almost a desert. Hearing of all this, the King settled that he would himself appoint an able man with a sufficient salary; and that he would abolish all the heavy taxes which weighed the people down. He found a just judge and put the matter into his hands. This officer administered justice without fear or favour, and life and property in Paris became perfectly secure. The same policy was pursued throughout the realm, and it is said that in a short time population increased so much from the justness and uprightness that reigned, that the estates, rents, and revenues of the kingdom were in one year nearly doubled, and the country very much improved.

One of the most notable passages in mediæval history is that in which Joinville describes an ever memorable scene in the following words :—

'Many times have I seen this holy saint after hearing Mass in the summer, go and amuse himself in the wood of Vincennes; when, seating himself at the foot of an oak, he would make us seat ourselves round about him, and everyone who wished to speak with him came thither without ceremony, and without hindrance from any usher or others. He then demanded aloud if there were any who had complaints to make; and when there were some he said, "My friends, be silent and your causes shall be despatched one after another." Then oftentimes he called to him Lord Peter de Fontaines, and the Lord Geoffrey de Villette, and said to them, " Despatch these causes"; and whenever he heard anything that could be amended in the speeches of those who pleaded for others, he most graciously corrected them himself. I have oftentimes seen this good king come to the Garden of Paris, dressed in a coat of camlet, and have carpets spread for us to sit round him, and hear and discuss the complaints of his people with the same diligence as in the wood of Vincennes.'

That picture is unique in European history—pure, clear-sighted justice and goodness at the head of the affairs of a great kingdom, and all men filled with trust and love. It is not only notable, it is prophetic. It carries our thought on to a time which is still in the far future, when '*A king shall reign in righteousness, and princes shall rule in judgment; and a man shall be as an hiding-place from the storm, a covert from the tempest; as rivers of water in a dry place, and as the shadow of a great rock in a weary land.*'

It has been said that St. Louis was a saint as holy, as unselfish, as St. Bernard, and yet he never seems to have been even tempted to turn monk. It is most significant of the change which in that thirteenth century was passing over European society, and with which St. Francis in the preceding generation had very much to do, that this eminently holy man felt that he could live the saintly life quite as well, perhaps better, on the throne. And yet he had a very deep reverence for the cloister. He ardently desired that his three dearest children should take the vows, and earnestly pressed it on them, but seeing at last that they felt no vocation to it, with that admirable wisdom which distinguished him, he renounced his project: and set himself at once to establish them suitably in life. And it is remarkable too that, devout as he was and wholly devoted to religious duty, no king of France ever met with calmer, firmer resistance the arrogant demands of the Church. Here is one notable instance, related by Joinville in the following terms:—

'The prelates of France once assembled at Paris to speak with the good St. Louis, and one of them . . . addressed the king, by the unanimous assent of the other prelates, as follows :—"Sire, know that all these prelates instruct me to tell you that you are ruining Christendom, and that it is sinking in your hands." The king upon this crossed himself and said, "Bishop, inform me how this happens and from what cause." "Sire," he said, "it is because no notice is taken of excommunicated persons ; for at this moment a man would rather die in a state of excommunication, than be absolved, and will in no way make satisfaction to the Church. Therefore command your bailiffs and provosts, that wherever they find a man who has been excommunicated a whole year and a day, they constrain him to be absolved by the seizure of his goods." The holy man replied that he would cheerfully order this to be done to everyone who should be found unjust to the Church. The bishop said it only belonged to them to be acquainted with their own cause of complaint. To this the good king said, that he would not act otherwise, for it would be blameable before God and against reason, to force those who had been injured by churchmen, to absolve themselves without being heard in their own defence. And he reminded them of a Count of Brittany, who was excommunicated by the prelates for seven years, and at last brought his cause before the Pope, who decided in his favour. "Now," said the king, "should I have compelled the Count to seek absolution at the end of the first year . . . I should by so doing have behaved wickedly towards God and towards the Count of Brittany." After the prelates heard this they were satisfied with the answer the king had made them.'

Here is something like the question between Becket and Henry, settled quite quietly against the Church. Why? Because there was that perfect justice in the secular power, that all knew that the best interests of men, secular and sacred, were safer in the hands of the King than in the hands of the priests.

There was, however, a certain strain of fanaticism in the character of St. Louis, which we must take as the drawback to an otherwise uniquely noble and beautiful life. It was utterly lamentable that he should leave all this lofty and fruitful work for France, to waste his strength and treasure in a Crusade. Of the Crusades at large something has been already said. None were more heroic, none more miserable in their issues, than the expeditions which Louis led to Egypt and to Tunis, where the Crusade as well as its captain died. St. Louis was an able leader and a gallant soldier. But he lacked the gift of a great commander; the enterprise was too vast and difficult for his hand, although, rightly handled, this of all the Crusades had perhaps the best chance of success. It was, however, managed miserably, and it as miserably failed. In everything with which the King had personally to do, his highest qualities revealed themselves. He fought with splendid courage and conduct: he suffered with noble patience and dignity. In defeat, pestilence, famine and captivity his spirit never stooped for a moment. Sick himself, he was foremost in cheering his starving plague-stricken soldiers, and with his own hands he helped to bury the dead. Nothing could induce him, by sea or by land, to leave his comrades when his life was in deadly peril; he had led them forth on this disastrous enterprise, he would not abandon them in life or in death. But it is a sad, sad history, a dark chapter in the record of what fanaticism has done for the wasting of the world.

Behind all this powerful and purifying political and social influence, we may be sure that there was a very pure, lofty, and gentle nature and a very noble and wisely ordered personal life. Joinville has this passage on his care of his children.

'Before this good king went to bed he was often accustomed to have his children brought to him, and then relate to them the brilliant actions and sayings of ancient princes, telling them to retain them well in their memory to serve as examples. In like manner he would tell them the deeds of wicked men, who by their luxury, rapine, avarice, and pride had lost their honours and kingdoms, and that their deaths had been unfortunate.'

Joinville, who was no saint, though a man of pure character and life, had once answered a question of the King, that he 'would rather have committed thirty deadly sins, than be a leper.' The King waited till the company left, and then took Joinville to task as he sat at his feet. 'Ah, you bad *musart, musart!* you are deceived; for you must know that there can be no leprosy so foul as deadly sin, and the soul that is guilty of such is like the devil in hell.'

He was singularly temperate and always mixed his wine with water, and asked Joinville why he did not do the same. He answered naïvely that he had a large head and a cold stomach, which would not bear it. Two were talking at table in a low voice. 'Speak aloud,' said the King, 'or your companions will think that you are speaking evil of them.'

The following anecdote reveals an exquisite courtesy and consideration for others. Robert of Sorbon once reproached Joinville for being more richly dressed than the King. Joinville turned the tables on him, saying that he wore the dress handed down from his ancestors, 'It is you who ought to be reprimanded, for you are descended from bond-men on both sides, have quitted the dress of your ancestors, and have clothed yourself in finer camlet than the King now wears.' The King, to Joinville's surprise, rather took the part of Robert. Afterwards St. Louis called Joinville and confessed that he had been wrong in taking his part, 'but I did it from seeing him so much confounded, that he had need of my assistance, and about dress the wise man says, "We must dress ourselves so that the elders may not think that we dress too grandly, nor the young ones that we dress too meanly."' This is worth quoting because it shews not only his courtesy, but his practical wisdom; unless we go to Polonius it would be hard to find a wiser remark about the seemly in dress.

It need hardly be said that there was peculiar tenderness in his consideration for the poor. He took into his household an old servant, whom his grandfather had dismissed because the fire crackled. Once he had an inflammation in the leg, which gave him great pain. He wished to examine it, and Jean held a lighted candle close to the limb. He let a drop of burning grease fall on it. Louis started up in agony. 'O Jean, Jean, my grandfather sent you away for a much less thing!' was his only rebuke. There were always some poor set down to dinner with the officers of his household. Three invariably dined in the royal apartment, quite near the King. Joinville says, 'I have often seen him cut their bread and pour out their drink.' Not seldom, when he had a little time on hand, he would say, 'Let us go and visit the poor of such a place, and give them a feast to their liking.' A poor woman stood at the palace door with a loaf. 'Good King,' she said, 'it is this bread, thy charity, on which my poor husband liveth, who is lying at home very ill.' The King took the loaf saying, 'The bread is hard enough,' and went with her to the house to see the sick man, and to take him in more senses than one, better bread. Once a leper on the other side of a muddy pool dared not approach, but tried to attract his attention. The King crossed over, gave him some money, and then took his hand and lifted it to his lips. '*Inasmuch as ye have done it unto one of the least of these my brethren, ye have done it unto me.*' Thus he bore himself through the noblest and most beautiful life lived during the Middle Age of Christendom. One word on the death, which fitly closed it, and we have done.

In 1270 he was so ill that discerning eyes might have seen that his end was near. He was 55 years of age, but he was never strong and he was worn out with toils and cares, and, let us add, the strain of such a lofty life. Then once more the Crusading passion seized him. *Seized him* is the appropriate word. St. Louis is hardly responsible for that last mad and fatal Crusade. He was like a man under the dominion of a fixed idea, against which reason was vain. His people, his barons, even the Pope, entreated him to abandon it. They pointed to the splendid progress and prosperity of the realm which his wisdom, firmness, and justice had created, and dreaded lest a hopeless enterprise, by robbing it of its head, should lay it in the dust. Joinville even flatly refused to sail. But it was in vain; nothing would turn him from his purpose, and we may trace in his determination something of the insane obstinacy of disease. His intellectual powers were evidently failing. The Crusade was nothing but disorder. There was no ruling mind anywhere. They directed their course to Tunis. There was no order in the fleet, no order in the camp, no order in the field; there were no stores, there was no food. Pestilence broke out in the army, aggravated by famine. The soldiers died like sheep, and their bodies rotted in the sun. Louis at last was stricken, and he knew, and knew joyfully, that the hour of his departure was come. He gathered about him those of his children who were with him, and laid his charge upon them as a dying Christian father, with pathetic emphasis and tenderness. Then, true to the habit of his life to devote himself to the service of the State and of Christendom, he received some ambassadors from Constantinople by his dying bed, and heard their requests. During his last night he frequently started up in bed and cried, 'O Jerusalem! O Jerusalem! we will go to Jerusalem!' At last he ceased to speak; but he had himself laid on a coarse sack covered with ashes with the Cross before him. Then the light died out of his eye, and the death shadow gathered over his brow. 'Father, after the example of the Divine Master, into Thy hands I commit my spirit,' was murmured from his stiffening lips. A moment more, and the most passionate desire of his heart was satisfied. He had passed to the Jerusalem on high.

X.

JOHN WYCLIF, AND THE DAWN OF THE REFORMATION.

X.

JOHN WYCLIF, AND THE DAWN OF THE REFORMATION.

THE Papal Empire touched the height of its power under Innocent III., who was reigning in 1200 A.D., when that great thirteenth century dawned, wherein all things in Europe began to be new. He realised the dream of Gregory VII.—a Papal Kingdom of Heaven. Gregory died in exile broken-hearted, but Innocent wielded imperial power over the kings of the world, in the name of Christ, their King. When John of England, lord of the freest and strongest realm in Christendom, accepted vassalage, the Pope felt himself substantially overlord of all the lordships of this earth. And this position is precisely what Innocent meant to claim, when he wrote—'The Lord committed, not the Church universal only, but the whole world to Peter's rule,' and formulated the thesis already referred to, that Pope to King is as sun to moon, and that as the sun sways his planets, so the Pontifical is set to regulate the Regal power.

There is a grand truth behind Innocent's words, to which hatred of assumption often blinds us: but it is a truth marred by a tremendous mistake. The secular needs the spiritual to enlighten and to rule it; the spiritual is its true light and lord. So far Innocent was right. But the sun which is to lighten the darkness and to rule the motions of the secular sphere, is neither Priest nor Pope,

but the Lord Christ working by His word and Spirit in
human consciences and hearts. Here is the deadly error of
the Papacy, in that the Pope 'as God, sitteth in the temple
of God, shewing himself that he is God.' And this is the
fatal root of all the shame which the institution has brought
upon the Gospel, and all the suffering which it has inflicted
on mankind.

Innocent realised the Papal dream for the moment, and
then from that moment the ecclesiastical dominion began
to decay. It came about in this wise. John of England
the Papal vassal, and Otho the Papal claimant of the
Empire, banded under Papal auspices against the French
King, Philip Augustus. The French people, and notably
the townsfolk, rallied round Philip, and on August 27,
1214, he gained the great victory of Bouvines. Neither
party probably mustered more than 20,000 men, but for
all that Bouvines was one of the most notable battles of the
world, and for this reason—a French nation gathered around
a French monarch, and held its own against Pope and
Empire. It was the victory of a nation wherein the common
people had their place and part, and it marks decisively
the rise of this new force in Europe, before which the
Papal tyranny was destined ultimately to go down.

If the *power* of the Papacy culminated under Innocent,
about the year 1200, its *splendour* shone out in 1300, at
the great Jubilee which was held in Rome by Boniface
VIII., the last of the great Imperial Popes. Splendour
always follows in the wake of power; an age of splendour
is always vitally an age of decline, and its glow is just
the fungoid brilliance of colour with which nature does her
best to cloak decay. Boniface, imperious perhaps rather
than imperial, conceived the grand idea of a Jubilee of the
Universal Church. A great crowd of pilgrims made their
way in that year, 1300, to Rome, and left their costly

offerings at the shrine of St. Peter. The ambassadors of the leading States of Christendom brought their homage, and Boniface, as he looked round on that vast and glittering throng, might well believe himself the one overlord and master of the world. Indeed he is said to have seized a sword, and to have crowned himself with the imperial crown, shouting, 'It is I who am Cæsar; it is I who will defend the rights of the Empire.'

Innocent had wielded the two swords, Boniface must display them, and flourish them before the eyes of men. The boast was a sign that the swords no longer rested firmly in his grasp. There were keen observers there who were noting everything—John Villani, and Dino Compagni, the founders of that intellectual school of historians and critics which was rising to power in Florence, and was destined to play such a part in the coming age. Compagni says that he conceived the first idea of his history at that Jubilee; one must read a good deal to understand how fatal honest history has been and is to Rome. A few months later Dante was in Rome; Dante, who in that transcendent poem which rounds the Middle Age and opens the Modern, pictures, with his terribly graphic pen, that very Boniface writhing and shrieking amidst the torments of the Inferno.

Soon after that Jubilee the Papal power bent to its fall. Philip le Bel of France was the bitter enemy of Boniface, as his ancestor had been of Innocent, and in 1300 Philip le Bel was already master. Three years after that splendid triumph, the Pontiff, who had seen the civilised world at his feet, was struck from his throne by the brutal hand of the emissary of the French King. Philip had assembled the States General to prepare himself for the conflict, and Michelet calls that the baptismal register of the nation. The most furious diatribes against Boniface were uttered, and Philip, having a nation thoroughly roused and resolved behind him, sent his representatives to summon the Pope before a Council. They found him at Anagni, and taking with them a member of the Colonna family and a troop of mercenaries, they broke into the town. William of Nogaret addressed him with fierce vituperations; Colonna struck him with his mailed hand, and would have killed him, but the more politic Frenchman forbade. Old and broken as he was with 86 years of toils and cares, the Pope bore himself bravely. For three days he remained in the hands of his captors, refusing all food for fear of poison, and then the people rose and rescued him; but it was too late. He was borne starving into the market-place. 'Whoever will give me the least morsel to relieve my wants,' he sobbed, 'I will give him absolution for all his sins.' Then he set out for Rome, which he entered only to die. Stories were current at the time that as the last hour approached, he became fiercely blasphemous. It is said that he drove from him the priests who came with the viaticum, and thus 'unhouseled, unannealed,' denying his Lord, execrating the Virgin, with oaths and curses which made men shudder, screaming with curious confusion of tongues, 'Allonta di Dio, et de Sancta Maria, Nolo, Nolo,' the imperious spirit of the last of the great Mediæval Popes passed up to its dread account.[1]

This striking and terrible history is the true prologue to the tale of Wyclif's life and work. The dishonour and decay of the Papacy was a fundamental condition of that new state of society in which he was to sow to such noble purpose the germs of the Reformation. The special

---

[1] Ferretus Vincentinus, *apud* Muratori, *R.I.S.*, vol. xii., col. 1008. It is fair to add that there are other accounts which give a more favourable picture of the last hours of Boniface.

characteristics of the new epoch which opened with the thirteenth century have been described in previous lectures. Among the features of the age which help to explain the growing resistance which men were disposed to offer and able to offer to the overweening claims of Rome, notice has been already taken of the rise of national feeling, of national monarchies, and of vernacular literature. The latter is so intimately associated with the name of the first translator of the Bible into modern English that it claims here a further word. One often hears hasty expressions used about the sin of burying the Scriptures in a learned language, which scholars only could understand. But while the modern languages were in process of formation, there was nothing else to be done. The Latin being a dead, and therefore a fixed, language, while living languages were rapidly changing and settling into shape, the use of the former served a purpose of incalculable importance to Europe during the era of transition; while at the same time it threw enormous power into the hands of the men who alone were familiar with it, the ecclesiastics of the Roman Church. We must clearly understand that this grew out of the necessities of things, not out of an ecclesiastical conspiracy against the liberties of mankind. Rome had no dread of the Scriptures until they were appealed to by the advocates of Reform. While during the thirteenth century the vulgar tongue was growing to form in all the western nations, Italy of course leading the way, in the fourteenth it was fairly fit for literary use. In the beginning of the century, Dante found, or made, his dear Italian the fit vehicle for his wonderful poem, while before the end of it, the vulgar English became suited in Chaucer's hands for the noblest artistic treatment, and in Wyclif's for the translation of the word of God.

We have seen Boniface VIII. overthrown in the plenitude

of his power. The work of Philip did not end with the outrage. He was strong enough to compel the removal of the Papal Court from Rome to Avignon in France, where the Popes became mere puppets of the French kings. For seventy years they remained in exile—Papal writers call it the seventy years' Captivity—then on the restoration to Rome in 1376, the Papist schism arose. The French and Italian parties set up their Popes against each other, and from 1378 to the Council of Constance, where in 1417 the scandal was put down with a high hand by the assembled prelates of Christendom, there were Popes and Antipopes fighting and cursing each other with the intensest fury, amid universal sorrow and shame. This captivity and schism were naturally attended by a frightful corruption of ecclesiastical society. It is a dark subject, but we must glance at it in order that we may fairly grasp the features of the age and understand the forces which were working for Reform.

No one who has not looked closely into the history of the times can imagine the horrible corruption that was covered by the splendid mantle of the Papal Church. The policy of Hildebrand had at last triumphed, clerical celibacy was the law, and society was reaping the inevitable fruit. As a political measure celibacy was in a sense a grand success. It gave the rulers of the Church an able, disciplined, and devoted militia, to fight its battles and to spread its net in every country in Christendom. Never in the whole course of its history has the world seen such a force at the absolute disposal of one will as the celibate priesthood of the Roman Church in the service of its head. The hierarchy gained its end triumphantly, and society, though it reaped some high advantages—for instance the priesthood was kept from becoming a caste—paid on the whole a fearful price for them.

It is no anonymous libeller, but a dignitary of the Spanish Church, who, writing in this age, declared that the bastards of the ecclesiastics were little inferior in number to the children of the laity. If we cast our eye over the legislation of provincial councils, we find damning proofs that the most fearful forms of vice ran riot in ecclesiastical society. An early Dominican retails the legend which represents the devil as thanking the prelates of the Church for conducting all Christendom to Hell. Innocent IV. left Lyons in 1251 after residing there eight years with his court. The farewell speech of Cardinal Hugo is significant. ' My friends, since our arrival here we have done much for your city. When we came here we found three or four brothels: we leave behind us but one, but it extends without interruption from the eastern to the western gate.' Perhaps the sternest condemnation of the morals of the Roman Court is to be found in the language of the noble and high-minded Bishop Grossetete of Lincoln in 1253. He quoted against it when dying the scathing lines:—

> ' *Ejus avaritiæ totus non sufficit orbis ;*
>
> *Ejus luxuriæ meretrix non sufficit omnis.*'

When the Papal Court was at Avignon, Petrarch was there to observe and to record. It would not be possible to quote here one-tenth of the terrible account which he gives of the sensual enormities which were mere pastime to Prelates and Popes, but here is the famous sonnet which embodies his tremendous denunciation of the corruptions and crimes of Rome, to which every country in Latin Christendom said, Amen :—

> ' Fountain of woe ! Harbour of endless ire !
> The school of errors, haunt of heresies !
> Once Rome, now Babylon ; the world's disease
> Who makest man to groan with mad desire !
> O Forge of Fraud ! O Prison dark and dire !
> Where dies the good, where evil deeds increase,

> Thou living Hell! Portents will never cease,
> If Christ move not to purge thy sin with fire.
> Founded in chaste and humble poverty,
> Against thy Founder thou dost raise thine horn,
> Thou shameless harlot! And whence comes this pride,
> Even from foul and loathed adultery,
> The price of lewdness. Constantine return!
> Not so : the craven world its doom must bide.'

Reference need hardly be made to the well-known catalogue of crimes which the Council of Constance laid to the charge of Pope John XXIII., when it deposed him. They include incest, violation, adultery, homicide, poisoning, simony, heresy, and materialism. John suffered judgment to go by default.

These terrible tales were freely repeated and firmly believed throughout Christendom; every point could be illustrated out of popular ballads, as well as from grave historians and doctors of the Church. 'How then,' it may be asked, 'did the system hold together? Why did not secular Christendom rise on it and sweep it from the earth?' Well, the system lived on partly through the tremendous strength of its organisation and the depth of its root fibres, partly through the vague and awful forces which were believed to be behind it, but mainly, let it be said in justice, through the good work which it did for the world. Now, as then, the strength of the Roman Church lies neither in the wisdom of its head, nor in the heavenly-mindedness of its hierarchy : if that had been all it would long since have gone down into the abyss. Remember Chaucer's noble description of the poor Parson :—

> 'That Cristes gospel trewely wolde preche.
> His parishens devoutly wolde he teche.
> Benigne he was, and wonder diligent,
> And in adversite ful patient :
>
> .   .   .   .   .   .
>
> To drawen folk to heven, with fairenesse
> By good ensample, was his besinesse :

> But it were any persone obstinat,
> What so he were of highe, or low estat,
> Him wolde he snibben sharply for the nones.
> A better preest I trowe that nowher non is.
> He waited after no pompe ne reverence,
> Ne maked him no spiced conscience,
> But Cristes lore, and his apostles twelve,
> He taught, but first he folwed it himselve.'[1]

Think of the multitudes of such men, quiet, holy, benignant village pastors, whom in all ages the Roman Church has scattered about Christendom. They have in all ages helped mightily to save the Church which Popes and Prelates have done their best to destroy.

One other feature of the Church of the period must be noted—its rapacity, which had much to do with Wyclif's life and work, and in this connection England appears on the scene. Papal dominion seemed to the Roman statesmen to carry with it the right of taxation. The expenses of the Roman Court were enormous, the waste prodigal. It was the rapacity of the spiritual rulers which at length brought them to the dust. The Pope had been allowed to shear his own sheep, the clergy, pretty closely, though with some limitation on the part of the secular power. But when he began to put forth the claim to tax the people as well as the priests, the hour of his overthrow drew near. There is a curious calculation of Bishop Grossetete of Lincoln in the thirteenth century, which Matthew Paris records :—

'Innocent, the present Pope, hath impoverished the Church more than all his predecessors since the first establishment of the Papacy. The revenues of foreign clerks appointed in England, and enriched by the Church of Rome, amounts to 70,000 marks. The clear revenue of the king was reckoned not to amount to more than a third of that sum.'[2]

In the Good Parliament of 1376—and men and bodies

---

[1] Prologue, l. 483 ff.   [2] Matthew Paris, ad ann. 1253.

got baptised 'good' in those times, very much on the ground of antagonism to Rome—the Commons say:—

'The taxes levied by the Pope amount to five times those levied by the King. . . . The brokers of the sinful city Rome promote for money unlearned and unworthy caitiffs, to benefices of the value of 1000 marks, while the poor and learned hardly obtain one of 20. So decays sound learning. They present aliens who neither see nor care to see their parishioners, despise God's services, convey away the treasure of the realm, and are worse than Jews or Saracens. God gave his sheep to be pastured and not to be shorn.'[1]

In England the extortion had filled the cup to the brim, and when Wyclif was young it was already beginning to overflow. England was then on the whole the most advanced of the European kingdoms, and most ripe for projects of Reform. Our commonalty, the yeomen and citizens of England, became a factor of recognised importance in the national polity long before the fourth estate grew to manhood in any other country of the West. The French wars made them a power in Europe, and filled those, at any rate, who met them in fight with a great dread of their powers. Moreover, the reign of Edward III. was a martial reign, in which constant wars necessitated constant appeals to Parliament. Seventy writs were issued during his rule of fifty years; and the representatives had already established the principle that redress of grievances must precede supplies. In England, therefore, there was a stirring active people, trained to judgment on weighty matters, ready to Wyclif's hand. It was a time, too, of intense fermentation. An old age was ending; men felt it tremblingly, and they were eager to hear what could be told them about a new. The fearful pestilence which wasted Europe about the middle of the century, and which is said to have destroyed one-half of the population, left behind it when its shadow passed away very important moral and economical results.

[1] See Milman, *Latin Christianity*, Bk. XIII., ch. 6.

In curious ways it opened that great conflict between capital and labour which has been a mainspring of human activity from that day until now. It left, also, a profound moral impression on the heart of the people, and had much to do with that deep sadness which overshadowed English society, when the old King was closing his long and brilliant reign in confusion and disaster.

It was in such a society, sick to the heart of the corruptions and extortions of Rome; emerging from the feudal order, but in sore perplexity as to what should succeed it ; seething with social discontents, groaning in social travail, and still quivering under the wave of moral emotion which had swept over it, that John Wyclif made the pure word of Christ's Gospel once more a power among men.

Before the death of Edward III. in 1377, Wyclif was already a noted and powerful man in England, and indeed in Europe, and had kindled that light which has burned, and must burn, brighter and brighter unto the perfect day. He was born somewhere about 1324, and was one of those ' Yorkshiremen stern of mood ' whom Scott celebrates— thorough to the backbone. We hear singularly little of his early history, but it appears that about 1340 he made his way to Oxford, where we find him connected with Balliol and with Merton, a college which could boast already many illustrious names.

In the twelfth century the Universities began their rise, and in the thirteenth they had become a leading power in Europe, planting throughout the West the *foci* of forces which would in time prove quite as deadly to the supremacy of the Church from the intellectual side, as, in the political sphere, the development of national institutions and national life. It was out of the University of Oxford, through Occam and subsequently through Wyclif, that the

first clear and Scriptural protest went forth, from teachers
of European reputation, against the Mystery of Iniquity
which was seated on the seven hills of Rome.   Occam,
who died in 1347, had spoken out with exceeding plain-
ness, and in one polemical treatise had proved the Pope to be
a complete heretic.   The ideas, therefore, which Wyclif was
about to promulgate to the world were not wholly strange
to Oxford ears.

We can form little idea in these days of the intense
interest which in the thirteenth and fourteenth centuries
gathered around the seats of learning.   Two hundred years
before, thousands of students, very poor most of them and
many of them very ragged, had streamed after Peter
Abelard, as he moved from town to town lecturing about
all things on earth and in heaven, and opening the living
intellectual springs.   Before the great plague 30,000
students are said to have resorted to Oxford, all passionately
eager to drink of the new fountain, and to arm themselves
with the new weapons of thought, the value of which in
the decline of feudal ideas they had begun to realise.
The University was from the beginning a commonwealth, a
republic of letters.   Prince, clerk, peasant, were absolutely
level on its floor; thought alone was king; all nations had
there one language and one interest.   Oxford has as grand
a record as any city in Europe, and a full history of
Oxford would be very largely a history of the higher
progress of Christian society.

In the University Wyclif achieved a very high reputation
as a scholar and teacher before he stood forth as a Reformer.
Probably about 1366 he became Doctor of Divinity and an
authorised public teacher, and he was soon distinguished as
the most popular and powerful disputant of his time.   Henry
of Knighton says of him, 'As a theologian he was the most
eminent of the day, as a philosopher second to none, and as

a schoolman incomparable.'[1] In 1375 the King presented him to a prebend in the diocese of Worcester, and about the same time to the rectory of Lutterworth, which he held till his death in 1384.

It was from his Doctor's chair at Oxford that Wyclif commenced his searching examination and rebuke of the tyranny, the superstition, and the profligacy of the Papal Church. One of the most conspicuous features in his polemic against Rome was his scathing denunciation of the Mendicant Orders, who, having been a century and a half before well-nigh the saviours of Christendom, had now become something much more like its pest. In a previous Lecture the rise of the Mendicant Orders was traced to the time of their first glory, and it was noticed how soon the inevitable corruption began to set in. Notwithstanding their vow of poverty, they grew enormously rich even in spite of themselves, and as they grew rich they degenerated. When once the spiritual fervour died down their wandering life demoralised them rapidly, and within thirty years of the death of St. Francis, Bonaventura thus writes of his Order:—'They are immersed in carnal repose. . . . such is their rapacity that it is no less terrible to fall in with them than with so many robbers,' while in Boccaccio and Chaucer 'friar' is the synonym for gluttony, rapacity, and lust.

These friars literally swarmed about Europe. They had landed in England in 1224, when the Order was in the first glow of its pure and lofty self-devotion. Their quaint attire led the dignified monks of the elder Orders to mistake them for buffoons, and they were even turned out of monasteries because they would not amuse the inmates by tricks. But monk and layman soon found that the new comers were terribly in earnest. They settled in the most wretched rookeries of the towns, and gloried in ministries from which all other

---

[1] *De Eventibus Angliæ*, col. 2604.

Christian charity recoiled. Wealth and converts flowed in upon them. They invaded the Universities and occupied the most distinguished chairs. They took the bread out of the mouths of the parochial clergy by their zeal, their preaching power, their cleverness, and the easy terms of their absolutions. In the Universities their proselytising influence was so disastrous that parents grew alarmed, and the Archbishop Fitzralph of Armagh declares that from this cause mainly the students at Oxford were, within his memory, reduced from 30,000 to 6,000. Against the friars Wyclif directed his fiercest assaults, and the points just touched on will explain why neither University, Church, nor Commonalty, was sorry to see them vigorously attacked. And yet, corrupt as they had become in the time we are speaking of, as they roamed about Europe with their sermons, their tales, their relics, their absolutions, their jests, and their tricks, they had done in their time a work of incalculable importance, and had at any rate mingled some Christian ideas once more with the daily life and the busy occupations of mankind. The monk, we have already seen, went *out of* the world, the friars went *into* the world, and as clever talkers, striking preachers, stirring newsmongers, they brought such truth as they had to offer into vital contact with the hearts and consciences of men. They stirred thus an interest and created a yearning which a purer truth alone could satisfy, and they made ready the path, though in ways which they knew not, for the preachers of the everlasting Gospel.

For a brief space, less than a generation, the first inspiration lasted, but when Wyclif opened his attack, the Christian work of the Order had long been done. It was corrupt to the root and was corrupting everything around. As a specimen of the way in which Wyclif handled the friars, the following may be quoted, and it will be observed that behind all his argument against them is the idea that the Order is condemned

because its authority is not in the Word of God.   The passage
runs as follows :—

'See now where these friars break falsely all the commandments of God.
If they choose to be ruled more after the ordinance of sinful men and
idiots, than after the clean ordinance of Christ ; and say that sinful man's
ordinance is better, and truer for man, and more perfect than is the clean
ordinance of Christ—then they worship false gods, and are heretics and
blasphemers, and so they break the first commandment of God.   If they
dread more, and punish more for breaking of sinful man's traditions, than
for breaking the commandments of God ; and study and love more their
private rules, than the hests of God, then they worship, love, and dread
sinful man, and, it may be damned devils, more than God Almighty—for,
as Austin saith, a man maketh that thing his God the which he dreadeth
most and loveth most.

'If they hinder curates and poor priests from teaching man God's law,
by hypocrisy and help of Antichrist's laws, for dread lest their hypocrisy
be perceived, and their winning and worldly pride laid down, they are
cursed manquellers, and the cause of the damnation of all the souls that
perish through their default in not knowing and keeping God's commandments.   If they preach principally for worldly muck and vainglory, and
so preach to be praised of men, and not simply and plainly the Gospel of
Christ for his glory, and gaining of men's souls, they are corrupters of
God's word, as Paul saith.'[1]

Another matter of large public importance which claimed
the Reformer's attention concerned the exactions of Rome,
and the true relations of the temporal and spiritual powers.
John of England had covenanted to pay 1000 marks per
annum as his vassal tribute to Rome.   It was paid at
intervals, but Edward III. when he came of age formally
discontinued it.   In 1365 Urban V. was foolish enough to
demand payment with arrears.   The demand was laid before
Parliament and sternly rejected by a unanimous decision of
the Lords spiritual and temporal and the Commons, to the
effect that King John had acted entirely beyond his right in
subjecting his country and people to such a feudal superiority
without their own consent.   They further declared, that in
case the Pope should carry out any hostile procedure against

[1] *Tracts and Treatises*, Lond. 1845, p. 8.

the King, they would place the whole powers and resources of the nation at the disposal of the monarch for the defence of his crown and dignity.

Wyclif, already at this time a celebrated man and a Royal Chaplain, struck into the controversy and struck home. His discussion of the Papal claim is thrown into the form of a report of sundry speeches, purporting to have been delivered by certain Lords in a debate, presumably in Parliament. If these speeches were, in substance, actually spoken in the Council, as is the opinion expressed by Dr. Vaughan in his most valuable Wyclif publications,[1] the fact would make Wyclif, among other things, a kind of father of Parliamentary reporting. In his tract seven Lords are represented as bringing forward seven different reasons for rejecting the Pope's demand, while Wyclif sums up the controversy in his own person, deciding that the agreement made by John was both immoral and without authority.

At a subsequent period grave disputes arose between Edward and the Pope about 'provisors,' by means of which the Pope secured for his creatures the richest emoluments of the Anglican Church. Wyclif was on the embassy sent to discuss it with Gregory XI., and at Bruges, where they met the Papal delegates, he saw with that keen eye of his something of the inner working of the Papal system.

Again at a yet later date this same question in a somewhat different form presented itself for discussion ; and there exists among the tracts of Wyclif one headed ‘ *Answer of Master John Wyclif to the question given below: it was propounded to him by our lord the King of England, Richard the Second, and by his great Council, in the first*

---

[1] *Life and Opinions of Wycliffe*, Lond. 1831; and *John de Wycliffe, a Monograph*, Lond. 1853. [The same opinion is held by Dr. Lechler in his more recent study of Wyclif, and by his translator Dr. Lorimer. See *John Wiclif and his English Precursors*, Lond. 1878. I., p. 247. Ed.]

year of his reign.[1]   The question concerned the right of
the Crown to impound and apply to national exigencies
English money which was claimed by, and on its way to,
the Pope, and Wyclif, who had already explicitly maintained
the right of the secular government to deal with clerks and
with their property as subjects of the Crown, now gives
his reply to the question of King and Parliament to the
effect that 'our kingdom may lawfully keep back and
detain their treasure for the defence of itself, in what case
soever necessity do require the same.'   The answer, which
extends to considerable length, is curious because of the
scholastic form of part of it, and the free Scriptural tone of
the rest.   It indicates Wyclif's true place as the great
link of connection, intellectually as well as spiritually, between the scholastic age and the age of the Reformation.
In culture and tone of thought he is at once the last of
the great schoolmen and the first of the greater Reformers.
Not his terms only but the form of his arguments are
strongly scholastic, while he mixes with them pointed and
vigorous appeals to the common understanding and the
plain meaning of Scripture, which make him the pioneer
of the great intellectual movement which was about to
shake and to renew the world.   As a specimen of the
first it may be interesting to quote the opening sentences
with their dry and formal argument, which runs as follows :—

'Every natural body hath power given of God to resist against its
contrary, and to preserve itself in due estate, as philosophers know very
well.   Insomuch, that bodies without life are endued with such kind of
power (as it is evident) unto whom hardness is given, to resist those
things that would break them, and coldness, to withstand the heat that
dissolveth them.   Forasmuch then, as the kingdom of England (after the
manner and phrase of the Scriptures) ought to be one body, and the
clergy with the commonalty the members thereof, it seemeth that the
same kingdom hath such power given it of God ; and so much the more
apparently, by how much the same body is more precious unto God,

<hr>

[1] Printed in the *Fasciculi Zizaniorum*, Rolls Series, p. 258.

adorned with virtue and knowledge. Forasmuch then as there is no power given of God unto any creature, for any end or purpose, but that he may lawfully use the same to that end and purpose, it followeth that our kingdom may lawfully keep back and detain their treasure for the defence of itself, in what case soever necessity do require the same.'

In other parts of the tract the argument is broad and natural. It is interesting to note that Wyclif supports his assault on Papal greed of wealth and power by a fine quotation from St. Bernard, whose constant and unsparing rebukes of the worldliness of the Church of his day have been referred to in a previous Lecture. Wyclif then proceeds :—

'From these words of a blessed man whom the whole Church hath agreed to honour, it appears that the Pope has no right to possess himself of the goods of the Church, as though he were lord of them, but that he is to be, with respect to them, as a minister or servant, and the proctor for the poor. And would to God that the same proud and eager desire of authority and lordship, which is now discovered by this seat of power, were aught else but a prelude, preparing the pathway of Antichrist. From the Gospel evident it is, that the children of Christ's kingdom were not produced by such means, but were the fruit of His poverty, His humility, and His suffering of injury.'

One sees at once where Wyclif stands in the matter of the true relation of the temporal and spiritual powers. The main feature of all his teaching is his frank and fearless resort to the Word of God. 'To the law and to the testimony' is his constant appeal. In all controversies he will ask, Is this in the order of things which Christ set forth in Scripture? No? Then it shall have no place among ourselves. Luther himself is not clearer than Wyclif as to the authority and the sufficiency of Scripture, and the complete discordance of the whole Church system of those times with the plain teaching of the Divine Word. The following noble passage illustrates Wyclif's view of the importance of independent study of the Word. We seem to see here the narrow end of the wedge which Luther was to drive

home.   Wyclif speaks of those who would reserve the
Scriptures as

'Antichrists, forbidding men to know their belief, and to speak of
Holy Writ. For they say openly that secular men should not intermeddle themselves with the Gospel, to read it in the mother tongue, but
attend to a holy father's preaching, and do after such in all things. But
this is openly against God's teaching. For God commandeth generally
to each layman, that he should have God's commandments before him,
and teach them to his children. And Peter biddeth us be ready to give
a reason for our faith and hope to each man that asketh it. And God
commands His priests to preach the Gospel to each man, as the reason is,
because all men should know it. Lord! why should worldly priests
forbid secular men to speak of the Gospel, since God giveth them great
wit of kind (by nature) and great desire to know God and love Him?
Since the beginning of the world none have heard higher craft of Antichrist whereby to destroy Christian men's belief and charity, than is this
blasphemous heresy—that laymen should not intermeddle with the
Gospel.'[1]

We are not able to trace with any accuracy the course
of Wyclif's instruction during his later years at Oxford;
though a fair notion of it may be gathered from a study
of his '*Trialogus*.' He went on applying the test of the
Word of God to the principal doctrines and practices of
the Church, kindling a burning enthusiasm in the one party,
in the other a vehement alarm and hate. About saints'
days, for instance, he says, 'Not a few think it would be
well for the Church, if all festivals of that nature were
abolished, and those only were retained which have respect
immediately to Christ.' The most important theological controversy in which Wyclif was engaged was that which he
carried on with so much vigour and earnestness in opposition
to the Romish dogma of Transubstantiation. Wyclif saw
clearly what it would be well for us to keep as clearly in
sight, that this dogma is at the heart of the sacerdotal
power of Rome. Sacerdotalists, if they want to uphold

[1] From the Tract *de XXXII Erroribus Curatorum*, in Vaughan, *John de
Wycliffe*, Lond. 1853, p. 526.

the office and power of the priest, are wise in their generation in maintaining the Real Presence; and in offering
their daily sacrifice—*theirs*, it is neither of the Father, nor
of Christ. This is the key to their position: while this
stands they may stand; when this falls, as fall it must,
they will fall. But if '*by one offering he hath perfected
for ever them that are sanctified,*' if '*the just shall live by
faith,*' not in the Christ of a priest's incantations, but in
the living and reigning Saviour who is in perpetual presence
with the believing soul; if the mission of the Church is to
preach '*Christ Jesus, and him crucified,*' then '*the truth
as it is in Jesus*' and Sacerdotalism are in deadly antagonism,
and if the Gospel is to triumph, Sacerdotalism must wither
before it, and perish out of that Christendom which it has
done so much in all ages to waste and to destroy. Wyclif
saw this and struck at once at the heart of the error of
Rome in a series of discourses and controversial papers
which may be studied in the '*Tracts and Treatises*' edited
by Dr. Vaughan for the Wycliffe Society.

Before, however, this controversy came to its height, Wyclif
had, as we may well imagine, attracted the hostile notice
of Rome, and the Pope felt that some action must be
taken. Just 500 years ago, in 1377,[1] three Bulls were
issued, to the King, to the Archbishop, and to the University,
commanding that proceedings should be instituted against
Wyclif, whose doctrines are thus described in the Bull to
Oxford, which Foxe has preserved :—

'Grievously it has come to our ears, that one John Wyclif, parson of
Lutterworth in Lincoln diocese, a professor of Divinitie (would God he
were not rather a master of errours), is runne into a kind of detestable
wickednesse, not only and openly publishing, but also vomiting out of
the filthy dungeon of his heart, divers professions, false and erroneous
conclusions, and most wicked and damnable heresies.'[2]

<hr>

[1] [The lecture was delivered in 1877.—ED.]
[2] Foxe, *Acts and Monuments*, 1632. I. 563.

Early in the year 1377, Courtenay, Bishop of London, had cited the Reformer to answer for his heresies. He appeared with John of Gaunt, Lord Percy the Earl Marshal, and a great throng of people. We have already seen enough to explain the sympathy with which Wyclif's views were regarded by laymen in high places. On that occasion, however, the popular feeling was with the bishop. The truth is that John of Gaunt, in the last days of Edward III., was in disfavour with the people. He was known to be ambitious and was suspected of designs against the interests of the heir of their darling Black Prince; John of Gaunt accordingly could lend no strength just then to Wyclif's cause. There was rough recrimination between the bishop and the secular lords, the meeting broke up in confusion, and nothing was done. In 1378, Wyclif was summoned before a synod at Lambeth, and at this meeting the people were tumultuously in his favour. The churchmen were cowed, and when a message came from the Queen Mother forbidding them to do anything against Wyclif, the synod was dissolved and again there was no result—except indeed a valuable paper which he drew up, answering *seriatim* the charges of heresy, and setting forth his views. After this great strain, the Reformer appears to have fallen ill. The friars, thinking that he was dying, exhorted him to repentance. But he was made of sterner stuff. Imagine their disgust and dread when the sick man, gathering up all his strength, and asking to be raised in bed, exclaimed, 'I shall not die but live, and shall again declare the evil deeds of the friars.'

There came then, as always comes in great movements, a pause in the onward progress, and there was heard the cry of Halt all along the vanguard of Reform. The misery of the poor broke out into rebellion; and men connected this with Wyclif's teachings—in one sense, not unjustly.

The truth previously indicated, that the friars were a living link of connection between the Middle Age and the preachers of the Reformation, is further established by the fact, that Wyclif organised and trained bands of 'poor priests,' who went about barefoot, staff in hand, everywhere preaching the Gospel—the Methodists of the fourteenth century. The common people heard them gladly—it always does hear such preachers gladly—and their words stirred a great hope in the heart of the starving and wretched poor. Their teaching, though they were no preachers of rebellion, added inevitably to the popular excitement. They were not backward—God grant that the vanguard of the Church may never be backward—in maintaining '*the cause of the afflicted, and the right of the poor.*' To the minds of men in high, and men in safe places, their purely Christian teaching seemed to be in some sinister connection with the popular discontent, and so for a time a cloud gathered round the Reformer and his work. The University silenced him in 1382. A synod was held by the Archbishop of Canterbury in which his tenets were formally condemned. Still, none dared to touch his person, and he retired unharmed to Lutterworth, where the last and the best part of his life's work was done. It is a noble testimony to the temper of England in those days, that he was able to continue this glorious work in peace at his country living, and that he died there peacefully in his bed in 1384.

A final word on his last and most honourable achievement, his translation of the Bible into the English tongue. A word will be sufficient, as it is the best known and the most valued of all the noble gifts which he bestowed upon the world. Though silenced at Oxford, he continued at Lutterworth to pour forth a copious stream of treatises on every manner of subject connected with the religious instruction and welfare of the people. Incomparably his greatest work, however, during these last years was the translation, which with the aid of coadjutors he was able to accomplish, and in part to revise, before his death. In writing of the use of the Scriptures in the vernacular, he utters the following noble vindication of the principles which inspired his own undertaking :—

'Seeing the truth of the faith shines the more by how much more it is known . . . that the truth may be known more plainly and diffusively, true men are under a necessity of declaring the opinion which they hold, not only in Latin, but in the vulgar tongue. . . Nor are those heretics to be heard who fancy that seculars ought not to know the law of God, but that it is sufficient for them to know what the priests and prelates tell them by word of mouth ; for the Scripture is the faith of the Church, and the more it is known in an orthodox sense the better. Therefore, as secular men ought to know the faith, so it is to be taught them in whatsoever language is best known to them. Besides, since the truth of the faith is clearer and more exact in the Scripture than the priests know how to express it ; seeing, if one may say so, that there are many prelates who are too ignorant of the Scripture, and others conceal points of Scripture, such, to wit, as declare the poverty and humility of the clergy, and that there are many such defects in the verbal instructions of priests, it seems useful that the faithful should themselves search out or discover the sense of the faith, by having the Scriptures in a language which they know and understand. . . . The laws, therefore, which the prelates make, are not to be received as matters of faith, nor are we to believe their words or discourses any further or otherwise than they are founded in the Scripture, since, according to the constant doctrine of Augustine, the Scripture is all the truth. Therefore this translation of the Scripture would do at least this good, that it would render priests and prelates unsuspected in regard to the words of it, which they profess to explain. Further, prelates, as the pope, or friars, and other means, may prove defective, and Christ and his apostles, accordingly, converted the most part of the world by making known the Scripture in a language which was most familiar to the people. For to this purpose did the Holy Spirit give them the knowledge of all tongues. Why, therefore, ought not the modern disciples of Christ to collect fragments from the same loaf, and after such example open the Scriptures clearly and plainly to the people, that they may know them.'[1]

The toil involved in this work of translation was enormous,

---

[1] *Tracts and Treatises*, p. lxii.

and there can be no question that it wore his noble life away. His tracts and translations were written in nervous, pithy vernacular, which stamps Wyclif as the true father of English prose. We learn that intense interest was taken in the work by the people, and indeed by all classes. One hundred and seventy MS. copies of his Bible are now extant, many of them bearing the names of the most eminent persons in the realm, amongst them those of four of our kings. Through Anne of Bohemia, Consort of Richard II., the *Tracts and Treatises* were carried to her native land, and lit up there the flame of the Reformation. In England the translation kindled a light which has never been extinguished, and, thank God, never can be extinguished while England endures. This was Wyclif's grand achievement, his crown of everlasting honour; and it was at the cost of life that his work was done. On December 29th, 1384, he was struck down by paralysis in his Church at Lutterworth, and on the 31st he peacefully expired.

After his death there came an era of reaction, which demands a closing sentence. This reaction may be accounted for in different ways. The fact is that the fifteenth century in England was a dark sad age, standing related to the glorious epoch that was to succeed it, much as the eighteenth century is related to this great nineteenth in which, let us thank God, we live and work. Men like Wyclif are like the fabled ninth wave of the flood tide: they leave a mark high up on the sand; the next wave recedes, the next, the next; but wait, soon the whole tide will be up to the limit and beyond. The key to the reaction may be sought, if we will, merely in the natural timorousness and sloth of the mass of mankind. There is, however, in addition to this a nobler reason. Reformation on a great scale is an awful work, and the most earnest feel this, and tremble before it. There exists deep down in the heart of Christian society an uneasy feeling that many things are wrong, radically wrong, in our attempt at a kingdom of Heaven, and that the righting them will be solemn and costly work; and so when a great power of God seems to be manifesting itself, men give pause, not ignobly altogether, but rather as Moses trembled before his mission, appalled by the magnitude of the task. These thoughts and feelings, with other influences that might be adduced, create, so to speak, the atmosphere in which the reactionaries work. In this case, there was a political *motif*, that was supplied by the defective title to the throne of the Lancastrian kings. Like Louis Napoleon and others of our own time, trembling for their power, they sought the sinister alliance of the Church. Frightened people soon get cruel, and the fires were quickly kindled in which Cobham and other noble martyrs perished. They dug up Wyclif's bones and burned them, and scattered the ashes to the winds and seas. Fools! The winds and the seas had already fulfilled a benigner ministry; they had borne his relics, the living germs of his intellect and spirit, and scattered them broadcast through Europe, the vital seeds of a lasting Reformation; and what cared he for his bones?

Through all the dark times, however, which followed on the age of Wyclif, his work remained as he had left it. There was the Book and the Tracts and Treatises of the Reformer in vulgar English, the tongue of the great English people, and these kept still glowing the embers which, when the days of the reaction were ended, leapt forth into such brilliant quickening flame. There was the Book! There is the Book! and while this Book abides the priest can never triumph in Christendom, nor the Gospel perish out of the world. Of all that the Reformation, and the Bible which it has put into the hands of the people, have done for England, we must hold John Wyclif to be the earthly parent, as fellow-helper on earth with Christ in heaven. The greatest Englishman of his time, and amongst the greatest of all times, foremost among the world's elect spirits, few even among its saints and martyrs will appear with more abundant honour in the day, when ' *The teachers shall shine as the brightness of the firmament; and they that turn many to righteousness as the stars for ever and ever.*'

INDEX.

THE END.